U.S. NUCLEAR WEAPONS IN CANADA

To:
T. Murray and Ollie

U.S. NUCLEAR WEAPONS IN CANADA

JOHN
CLEARWATER

THE DUNDURN GROUP
TORONTO · OXFORD

Publisher: J.Kirk Howard
Editor: Wendy Thomas
Design: Jennifer Scott
Printer: Transcontinental Printing, Inc.

Canadian Cataloguing in Publication Data
Clearwater, John
U.S. nuclear weapons in Canada
Includes bibliographical references and index.
ISBN 1-55002-329-2

1. Nuclear weapons — Canada — History. 2. Nuclear weapons — United States —
History. 3. Canada — Military relations — United States. 4. United States — Military
relations — Canada. I. Title.

U264.5.C535 1999   355.8'25119'0971   C99-932276-1

1   2   3   4   5   03   02   01   00   99

THE CANADA COUNCIL | LE CONSEIL DES ARTS
FOR THE ARTS | DU CANADA
SINCE 1957 | DEPUIS 1957

Canadä

We acknowledge the support of the **Canada Council for the Arts** for our publishing
program. We also acknowledge the support of the **Ontario Arts Council**. We
acknowledge the financial support of the Government of Canada through the **Book
Publishing Industry Development Program** (BPIDP) for our publishing activities.

Printed and bound in Canada. Printed on recycled paper.

www.dundurn.com

Dundurn Press	Dundurn Press	Dundurn Press
8 Market Street	73 Lime Walk	2250 Military Road
Suite 200	Headington, Oxford,	Tonawanda, New York
Toronto, Ontario, Canada	England	U.S.A. 14150
M5E 1M6	OX3 7AD	

Table of Contents

ANNEX

Acknowledgments

I am indebted to the staff of the National Defence Directorate of History and Heritage (DHH) in Ottawa for allowing me access to their superb collection. My special thanks go to Isabel Campbell, who is not only a fine historian of military activities, but is also a Newfoundlander, and who was able to provide valuable insights.

Very important in the formulation of this book were BJ Petzinger, DAIP, and all her staff at National Defence Headquarters in Ottawa. I give thanks to all of them, and gratefully acknowledge their assistance in the first and second volumes of this series.

I appreciate the work done on my behalf by the Government Archives Division of the National Archives of Canada. The staff in the Reading Room at the Archives has also been terrific in putting up with myriad requests. However, the Access to Information staff at the Archives has recently adopted a policy of charging applicants for all manner of document processing, thereby cutting off all but the richest requesters from the use of the so-called national historical records. This policy has been supported by the Minister for Canadian Heritage, Sheila Copps. In the course of writing this book, I brought a federal court case against the minister for obstructing access to vital records of the government under the Access to Information Act.

The Department of Foreign Affairs, formerly External Affairs, provided me with superb support. Most External Affairs documents used in this study were gathered for my previous book, *Canadian Nuclear Weapons*, when I was accepted into their Academic Access Programme. I give great thanks to Saul Grey for his perseverence in seeking both Canadian and U.S. release of the documents.

The Access to Information section in the Prime Minister's Office and Privy Council Office provided a great deal of help to this project. They were able to give me minutes of both full cabinet meetings and of Cabinet Defence Committee meetings at which nuclear weapons for both Canada and U.S. forces in Canada were discussed. Cuiuneas Boyle, another Newfoundlander, and her staff have never been anything but completely forthcoming with aid and information. I appreciate all their hard work and note that important sections of this book would not have been possible without their input.

I thank the DND Public Affairs office and National Defence Photo Unit for the use of the photographs in this book.

In the United States I received assistance from three vastly different sources. The U.S. National Archives and Records Administration was able to provide State Department records for the 1950s and 1960s, while the non-governmental National Security Archive in Washington allowed me to browse their files on their past and upcoming nuclear weapons history project. The U.S. Air Force was also helpful in that the staff at the USAF Historical Research Agency in Montgomery, Alabama, showed me files on USAF nuclear support units.

On the non-governmental side, I thank Pablo Zeiss of Winnipeg for his wonderful line drawings of airfields and bunkers. He is a skilled draftsman and gentleman.

Last, I express my gratitude to "Sharpsword."

Acronyms

ADC	Air Defence Command (RCAF or USAF)
AFB	Air Force Base (USAF)
ALCOP	Alternate Command Post
AOC	Air Officer Commanding
ASW	Anti-submarine warfare
AUW	Advanced Underwater Weapons
BMEWS	Ballistic Missile Early Warning System
BUIC	Back-Up Interceptor Control
CAF	Canadian Armed Forces
CAS	Chief of the Air Staff (RCAF)
CDC	Cabinet Defence Committee
CDS	Chief of Defence Staff
CF	Canadian Forces
CFB	Canadian Forces Base
CGS	Chief of the General Staff
CI	Capability Inspection
CINC	Commander-in-Chief
CONAD	Continental Air Defense (USAF)
DefCon	Defense Condition
Det	Detachment (USAF)
DEW	Distant Early Warning (Line)
Dhist	Directorate of History
DND	Department of National Defence
FIS	Fighter-Interceptor Squadron

GADS	Goose Air Defence Sector
ICI	Initial Capability Inspection
kt	kiloton
Mk	Mark
Mt	megaton
MMG	Munitions Maintenance Group (USAF)
MMS	Munitions Maintenance Squadron (USAF)
MUNS	Munitions Maintenance Squadron (USAF)
MND	Minister of National Defence
NATO	North Atlantic Treaty Organization
NORAD	North American Air/Aerospace Defence Command
NFLD	Newfoundland
NSI	Nuclear Safety/Surety Inspection
PCO	Privy Council Office
PJBD	Permanent Joint Board on Defence
PMO	Prime Ministers Office
QRA	Quick Reaction Alert
RCAF	Royal Canadian Air Force
RCMP	Royal Canadian Mounted Police
RCN	Royal Canadian Navy
SAC	Strategic Air Command (USAF)
SACLANT	Supreme Allied Commander Atlantic (USN)
SAGE	Semi-Automatic Ground Environment
SAS	Safe And Secure (or) Special Ammunition Storage
SOSUS	Sound Surveillance System
SSEA	Secretary of State for External Affairs
USAF	United States Air Force
USN	United States Navy
ZED	classification for nuclear documents

Introduction

This is the second volume in the nuclear weapons in Canada series which began with the 1998 book *Canadian Nuclear Weapons*. I found that the basic research for the first book had also produced a tremendous amount of never-before-seen material on strictly U.S. activities in Canada. As this material was not directly applicable to the earlier book, it was simply held for later use. Further research in both the United States and Canada brought the entire story into focus, and that is what is presented here.

The purpose of this volume is to bring together until-recently secret information about the nature of the nuclear weapons stored, stationed or lost in Canada by the United States Air Force and the United States Navy and combine it with known information about the systems in the U.S. nuclear arsenal.

The history of bringing the atomic bomb to Canada goes back to the first years immediately after World War II when the U.S. government, under the prodding of the newly created Strategic Air Command, began a slow and steady process of talks designed to allow Goose Bay to be groomed for the eventual acceptance of nuclear weapons. An entire chapter is devoted to the political and military actions over this most strategically placed site. See Chapter 5 for the complete story of nuclear weapons in Goose Bay.

So complete was the inclusion of Canada in the nuclear web of the United States that the complicity was taken for granted for several years. The U.S. embassy in Ottawa reported to Washington that "there are no real problems, either with respect to the Canadian Government or the population, arising from the presence, activities, or conduct of United States forces in Canada."[1] So close was the military and political relationship, with the possible exception of the Diefenbaker and Kennedy years, that there was never any question of Canada pursuing an independent defence policy. In fact, nothing was done without first informing the United States and seeking permission. This even extended to the mundane. Before the issuance of the 1964 White Paper on Defence, Paul Hellyer sent a copy to Robert McNamara, the U.S. Secretary of Defense, asking for his concurrence in the document. Hellyer hoped that McNamara would not "find anything in these references contrary to any views you may have expressed."[2] Canada, by choice of politicians and actions of military leaders, had little strategic room for movement.

Not only was the U.S. Air Force and the U.S. Navy represented with nuclear weapons systems, but the U.S. Army managed to bring in at least one item. During the late 1950s and early 1960s, the U.S. Army tested their Nike-Hercules air defence missile at Fort Churchill, Manitoba.[3] The Nike-Hercules could carry a W-31 nuclear warhead for intercepting bombers. Although the warhead was never deployed to an operational system in Canada, the system was tested here for use in the United States and abroad.

The first known presence of nuclear weapons in Canada came in September 1950, when the USAF stationed eleven Mk4 "Fat Man" style atomic bombs at Goose Bay, Newfoundland. Although the deployment went well, one of the bombs was lost over the St. Lawrence River while being ferried back to the United States. Details of this and other accidents can be found in Chapter 4.

It was not only the weapons themselves which came to Canada: there was also the export of radiation from the United States. During the Cold War, the U.S. government engaged in a great deal of lying and

WEAPON	INITIAL ENTRY	WITHDRAWN
W-54	Jul 1965	Dec 1966
Mk-101 or Mk-57 (depth bomb)	Feb 1968	Jun 1970
various nuclear gravity bombs	Jul-Dec 1950	Jun 1971

manipulation of public opinion. This was especially true during the nuclear weapons test moratoriums and the test ban treaty. While the United States was usually busy accusing the Soviet Union of all sorts of violations, the weapons laboratories and the government were testing nuclear weapons, and this had an effect on Canada. The State Department feared that given the large amount of radioactivity produced by Project "Schooner" near the Canadian border, the public would find out and the United States "would doubtless face criticism in the public media." Clearly, the violation was not the problem; people finding out about it was the problem. The State Department went on to comment that "we cannot expect the Government of Canada to connive with us in hiding the fact of a violation."[4] This was all part and parcel of the nuclear mess in which the Canadian public found itself by virtue of the U.S. hegemony in Canadian military and political affairs which dated back to the end of World War II.

One thing that was not exported from the United States to Canada was racism: Canada already had enough. Deterioration of airfield facilities since the end of World War II was of concern to the USAF, and in 1948 they asked Canadian permission to send engineering troops to four locations in the Northwest Territories and Quebec to perform necessary maintenance work. The problem as Lester Pearson, the Under-Secretary of State for External Affairs (SSEA), saw it, was that the United States intended to use "negro engineering troops" for this work. While there was little problem with the sites in the Northwest Territories, provided that the blacks were free of venereal disease, the question of Quebec was very problematic. So racist and xenophobic and parochial was Quebec in 1950 that it was almost impossible for the federal government to handle defence matters on a purely practical basis. Pearson wrote to the SSEA that they should "*not* use coloured troops" in Quebec, "where the presence of US coloured troops in peace-time might be misunderstood and misrepresented." Louis St. Laurent, the SSEA, wrote "I agree" in the margin and returned the memo.[5] St. Laurent, soon to be Prime Minister, also noted that "the presence of coloured troops of US in any part of Quebec would expose us to undesirable criticism especially in light of present relations between us and the government of Quebec."[6]

The late decision to also remove Fort Chimo from the list of approved sites for blacks was not communicated fast enough, and it turned out that the USAF had already moved well into the process of sending the troops. This emergency note was conveyed to the U.S. authorities, who asked that they be kept informed through political channels in the future. The situation worsened by the 1950s, as the

United States had formally desegregated their military. This meant that there now were blacks in regular units, and that these units could be posted at any time to Canada. In the past, it was relatively easy to keep "negro units" out of Canada, but the ban could not apply to all units which had black troops. USAF General Whitten informed the Permanent Joint Board on Defence (PJBD) that in early 1950 he had already received 45 black troops for stationing in Newfoundland, and that the Newfoundland government was none too pleased with this situation.[7] However racist the Newfoundland government may have been, they were not about to jeopardize the flow of U.S. money into the province and therefore found it desirable not to raise any objections.

Nuclear weapons had never been wildly popular with the Canadian public, and it was this thin line of marginal support which both the Diefenbaker and Pearson governments had to tread. No one ever enjoyed full support on the nuclear question, and for this reason, the security apparatus of the state was brought into action to protect the government. Threats and subversion were seen everywhere, and the highest levels of government were constantly kept informed of the slightest bit of dissent. So sensitive was the state to criticism that every utterance of the local communist party and many lesser organizations were digested by the secret police and forwarded to no less than the Under Secretary of State for External Affairs for transmission to the Secretary of State.[8] If more than a few Communist Party of Canada members got into a car, the RCMP was there to write an informational memo to file on the event.[9]

No one was safe from being observed and photographed and spied on. Even the liberal Voice of Women organization had most of their regional and national meetings attended by undercover agents spying for the government.[10] In some cases, one infiltrator was not enough, and the RCMP would send an entire "surveillance team" to meetings or demonstrations or talks.[11] Despite the size of the operations against so many people and groups, the RCMP had an impressive record of keeping their agents and spies and provocateurs hidden. As Assistant Commissioner W.L. Higgitt, the director of Security and Intelligence for the RCMP wrote, "Please take no action which might jeopardize our source."[12]

The subject of NORAD itself was so sensitive that the Royal Canadian Mounted Police were directed to open a special investigation surveillance file on any protests over the continuation of NORAD.[13] A letter from the National Women's Committee of the Association of United Ukrainian Canadians, endorsed by the Women's Gathering at Tea and Shower in Toronto in Aid for the Vietnamese Children in February 1969, went unanswered by the prime minister. In fact, the letter was stamped "Reply Not Recommended 13/3/69." While Prime Minister Trudeau never replied, his office was considerate enough to send the letter to the secret police for inclusion in the surveillance files.[14]

The reality was that after 20 years of trying to get Canadian permission to emplace defensive nuclear weapons in Canada, the United States Air Force and Navy stayed only two years. All the military and diplomatic effort required through four different governments would result in the United States keeping nuclear weapons for ready forces in place in Newfoundland for only two years. By 1970 it was all over.

The reader will see for the first time the minutes of cabinet and Cabinet Defence Committee meetings in which the storage of nuclear weapons is discussed. Also printed here for the first time, in the Annex, are the agreements and arrangements between Canada and the United States for the storage of both USAF and USN nuclear weapons, and for overflights with nuclear weapons on bombers and interceptors.

Much of the material presented in this book is of a purely documentary nature. Many days, weeks, months, and even years have been spent trying to have secret files opened for examination. For this reason, the text of this work is heavily based on original wording of documents written in the 1940s through 1960s. By using this technique, it is hoped that the feeling of the time in dealing with U.S. nuclear affairs in Canada will be accurately conveyed. Rather than heavily edit their words, I let the authors and their papers speak for themselves. Most of the documents presented here were until recently classified as secret, and many were top secret.

Researchers wishing to continue this important work should find the documents and analysis presented here of great use. What they will also find appealing is that Chapter 9 is devoted to a short discussion of the sources available and the location of sources yet to be fully exploited. I would hope that someday soon a military historian would undertake a comprehensive study of Goose Bay all by itself, and that another would tackle the question of Argentia, and another the radar lines. It is my hope that this work will give people a firm grounding for further exploration of the topics presented.

I am always seeking more information on the subject of nuclear weapons in Canada, whether deployed by the United States Air Force, the United States Navy, the RCAF, the RCN, the Canadian Army, or the Canadian Forces. This continues to be a grey area of Canadian history, and much work needs to be done. If you have any facts or memories or items of interest, I would be most pleased to hear of them.

Lastly, while every effort has been made to ensure that all the facts presented here are accurate and reflected in the documentary record, any mistakes or omissions are entirely the fault of the author. If you have corrections, I would be grateful to receive them and thereby add to our knowledge of Canadian and U.S. nuclear affairs in Canada.

John Clearwater
Ottawa
da710@ncf.ca

Chapter One

CONSULT AND AUTHORIZE

Canadian authorization for the use of nuclear weapons by the United States

The central question in nuclear weapons theory and practice is not how the bomb works, but how the use of the bomb is controlled by those in command and by those who think they are in command. This becomes even more important when the bomb is housed in other than its home country. Because Canada hosted U.S. nuclear weapons for its own forces, for U.S. forces based in Canada, and those flying over Canada, the question of consultation and authorization was especially important. By examining this unique aspect of nuclear history, we are able to learn a great deal about the workings of the U.S. political and military system for controlling the use of nuclear weapons.

Although this book is about U.S. nuclear weapons for U.S. forces which were either based in Canada, temporarily deployed to Canada, or simply flew over Canada, it is impossible to understand the convoluted processes for consultation and authorization by examining only the U.S. side of the equation. Canada was also acquiring the use of U.S. nuclear weapons for various defensive and offensive weapons systems, and the question of consultation and authorization had to be dealt with as laid out in the August 1963 agreement. Because most weapons to be deployed to Canada were for air defence, and because this fell under NORAD control, and as NORAD is a bi-national command, consultation for one automatically became consultation for both. There would then be a spill-over effect when the U.S. Navy moved nuclear anti-submarine weapons to Argentia, as the Canadian government used the older air defence formula as the consultation understanding for the USN. Overflights had a far older history and will be dealt with separately in Chapter 3.

By 1951 Canada already had the experience of the United States operating atomic bombers over Canada, and even of the USAF losing two atomic bombs in Canada. For this reason, the concept of control was important to Ottawa. In January 1951 U.S. President Truman assured Ottawa that the same commitment he made to British prime minister Clement Attlee on consultation would apply to Canada. This meant that Truman would inform both the British and Canadians of any possible use of the atomic bomb. The U.S. Joint Congressional Committee on Atomic Energy insisted that there be no limitation on the U.S. use of the bomb, and therefore the president could commit only to "inform," and not "consult" the chief allies. Even if there was consultation, this in no way implied that the United States required "consent" from Canada.[15] Curiously enough, even though the first experience Canada had of nuclear weapons complicity involved strategic overflights, the focus of negotiations on consultation and authorization would eventually move away from this still important area into the field of air defence.

The Canadian government had insisted that "when the deployment of nuclear components to or over Canadian territory or the use of Canadian bases for actual strikes is involved, [they] required that it be approached on a Government-to-Government basis."[16] The British permission formula was set forth in the joint communique of the Truman-Churchill talks of 09 January 1952 and stated that "the use of these bases in an emergency would be a matter of joint decision ... in light of the circumstances prevailing at the time." On this basis an accommodation was reached under which Canada was extended the same courtesy as the British at the same time.[17]

The issue sat dormant for several years until 1956 when the United States became concerned about the increased capability of the Soviet long-range bomber force and the impact that would have on both air defence and retaliatory forces in North America. The United States, now more than ever concerned about getting the bomber force airborne and off towards the Soviet Union via Canadian air routes, opened discussions with Canada on various alert measures. Through 1956 secret high-level talks, of which little is known, took place on the question of raising alert levels, and by 1957 this had produced an initial agreement.

In March 1957 the Canadian government formally recognized that an occasion may arise where time did not permit consultation.[18] Normally, consultation was to precede alert measures except when either government considered an attack on North America to be imminent or probable in a matter of hours rather than days. In this case, consultation might coincide with or even follow the institution of separate alert measures by either government.[19] However, with air defence forces which were still nominally separate, there were still separate alerts.

The Canadian government thought that separate alerts by either country would soon be a thing of the past, as a joint air defence command, NORAD, was soon to be formed. In talks with the United States, Canada was thinking ahead to a time when there would be a joint command of air defence and wanted to ensure that there would be consultation at the highest level, not command level, and that the only circumstance of importance was one of time.[20] Ottawa wanted consultations at least at the Chiefs of Staff level.[21]

The Canadian request for talks at the Chiefs of Staff level fell flat in Washington. The U.S. military would not allow the consultations to include the Joint Chiefs themselves. Rather, they wanted any agreement to state that talks would be conducted at the "level" of the joint staffs. The military required that the State Department consult the president on the proposal before finalizing it with Canada. Lastly, the military wanted State to take the requisite steps to have appropriate White House emergency action checklists prepared which would reflect the commitment to the Canadian government.[22] Always helpful with civilian affairs, the Pentagon included a draft reply for the State Department incorporating these elements.

In June, Dulles told Eisenhower that the Canadians wanted to ensure a high level of consultation, and that they were looking forward to joint command. Also, only time was a factor in allowing for non-consultation.[23] The document Dulles gave to Eisenhower had all of the long wordy bits from the Pentagon removed.[24] The document was then transmitted to Canada, and it was not well received.

Ottawa was uneasy over the language which it felt implied that high-level consultations would take place after declaration of a national emergency and after civil defence measures. They felt that consultation at that stage might be too late or merely pro forma.[25] The Canadian viewpoint was that for consultation to be genuine it should take place upon receipt of intelligence that a possible attack was imminent and before declaration of a national emergency and civil defence measures. This explained the Canadian interest in high-level consultation at the early stages of world events, and especially before a situation deteriorated to point where the United States felt it was under imminent risk of attack.[26]

Prime Minister John Diefenbaker was long disturbed by the fact that

Canada might have an inadequate voice or no voice at all in setting into motion actions which rendered war in North America inevitable. He therefore believed it was essential for a high-ranking Canadian officer to be placed in a senior position in the USAF or joint air defence headquarters. To this end Air Marshal C.R. (Roy) Slemon, then the chief of the Air Staff, was to be named as the Canadian deputy to the newly formed NORAD command.[27] Slemon would be the eyes and ears of Diefenbaker when it came to controlling how the US used nuclear weapons in and over Canada.

A revolution of sorts had occurred in the air defence realm in 1957. There was now a nuclear air-to-air rocket, and the MB-1 Agreement (discussed in Chapter 2) would soon bring it into Canada onboard USAF fighter-interceptor aircraft. Due to initially restrictive rules, and due to the inherently unsafe nature of the weapon, there was really no chance of carriage over Canada short of actual war. However, by January 1958 the USAF had modified the operational and safety rules to allow USAF fighters to carry the MB-1 under conditions of air defence readiness or higher state of alert. This meant that although the provisions of the MB-1 Agreement applied, the weapon could now be carried upon declaration of air defence warning yellow or red.[28]

This was now becoming a very important topic in Ottawa. In April the chairman of the Chiefs of Staff briefed Cabinet about the machinery for assessing the intelligence relating to a possible attack, and that for communicating with the prime minister and Ministry of National Defence (MND). The prime minister noted that his experience taught him that he could not be reached at many hours of the day and night, and that a full test of all the channels should be done.[29] At this meeting the Cabinet Defence Committee (CDC) approved a letter which, together with previous letters, would form a bilateral interim agreement on consultation prior to alerts.[30] The text has not been declassified; however, it was only a beginning in the Canadian quest for more equitable treatment by the White House and Pentagon in dealing with control of nuclear weapons in and over Canada.

It was a failed experiment, as within months Diefenbaker learned through the press that NORAD had gone on alert during the Lebanon crisis. It seems that the Canadian military had neglected to inform Ottawa of any of the actions taken by the United States which affected the Canadian military with regard to putting Canadian forces on a higher alert.[31] Diefenbaker voiced his opinion that the commander in chief of NORAD (CINC NORAD), General Earle Partridge, might raise the NORAD alert level over the Formosa Strait situation. External

Affairs said they assumed that alerts should be increased only when really necessary, and that if the United States wanted to increase the alert level of a bi-national command, it should consult Canada first unless global thermonuclear war was actually underway.[32]

Given how upset Diefenbaker was at this time, it was probably in the U.S. interest not to tell the prime minister the full details of the powers of the U.S. air defence commander. Ottawa had suspected that CINC NORAD had prior permission from the president to use nuclear weapons, and directly asked if this was true. In the autumn of 1958 Robert Murphy from the State Department declined to tell the Canadian government that the president had already delegated authority to CINC CONAD (Continental Air Defense Command) for the use of nuclear weapons in air defence. This was the same person as CINC NORAD, and Murphy was willing to tell Canadians only that CINC NORAD had no such authority.[33] It was a technical truth concealing a real truth, but it served to quiet Ottawa for a time.

At the urging of the Pentagon, Canada was being kept at a distance from real control. Throughout late 1958 the State Department attempted to water down the Canadian desire for an explicit commitment to consultations in all circumstances. Murphy explained that "under present arrangement, we must assume that [in view of the complete interchange of tactical data between the Air Defense Commands of the two countries], the decision made by both Governments would probably coincide."[34]

Probably was not good enough for a newly resurgent Ottawa, and the negotiations suffered due to U.S. intransigence.

On 15 December 1958 the Canada-U.S. Ministerial Committee on Joint Defence had agreed to parallel civil and military consultations for increasing the NORAD alert over the Berlin situation. In the spring of 1959 Foy Kohler from the State Department asked Saul Rae from External Affairs to bring all of this to the attention of the Canadian government as the United States was now actively considering raising the NORAD alert level. Rae said he would, but cautioned that the Canadian government still felt that CINC NORAD should only be able to increase the level of alert for exercises and real emergencies.[35] Kohler handed over an aide-memoire which read distinctly like an ultimatum.

> The United States Joint Chiefs of Staff have initiated military consultations with the Canadian Chiefs of Staff Committee concerning the question of directing CINCNORAD to increase the operational readiness of his forces in the event

access to Berlin is denied the Western Powers. Therefore, in the interest of ensuring that NORAD forces are properly prepared for any contingency, the United States Government urges the Canadian Government to give early concurrence to increasing the operational readiness of NORAD forces at such time as access to Berlin may be denied the Western Powers.[36]

Within a month Ottawa had decided that there was nothing much that could be done about situations already under way. They agreed to placing NORAD on a prudent higher alert if the Berlin situation deteriorated. However, Ottawa still insisted that Washington undertake consultations with a view to defining the precise conditions under which the Berlin situation would warrant such actions in North America. Ottawa then wished to consult should a defined situation arise.[37] The Canadians were now planning to put in place a system which could be invoked at a future crisis rather than having to manage each crisis separately and with no fixed agreement.

Of course, the U.S. government would not accept the Canadian request for definitions of circumstances, as they stated that these were being worked out by the western powers responsible for Berlin (U.K., France, United States), and would not agree to have parallel definitions with another country. The United States then stated that they would tell the Canadians the outcome of the Berlin talks, but that time would then be short. Washington was hoping that Canada would agree that the alert could be raised without awaiting the outcome of further bilateral political consultations on the over-all situation, "which, of course, [stated Washington] the United States would desire to hold immediately with Canada."[38] Ottawa was not pleased.

The Canadian ambassador in Washington, A.D.P. Heeney, lectured the State Department about the fact that the NORAD treaty called for the fullest possible consultations between the two governments. Ottawa felt that consultation on raising the level of readiness in a period of international tension was highly desirable, especially as this action had a political as well as military significance, especially if during a time of international tensions such military activity could be misinterpreted.[39]

Heeney told State of the Canadian proposal that CINC NORAD be limited in his ability to increase the readiness, as he was "not in a position to assess all the political factors available."[40] This was especially important when factors of overriding political significance were involved. Always a creature of Ottawa, Heeney said that any increase in readiness level would have to have an accompanying public communications plan. In closing, Heeney told State that Ottawa was concerned with the lack of notification given for various events. Cabinet wanted to know, through the Chiefs of Staff, when and where there would be training exercises, as these could potentially cause public relations problems for the government.[41]

Strangely, the United States immediately agreed to the contents of the Heeney proposal and on 2 October 1959 made it a formal agreement.[42] This, along with various other letters of understanding and the MB-1 Agreement, would form the basis for the consultation and authorization agreement of 1965. In the meanwhile, Washington was pushing for more frequent and consistent consultations with various levels of government. Cabinet did not want to establish any more committees which would further isolate them from real information. The discussion therefore went nowhere.[43]

Relations between Diefenbaker in Ottawa, and Eisenhower and later Kennedy in Washington continued to deteriorate. A lack of real willingness to include the Canadian civilian government in the bilateral military affairs of the two countries had completely alienated the Progressive Conservative government of John Diefenbaker. Negotiations slowed to a crawl, only becoming obvious again at the time of the Cuban missile crisis.

In the immediate aftermath of the most serious crisis of the Cold War, External Affairs examined the status of the consultation question. They discovered anew that the wording of the 1 March 1957 and 10 November 1958 exchanges of letters on prior consultation for raising the level of alert stipulated that they "should" consult at both the political and military levels; that it would pertain only to the full-scale alert of the national forces; that each had the right to increase their own alert; and that the alert could be increased without consultation due to a time factor of pressing international urgency.[44] The agreements seem to have been designed with situations such as the Berlin crisis or a direct attack on NATO in mind. The situation in Cuba did not fit in well, and this would be a problem.[45]

Central to the problem was the fact that the Canadian military had been placed on a higher alert by the United States military command, without the knowledge or concurrence of Cabinet. External Affairs concluded that the United States had no real obligation to consult with Canada during the Cuban missile crisis. "It seems that this agreement [embodied in the exchange of notes in 1959] is not entirely applicable to the Cuban situation insofar as the agreement was designed to provide for consultation in a period of increasing international tension. Emphasis also appears to have been laid on the responsibility of the respective national

Chiefs of Staff, in consultations with their respective political authorities, to reach agreement for increasing states of readiness for NORAD forces. Insofar as a request was made to Canada through military channels to increase the state of readiness of NORAD forces, it might possibly be argued that the United States had fulfilled its obligation under the agreement."[46]

The supplemental classified exchange of letters in January 1960 between the embassy and the U.S. State Department provided for consultation channels both military and civilian. The civilian channel was to be between the Canadian embassy and the U.S. State Department Bureau of European Affairs, or if more urgent, direct telephone contact between External Affairs in Ottawa and the U.S. State Department in Washington.[47]

In the spring of 1963 the Diefenbaker Tories were defeated by the Pearson Liberals with the assistance of the public relations firm which worked for the Kennedy White House. Although Kennedy no longer had to deal with Diefenbaker, the problem of consultation would not go away even with the far more accommodating Pearson government. Kennedy asked General Gerhardt, CINC NORAD, "if short of DefCon 1, the prime minister could withhold permission for Canadian units to observe, for example, DefCon 3 or DefCon 2." CINC NORAD told Kennedy that the prime minister was "not supposed to" do so. Gerhardt said that prior to DefCon 1 he would propose to consult both governments through his military channels of the U.S. Joint Chiefs of Staff and the Canadian Combined Chiefs of Staff.[48] It was this channel which had caused the troubles during the Cuban crisis.

Nuclear warheads for the Bomarc air defence missiles arrived in Canada beginning on 31 December 1963, and as a result of what was characterized in Ottawa as their "sudden arrival," there was an increased need for a consultation agreement. There were three weeks between the initial arrival and the Lester Pearson-Lydon Johnson summit meeting in Washington, and External Affairs proposed that Pearson and Johnson take note of an interim arrangement to cover the operational use of these weapons in a situation of surprise attack, provided that it could be completed by the time of the meeting.[49] External Affairs concluded that it would be wise to leave the comprehensive agreement negotiations in abeyance and to work on the interim arrangement in order to get some control over the U.S. weapons in Canada.

The two exchanges of notes in August and September 1963 had provided for the storage and operation of nuclear weapons by both U.S. and Canadian forces when authorized by both governments, but neither dealt with how or in what circumstances this would be done. Both countries' forces in Canada represented elements of the same problem, as they were all air defence forces under the unified NORAD command, and under the operational control of CINC NORAD.[50] Had there not been these two agreements, there would have been little need for Washington to extend any more than token consultation to Ottawa. However, with nuclear weapons now to be based on Canadian soil, the need was great indeed.

Secretary of state for External Affairs Paul Martin had been informed that the White House thought the procedural arrangements for consultation might be a good subject for talks between the prime minister and president at their upcoming summit. Martin played it down to Pearson, saying there was no time to prepare a position. However, Martin did tell Pearson that the recent unexpected arrival of the Bomarc warheads made the requirement for interim procedures more urgent. This was to be worked out between External Affairs and National Defence, and it might be ready for the prime minister to discuss with President Johnson.[51]

In Washington the White House was becoming more and more involved due to increased Canadian interest and willingness to work together. Johnson expressed his desire to personally "consult further with Pearson to make certain that the PM knew all about DefCon 1 and the like."[52] The president was advised to tell Pearson of his desire to discuss these matters after the negotiations progressed further. The White House National Security staff concluded that this would demonstrate presidential interest in this very important matter as well as a sympathetic concern for the interests of the prime minister. It would also alert the highest levels of the Canadian government to the fact that the negotiations were under way.[53]

The 14 March 1964 Lyndon Johnson letter to Lester Pearson was meant to be reassuring, while not conveying much information.

> I have been reviewing proposals put forward by our Department of Defense concerning the detailed procedures for the control of nuclear weapons assigned in support of NORAD air defense units in Canada, and I have asked Secretary McNamara to inform our General Gerhardt at NORAD that he should initiate discussions with your government on this subject.[54]
>
> I send you this note so that you will be sure to know of the initiation of these discussions, even though in their initial phases they will probably proceed at a military level. Later on, when the discussions are further advanced and you have had

an opportunity to inform yourself on the matter, I think it might be helpful for the two of us to have a discussion on procedures themselves and on any needful arrangements for intergovernmental consultation before their adoption.[55]

What had happened in Washington was that Johnson had approved in principle the release of nuclear weapons from U.S. custody to Canadian fighter units under conditions of surprise attack or upon the declaration of DefCon 1 or higher. Secretary of Defense Robert McNamara was now to authorize General Gerhardt, CINC NORAD, to negotiate procedures with the Canadian Air Defence Command and Chiefs of Staff to govern the operational use of nuclear weapons in the Canadian NORAD regions. In Washington, all higher consultation arrangements would be personally reviewed by Johnson.[56] As the National Security staff noted for LBJ, "Given the legal and constitutional significance of this matter, it seems desirable to have the memorandum signed by you."[57]

In Canada, similar provisions were being made by the Minister of National Defence, Paul Hellyer. On 16 March 1964, Hellyer issued interim instruction on authorization for the use of NORAD nuclear weapons, apparently without telling the rest of Cabinet that he had done so or of the contents of the instructions. The gist of the interim instruction was that prior authorization for the use of nuclear weapons by NORAD forces was given in an emergency. This was defined as an event "where warheads have impacted or where there is other clear and unmistakable evidence that an attack against the North American region has been launched."[58] This action by Hellyer and his staff would come back to haunt the negotiators during the final phases of the talks on the 1965 agreement.

External Affairs and National Defence had each prepared their own draft agreements which External Affairs would then use and form into one negotiating text. However, the DND draft was "not entirely satisfactory," as it was in technical form exploring the problem and not written as an agreement.[59] In the end, only the 4 May 1964 External Affairs draft was used. This document formed the solid basis for the final agreement and remained little changed over the next year. The Canadian draft agreement was to supplement but not nullify existing arrangements.

Meetings were to be held by senior political and military officials twice a year. In a rapidly developing situation in which a meeting was not possible, either party could initiate talks by telephone: this would be known as "emergency consultation."[60] Rapid and reliable systems for communication would be provided which would allow the simultaneous consultation of the prime minister, the president, the secretary of state for External Affairs, the U.S. secretary of state, the minister of National Defence, the U.S. secretary of Defense, and the two chairmen of the two Chiefs of Staff.

The Canadian position was that CINC NORAD should not be able to increase the state of readiness or release nuclear weapons until after consultation had taken place. However, there were exceptions to this rule. If an attack seemed imminent within hours, consultation might coincide with or follow an increased alert. The government increasing the alert was to promptly inform the other government of the action.[61] In reality this meant the United States would inform Canada, not the other way around.

While an increase to the highest state of alert and the release of nuclear weapons was not within the authority of either government alone (according to the Canadian government), circumstances might make this untenable. CINC NORAD's terms of reference and the exchanges of letters of 30 September and 2 October 1959, and of 11 January and 14 January 1960, governing the increase in alert status, were therefore reaffirmed, so the alert level could be increased without prior consultation.[62]

The draft was promptly sent to Washington for the embassy to show to the State Department.[63] Although the draft annexes were not yet finished, Ottawa hoped to send a team to Washington on about 21 May 1964 for further discussion with the U.S. side. Back in External Affairs there was a discussion about the need for the annexes and the relevance of the prior arrangements. Ross Campbell, the chief negotiator and assistant undersecretary of state for External Affairs, wanted a text which would specifically supersede some of the older agreements. However, this was not possible to do, as it would have meant incorporating all the prior language in the new agreement.[64]

Since the Canadian embassy in Washington was intimately involved with the negotiations, Ottawa took seriously any comments. The embassy suggested that the final agreement be signed by the prime minister and president. This would give it a much higher profile in official Washington. Such a move could serve Canadian interests by increasing the likelihood that the terms of the agreement would be brought to the attention of a wide number of senior U.S. officials. The embassy commented in a telex to Ottawa that "there is some evidence that at time of [the] Cuban crisis White House officials were not repeat not aware of existing arrangements with Canada for consultation prior to any increase in NORAD states of readiness."[65]

In addition, the embassy pointed out that it would be wise to remove reference that an objective of the regular consultations was to consider and to coordinate possible courses of action. This was because Canada might still wish to distance itself from certain U.S. actions such as those over Cuba, and especially in Indo-China as Canada was on the supervisory commission. They instead suggested that it be reworded to make the purpose an exchange of ideas and information, rather than coordination.[66]

The 19 to 20 May meeting never happened as there was no time for preparation. The following week was also no good due to the visit of the UN secretary general to Ottawa, so External Affairs aimed for 2 to 3 June.[67] Kirkwood at External worked out a lower-level meeting between himself and Cameron and Sheffield for Canada, and Barrett, the State Department desk officer for Canada, and other U.S. representatives on 27 May. This allowed administrative matters to be handled prior to the higher-level meeting headed by Campbell on 1 and 4 June.[68] All indications at this early date were that the State Department was positive about the Canadian drafts.[69]

The 27 May meeting in Washington was an important marker on the road to an agreement. The Canadian team was Kirkwood, Cameron, Shannon, Van Camp, and G/C Shaw. The U.S. team was headed by Barrett. The Canadian team started off by stressing that the authorization to CINC NORAD to use nuclear weapons operationally should apply throughout his command without distinction of nationality or location of forces concerned, and should come on a basis of equality from the prime minister and president.[70]

> The problem of substance concerned the definition of the circumstances constituting a surprise attack, a matter essential to the whole concept. The philosophy underlying that language [Canadian draft paragraph 4,V(d)] that, broadly speaking, prior authorization should be limited to situations involving actual or anticipated massive attack upon North America was not accepted by the US side. They wanted a definition so phrased as to leave much broader discretionary authority to CINCNORAD to deal as he saw fit with a sudden risk of attack in almost any form on North America. They pointed out that this is in fact what applies under the MB-1 Agreement, and it emerged in discussion that it is also embodied in Mr. Hellyer's "interim procedure" where the definition is "an emergency where warheads have impacted or where there is other clear and unmistakable evidence that an attack against the North American region has been launched."[71]

At this point the Hellyer interim arrangement came back to bite External Affairs. The team found it a little embarrassing to indicate that they were unable to accept the approach embodied in the interim instructions and the MB-1 Agreement. The team said that it was doubtful whether the prime minister would be prepared to give prior authorization on such terms or indeed perhaps in any terms not primarily dealing with massive or general strategic attack. They had to state that the Hellyer note was a purely temporary document meant to meet an urgent operational need. Kirkwood then told the State Department that as far as he knew it had never been endorsed by Cabinet."[72] At this point the U.S. side was now concerned that Canada might propose amending the MB-1 Agreement so as to restrict CINC NORAD's discretionary authority.[73] This was an issue which would have to await the higher-level meetings.

Although Paul Martin and Paul Hellyer had agreed to a renewal of the MB-1 Agreement for another year as of 1 July 1964, External Affairs now felt that this should not be communicated to the United States, as it could be used as a bargaining chip.[74] But the bargaining chip was only useful if there was a document on the table. By the end of May, Ottawa had provided the embassy in Washington with a new draft based on the administrative negotiations on 27 May.[75]

The question of prior authorization and the circumstances which would constitute an emergency were central to the Canadian team's position in the negotiations. Ross Campbell was told that there was no precise and formal definition of the circumstances under which CINC NORAD could declare DefCon 1.[76] "The restriction on CINC NORAD's authority to act on his own responsibility rested on the possibility of consultation and hence that when consultation was not possible the restriction did not apply."[77] Earlier exchanges of letters established that the Chiefs of Staff would consult with the MND, secretary of state for External Affairs and prime minister prior to a decision to raise the alert: however, this was based on there being time for such consultations.

CINC NORAD already had the authority from both governments to declare DefCon 1 on his own responsibility in an emergency, using his own judgement of what constituted an emergency. The problem Canada faced was of a U.S. domestic system of alert which had been rolled over into NORAD. "By virtue of its acceptance for NORAD, and the terms of the MB-1 Agreement, CINC NORAD's judgement that an emergency exists is legally sufficient to permit US interceptors to carry nuclear warheads over Canada under agreed rules of engagement and to land at, or take off from, Canadian bases."[78]

Campbell wrote Air Chief Marshal F.R. Miller a detailed memo explaining the problems and various aspects of the negotiations.[79] He wrote that the MB-1 Agreement provided that under DefCon 1 U.S.-based NORAD interceptors could enter Canadian airspace with nuclear weapons and use Canadian facilities. That agreement said nothing about authorization for the use of nuclear weapons, and it was left to the U.S. national mechanism. What this meant was that CINC NORAD could raise the alert on his own authority in an emergency, and the term emergency was not defined.[80] A 1963 agreement between Canada and the United States, the Goose Bay and Harmon agreement, provided for use of these nuclear weapons only when authorized by both governments. However, the aircraft could take off under orders from CINC NORAD armed with nuclear weapons. External Affairs desired that Paul Hellyer's interim instruction of 16 March 1964 be superseded as soon as possible.[81]

The U.S. position was that CINC NORAD would probably only have to use nuclear weapons in a situation of general and massive attack, and that CINC NORAD should have a broad enough latitude of action to allow for use against single targets. It was the option under the broad latitude which might not allow time for consultation. The U.S. side felt that a single aircraft might be the spearhead of a general assault and that as this would not be immediately clear, it would be better to use nuclear weapons from the very beginning just in case. Campbell and his team again responded that prior authorization should apply only in situations of actual or imminent general attack, and that there should be restrictions on any nuclear response to local or accidental intrusions.[82]

Miller was told that this fundamental difference of opinion meant that Canada may well have to define on its own the concept of surprise attack for the purpose of prior authorization. This would lead to a situation in which NORAD would no longer respond regardless of nationality or geography, but be hampered with two different operational requirements. This would also mean revising the MB-1 Agreement. It could also affect the way in which the USAF forces in Goose Bay and Harmon could be used, as there would be different rules for U.S. forces in the United States and those in Canada. This format would also be a retreat from the Hellyer instructions. Campbell noted that this would also demonstrate a lack of confidence in the responsibility and restraint which might be shown by CINC NORAD in times of emergency.[83] He said that it would be best to define it in a way mutually acceptable, thus permitting an international response by CINC NORAD. However, a definition acceptable to the United States would of course be more than Canada might wish. What

Campbell therefore hoped to do was append a cautionary passage asserting that authority was tempered with moderation: "Therefore, the utmost restraint and with full cognizance of the dangers of hasty or unnecessary resort to nuclear weapons, must be exercised in dealing with situations which might prove to be local or accidental."[84]

The letter went on to offer the External Affairs definition of an emergency situation: a surprise attack in force or unequivocal evidence that such an attack had begun. Such an attack would have multiple missiles on trajectories ending in North America, and/or multiple bomber tracks heading for the region. In addition, clear evidence of multiple launches and/or take-offs would suffice. It could also mean several nuclear bursts in the region of unknown origin within the space of a few minutes. Proper information from NATO or a major U.S. command that it had come under nuclear attack would also suffice. Lastly, Campbell proposed to say that an emergency could also be defined as "any circumstances which in CINC NORAD's judgement involve a clear and present danger of imminent attack upon one or more important targets in North America, in which delay might seriously prejudice the defence of Canada or the United States."[85] External Affairs proposed that this definition be added to the CINC NORAD terms of reference to show the precise definition on which he could act to raise the alert to DefCon 1. It would also have the additional advantage of tying the MB-1 Agreement into the new proposed general agreement.[86]

The higher-level meeting was finally held on 9 June in Washington, and the new U.S. proposal was that:

> neither USA authority for release nor authorization for use of nuclear weapons allocated to NORAD forces [in Canada] by the Canadian and USA Governments will be effected except in emergency circumstances or upon declaration of Defense Condition one (strategic attack against North America is imminent) or Air Defense Emergency (strategic attack against North America is occurring), as indicated in 7(c) and (d) below. In the case of the need for use arising suddenly in emergency circumstances as set forth in (d) below, it is agreed that the President of the USA will provide for the timely release of nuclear weapons to Canadian NORAD forces, and that the Prime Minister, acting on behalf of the Government of Canada, and the President will provide timely authorization to employ operationally nuclear armed NORAD forces (based or deployed

in Canada), including the flight in Canadian airspace of USA
air defense weapons carrying nuclear warheads.

The U.S. team had not been impressed with the restrictive wording
on the freedom of action for U.S. forces under NORAD contained in the
Canadian draft. They proposed to add a paragraph stating that "national
elements previously committed to NORAD shall be exempt from the
provisions of this agreement" in cases of national need.[87]

The root of the problem was a basic disagreement between Canada and
the United States as to whether the agreement should apply to NORAD as
a whole (Canadian position), or apply only to the Canadian regions of
NORAD (U.S. position).[88] Ottawa's position was that an agreement be
based on the idea that a single authorization process should apply
throughout NORAD. Canadian agreement was linked to acceptance of
this concept by the United States, which was inherent in the NORAD
agreement but which could not be brought to full realization until the 16
August 1963 agreement removed the differences in weapons systems
available to the two national components of NORAD.[89]

Despite the significant theoretical clash, Paul Martin went to the
Cabinet with a proposal to initial the draft agreement at the forthcoming
summer 1964 meeting of the Canada-United States Ministerial Committee
on Joint Defence. At this time it was thought that the prime minister and
president would later meet and together agree on the form of the final
document.[90] He told the Cabinet Committee on External Affairs about the
provisions of the draft and said that he would later ask Cabinet for
permission to sign the final agreement.[91] As Martin explained, the
Canadian draft provided a single system of consultative arrangements and
operational procedures applicable to NORAD as a single integrated
command. "Hitherto NORAD has been regarded as a joint command for
certain purposes, but for others, when it has been convenient to the U.S. it
has been used in practice very much as if it were an institution at the direct
disposal of the U.S. Government."[92] The problem with this position was
that "we still have no assurance that the basic concept embodied in the
Agreement, namely, that a single set of rules should apply throughout the
entire NORAD command, is acceptable to the US Joint Chiefs of Staff,
who were to consider this matter yesterday."[93]

The State Department and Pentagon had trouble with the wording,
especially as they considered their Alaska forces to be a totally separate
operation from NORAD. They pointed out that those aircraft regularly flew
with nuclear weapons sometimes under DefCon 5, and that these weapons

could have been used immediately.[94] The response from Washington was just a little looser than the Canadian wording, allowing greater latitude to CINC NORAD in raising alert levels and employing nuclear weapons. In the U.S. view, consultation would be done when there was time, and if there was no time then the president and prime minister would provide timely authorization for the use of these forces and weapons.[95]

By the end of June 1964, the final nail had been driven into the Canadian concept by the U.S. Joint Chiefs of Staff (JCS). The U.S. JCS had declined to approve the equality and reciprocity concepts underlying the draft agreement.[96] The Pentagon was determined to maintain the existing practice in which there was dual responsibility in Canada alone, while the United States continued to exercise complete unilateral freedom.[97] This was not a problem of wording, but a matter of principle. The United States had never played well with others or considered that international relations should be a level playing field. The joint chiefs simply would not accept a situation in which Canada became involved in the air defence questions of the United States, even though the opposite was already true. The JCS said that it would have to be resolved at the ministerial level on 25 June 1964. The JCS wanted the agreement worded to reflect a situation in which the United States and Canada consulted and authorized forces in Canada alone, while leaving other U.S. forces completely out of the picture. This intransigence may be a reflection of the failure of talks on dispersal of fighters to Canada (see Chapter 3) and basing of United States Navy anti-submarine warfare (ASW) weapons at Argentia (see Chapter 8).[98]

Because this was completely inconsistent with the NORAD concept as an integrated command jointly responsible to both governments, Pearson and Martin chose to direct Ross Campbell to again make the case for a single regime governing NORAD forces. The new agreement would supersede the MB-1 Agreement and the Hellyer interim instruction. If it was impossible, it would be referred to the prime minister and the president.[99] However, before the matter could be discussed by the Campbell team, Paul Martin would personally try to sell it to U.S. Secretary of State Dean Rusk at the 25 June ministerial meeting.

This was the first joint ministerial meeting in four years, as the animosity between Kennedy and Diefenbaker was unequalled in modern Canada-U.S. relations. With the negotiations stalled over the philosophical difference,[100] it was hoped that the ministers themselves could break the deadlock. The actual discussions within the meeting are still classified 35 years later. However, the State Department record of the meeting was partially declassified, and the severed parts are currently under appeal.[101]

The meeting did prompt the U.S. side to produce and present another draft of the problem section. U.S. Deputy Assistant Secretary of Defense W. Lang presented an informal proposal which he hoped could help bridge the gap between the Canadian and U.S. positions.

> CINC NORAD is authorized to employ nuclear weapons in accordance with his agreed terms of reference and his other agreed procedures. The two Governments recognize the limitations of the United States Atomic Energy Act regarding the transfer of nuclear weapons. The President will take such steps as may be necessary, acting within his Constitutional powers as Commander-in-Chief to authorize military action in emergencies, to make nuclear weapons available for employment by Canadian units under operational control of CINC NORAD in emergency circumstances or upon the declaration of Defense Condition one or higher state of readiness. Similarly, the Prime Minister shall take such steps as may be necessary to authorize the United States units equipped with nuclear weapons to be employed under the operational control of CINC NORAD in Canadian territory, including its airspace, under the emergency circumstances or upon the declaration of Defense Condition one or higher state of readiness.[102]

As the talks had progressed as far as they could without ministerial-level decisions, the embassy in Washington simply delivered the draft to Ottawa and requested a swift response,[103] as the United States had requested that talks resume on 9 July.[104] Campbell immediately asked the chiefs' views.[105]

Ottawa had rejected the Lang wording as being too vague and still allowing the complete and one-sided actions which the United States was then exercising over Canada, and which were contrary to the Canadian understanding of the spirit of the NORAD agreement.[106] External Affairs worked through Canada Day, then known as Dominion Day, to produce the response, and it was delivered to Washington on 3 July. Ottawa specifically spelled out the "national option procedure" which included the references to NORAD as having forces from both countries, but noting that situations might arise in which the vital interests of only one party were at stake, and in this case there would be a national use of forces without the participation of the other. Nuclear use was to be authorized by the president and confirmed for forces in Canada by the prime minister. This authorization could be provided prior to the event for use in case of emergencies. The text then delineates what constitutes emergency circumstances. The last section outlines that there might be hostilities in North America involving only one party and not involving a strategic attack on the continent. In this case, each would retain command of their own forces.[107] The document was in the hands of the State Department by 6 July.

In the week following the Canadian decision on the redraft of the contentious section, Ross Campbell's team rewrote the entire proposed agreement. The 10 July 1964 redraft of the proposed Canadian Note on Consultation and Authorization became the standard working document and would form the basis, with few changes, of the final agreement. The complete text is reproduced in Annex D at the back of this book. That day the teams gathered at the State Department in Washington to work out the final details.

Canada was represented by the able Ross Campbeil and Arthur Menzies from External Affairs, and Air Commodore Austin and Group Captain Sheffield from the RCAF. The U.S. team consisted of W.R. Tyler (assistant secretary of state for European Affairs), W. Lang (deputy assistant secretary of Defense), R.H. Davis (deputy assistant secretary of state for European Affairs), H.R. Brandon and R.J. Barrett (Canadian Desk), and J.C. Trippe (Legal Advisor's Office). Tyler opened the meeting by stating that the central question touched on some of the most sensitive areas in United States constitutional practice and that the White House had taken a close interest.[108] The U.S. side wanted to avoid having a situation in print in which it appeared that the two countries might pursue separate directions in air defence in North America.

Campbell pointed out that with the acquisition of nuclear weapons by the RCAF, there was no longer a distinction and that NORAD had to now be treated as a whole, not as two regions. This did not mean that Canada desired total unity of responsibility but was rather interested in a more unified concept of single command with involvement of both governments. The preferred method was to spell out in some detail the circumstances which would be required to allow raising the alert or using nuclear weapons. As he pointed out, more detail on agreed procedure meant less briefing of Cabinet on the internal workings of the U.S. system of command and control.[109]

Lang said he felt that the Canadian side was concerned over possible insufficient control over nuclear use by CINC NORAD, so he had reviewed the controls and found them to be stringent. He did not want it to sound as if there were two classes of citizenship in the NORAD family or that there was the possibility of divergent responses during a crisis.[110] Campbell responded that only the U.S. president could authorize the use of nuclear weapons, as Canada had none. It was their responsibility to protect the interests of the prime minister who would have to provide permission in case of an attack. The United States then tried to put off the discussion, but Campbell said that this was the heart of the unresolved portion of the agreement, and he would be distressed if it was left until later. He pointed out that it was necessary to have a clear understanding on both sides of the relative and respective responsibilities as had been shown during the Cuban missile crisis. Campbell went on to mention that the president had expressed a desire to meet with Pearson, and that they would have to finish the draft before this could happen.[111]

Prior to the 1963 agreements, CINC NORAD could order nuclear armed aircraft into Canada and the president could authorize nuclear use. Under the 1963 agreement, the use of the weapons over Canada required the prior authorization of the prime minister .[112] The need created by the 1963 agreement had been filled by the Canadian paragraph 7, which was intended solely as descriptive, while paragraph 8 was to define the means of approaching DefCon 1 by either consultation or through emergency circumstances. The U.S. team had completely misunderstood this distinction and interpreted paragraph 7 as being substantive rather than descriptive.[113] Changes to paragraph 7 turned it from descriptive to substantive by adding an "including" clause to the end.

The United States was using the term "timely" to refer to prior permission. Campbell wanted to call "prior" permission for the use of nuclear weapons what it was, instead of the U.S. euphemism. Both wordings would remain in active use, although the official wording became the U.S.-preferred "timely." Another wording problem arose over the Canadian unwillingness to refer to paragraph 9 as an escape clause. The term was to be "national defence clause." Eventually it was moved and gained a new header, but retained the Canadian wording.[114] With this "Mr. Campbell remarked in conclusion that there now appeared to be no remaining obstacles to making the final agreement on this subject."[115]

Ross Campbell was very wrong in stating that there was no remaining obstacle to the finalization of the agreement. Within a month, the Pentagon had agreed and sent the document to the White House for presidential approval. However, there was no time for a decision with the presidential election looming, and the latest crisis in Viet Nam occupying all the White House time.[116] "It was now highly unlikely that the White House would consider the draft before the November election. This did not mean a rejection, only a delay. This was communicated verbally, as U.S. officials would have a difficult time in explaining on paper why there was to be at least a three month delay."[117] Mr. Brubeck of the White House said that the president would be reluctant to authorize anything before the elections because of recent Goldwater statements on defence issues.[118] The process now came to a complete halt, even as nuclear weapons were being introduced into Canada for both U.S. and Canadian forces.

Each side now awaited the outcome of the White House review. Pearson was told that they were awaiting the personal review by Johnson, but that this would not happen until after the election, so in the interests of courtesy Pearson was to refrain from mentioning it.[119] Johnson was told by Dean Rusk that Pearson might raise the subject of the draft as Ottawa was awaiting the White House response. Rusk advised Johnson to assure Pearson that the matter was under urgent consideration.[120]

Immediately after Johnson was again sworn in as U.S. president, R.J. Barret from the State Department delivered a new set of concerns to the Canadian embassy. While the draft text was acceptable to all departments and offices involved, the United States wanted to add four points of clarification.[121] They wanted the Canadians to review the points and suggest the format in which they should be included.

1. Nothing in the agreement was intended to limit CINC NORAD in conducting exercises.
2. Consultations with CINC NORAD would be conducted through the normal operational channels of the Chiefs of Staff and the Joint Chiefs of Staff.
3. Measures of a precautionary nature included the dispersal and conduct of identification missions by U.S. aircraft carrying nuclear weapons in U.S. airspace.
4. The freedom of action of either government to take unilateral action extended to all situations short of an actual strategic attack responded to by NORAD.

In addition to the four points, Barrett also noted that the MB-1 Agreement was to expire on 31 January and asked that consideration be given to a one- or two-month extension.[122] Martin recommended to MND that the MB-1 Agreement be extended by two months. The previous extension had been for four months instead of the standard six in order to keep up the momentum of the negotiations.[123] External Affairs was now putting on the pressure to move quickly to the endgame.

Marcel Cadieux, under-secretary of state at External Affairs, asked for the DND view on the four points and said that they would have a meeting with the U.S. team to determine the actual nature of the items. Ottawa was concerned that the four points might conceal a hidden agenda which Canada would find difficult.[124] Air Marshal Miller replied that DND saw nothing odd, and he hoped that the agreement could be quickly signed as the MB-1 Agreement was to terminate on 31 March, and the CF-101 squadrons would be approaching operational readiness.[125] Ottawa therefore told the embassy that the language seemed acceptable, but as it was general, Ottawa was unsure of the actual meaning and wished the embassy to look into it. Additionally, Pearson and Martin wanted the agreement to be an exchange of letters and to be signed by the Canadian ambassador and the U.S. secretary of state in Washington.[126]

Quick discussions with Washington revealed that the new points were to ensure that CINC NORAD was not interfered with in conducting current exercises. The U.S. side pointed out that CINC NORAD and the USAF held operational readiness exercises where USAF forces under the operational control of CINC NORAD actually carried nuclear weapons or moved them from one place to another.[127] This was acceptable to Ottawa, and Cadieux recommended to Paul Martin that he and Hellyer present the draft agreement at the Cabinet Committee meeting within a week, even though it is not on the official agenda. "In my view, and in that of the Defence Staff, it amounts to a very satisfactory solution to one of the principal problems in implementing the nuclear agreements."[128]

With all the seemingly loose ends tied up, Paul Martin prepared to inform Cabinetof the results of the negotiations and to seek their approval to sign the agreement. He first brought it to the Cabinet Defence Committee and gained their approval .[129] On the advise of Basil Robinson, information for the full Cabinet was kept purposefully brief and the full memo was not circulated in advance. The full Cabinet would be briefed only on the larger memo, and they would not be shown the draft agreement.[130]

Martin explained the thrust of the draft agreement and set out the history of the talks and formulation of the document. He then explained the provisions of the agreement, concentrating on the procedures for consultation and authorization in the cases of a gradual build-up of tension or a sudden attack.[131] External Affairs wanted the agreement to apply throughout NORAD, and the United States refused to consider this. This explained the national defence clause. The United States wanted it to apply only for forces in or over Canada, while the Canadian side saw no reason for this, and insisted that as NORAD was a bi-national command the provisions of the agreement applied to both parties throughout the command. The problem was that Canada had discovered that NORAD was used for U.S. control of Canadian activities, while there was no analogous Canadian input to U.S. activities. This was the way the United States wanted it.[132]

The crux of the Canadian argument and position was tied up in the question of the applicability of NORAD rules to NORAD as a whole. The U.S. position was that what was Canadian was NORAD-controlled, and what was U.S. was U.S.-controlled. There was no inherent reason for this, since the nuclear weapons would be used by both forces, and since NORAD was supposed to be a joint command. "To accept an agreement applicable to forces stationed or operating in Canada only would have involved an acceptance by Canada that NORAD operations in the USA were matters for US determination alone. Acceptance of such a distinction would have vitiated the basis on which NORAD was established, and would have been extremely difficult to explain to the Canadian public should that ever become necessary."[133]

Prior authorization was a problem because they would have to define the circumstances under which it could be used, and the U.S. side was initially unwilling to do so. The agreement adequately does this, and provides for the prime minister and president to issue prior authorizations to CINC NORAD for use in emergency circumstances as defined in the agreement.[134]

Before asking for Cabinet approval of the agreement, the secretary of state for External Affairs asked for permission to send a small fact-finding team to Washington to seek information about the arrangements for consultation between the United States and other governments.[135] Some members had doubts about the desirability of signing an agreement at this point, but all agreed that it would have to eventually be done. Martin pointed out that the essential merit of the agreement was that it gave the prime minister the same political authority as the U.S. president over the use of nuclear weapons, as far as Canadian NORAD forces were concerned.[136] Cabinet gave its approval on 23 March 1965[137]: Ottawa told the embassy to proceed with the State Department to prepare to finalize and sign the agreement.[138]

The only last-minute change was that the State Department wished to add all of the prior notes to the end of the agreement as an annex.[139]

This was acceptable to Ottawa, and the State Department continued seeking an appropriate signing date. In Ottawa the governor general signed order in council No. 595 on 1 April allowing the draft document to be signed by Ambassador Charles Ritchie or George Kidd of the Canadian embassy in Washington.

The final agreement on the procedures to be followed for the authorization of the use of nuclear weapons in the NORAD theatre of military operations came on 17 September 1965, when Canada's ambassador to the United States signed the note. There is no public copy of the signed document. In Washington, R.C. Bowman of the National Security Council wrote to McGeorge Bundy, the National Security Council advisor to President Johnson, "Today is the day of jubilee! The notes of the nuclear agreement with Canada were exchanged this morning. Please sign the attached memorandum delivering Presidential authorizations to the Department of Defense."[140] The extremely secret world of prior authorization for the use of nuclear weapons was again on the president's desk.

PRIOR AUTHORIZATION

The very idea of the prior permission for the use of the ultimate weapon goes to the heart of the question of constitutional chain of command in the United States. The public has always been told that only the president carried the constitutional authority to order the use of nuclear weapons, and this was always phrased in such a way as to indicate that this permission would be given immediately before any use. In reality, permission had often been granted either early in a crisis such as the Kennedy orders over Berlin, or as part of general preparedness of Continental Air Defense Command and NORAD. With the weapons now stationed in Canada for both U.S. and Canadian forces, the question of prior permission had to be dealt with by the prime minister.

As the consultation and authorization agreement neared fruition, the secretary of state for External Affairs was told that President Johnson intended to tell Pearson on an informal and personal basis of the nature of his understanding with CINC NORAD so that the prime minister could take this into consideration in drafting his own understanding. The deputy minister told the secretary of state for External Affairs that if the understanding was written, the Canadian one should also be in written format.[141] The Canadian embassy in Washington was instructed to find out what the State Department thought about a summit meeting, as the agreement could not be signed until after the prime minister and president had met to discuss prior authorization.[142]

The problem now was that part of the negotiated settlement required that Johnson meet with Pearson for this personal talk. However, there was no time in the immediate future for such an activity prior to the planned signing of the agreement. The State Department was now looking for an interim arrangement for the provision of authority passing from the prime minister to CINC NORAD as set out in paragraph 8(b). The State Department suggested that the prime minister could tell CINC NORAD that the terms were in the process of being drafted, and as part of this process the prime minister would speak with the president soon. Pending this final outcome, the United States suggested that the prime minister give CINC NORAD the same authorization to use nuclear weapons operationally in emergency circumstances as was now given by the president. This would create a situation of symmetry of instructions to CINC NORAD.[143]

Due to the timing difficulties, and because it was becoming obvious that the agreement was not to be signed immediately, the MB-1 Agreement was extended "from March 31 for a further period" pending the entry into force of the new agreement.[144] Paul Martin had to tell Cabinet that the agreement would not be brought into force until the prime minister had met with the president and discussed the form of timely authorization to CINC NORAD to use in the event of a surprise attack.[145]

In the end, Pearson never met with Johnson on this topic, and finally the agreement was simply signed to prevent the unguided situation from continuing any longer. Pearson and Johnson both provided the required permissions to CINC NORAD. A memo from the summer of 1967 notes that "in the case of imminent attack, it has been agreed that the PM and President will grant authority to CINC NORAD without consultation."[146]

This was an extremely sensitive topic, and the military cautioned that all references to prior authorization in any public affairs communications plan be stricken. "Its public release could cause an airing of the question of prior authorization"[147] which was desired by neither Cabinet nor the White House. As will be seen in later chapters, this was only one example of the Canadian government's fetish for secrecy as far as their complicity with the U.S. nuclear infrastructure and operations was concerned.

In Washington, the State Department, Pentagon and National Security Council (NSC) staff were working on a prior authorization document. The State Department felt that since the agreement included reference to prior authorizations, these should be worked out before the agreement was signed. The memo and drafts were then provided to U.S. Ambassador-at-Large Tommy Thompson to send to J.T. John McNaughton, assistant secretary of Defense for international security affairs at the Pentagon. These would remain extremely sensitive and secret documents until the late 1990s; "however, the Presidentially approved authorizations would be shown informally to the Canadians to enable them to complete internal [text fragment missing from released copy]."[148] By June Thompson (State) had told McNaughton (secretary of Defence) that the State Department had prepared a draft memo for McGeorge Bundy (NSC) to give to the president. The State Department also prepared to draft authorizations for the president to sign and give to CINC NORAD and CINCONAD.[149]

In order to keep Canada at arm's length and to not reveal too much of the shady world of prior authorization, the State Department drafted two slightly different prior authorizations for Johnson to give to CINC NORAD and CINCONAD, who were always the same person. "The use of two authorizations is desirable in order to keep within US channels those aspects which Canadian officers in the NORAD chain do not need to see. These authorizations would discharge our commitments in paragraphs 7(b) and 8(b) of the draft agreement. They would also provide a formal basis for the NORAD nuclear weapons employment procedures."[150] The concept of emergency circumstances is confined to conditions under which prior consultations are not practicable.[151]

McGeorge Bundy recommended that the president accept the negotiated consultation and authorization agreement, and then sign two authorizations for use by CINC NORAD and CINCONAD.[152] One of the two permissions has been released and is printed here for the first time.[153]

President Lyndon Baines Johnson to CINCNORAD.
Authorization for the Employment of Air Defense Nuclear Weapons by United States and Canadian NORAD Forces under the Operational Control of CINCNORAD.
17 September 1967.
Top Secret.

The establishment of the North American Air Defense Command (NORAD), which placed air defense forces of the United States and Canada under the operational control of a single commander, CINCNORAD, recognized that the air defense of the United States and Canada must be considered

---

as a single problem and that it was essential to have in existence in peacetime an organization, including weapons, facilities, and command structure, which could operate at the outset of hostilities in accordance with a single air defense plan approved in advance by national military authorities.

An agreement was concluded on August 16, 1963 with the Canadian Government providing for the nuclear support of certain Canadian forces, including Canadian air defense forces under the operational control of CINCNORAD. A further agreement has been concluded today between the two Governments concerning inter alia the conditions governing the use of nuclear weapons by both Canadian and United States forces under the operational command of CINCNORAD. In furtherance of these agreements, and acting on behalf of the Government of the United States of America, I hereby authorize the Commander in Chief, North American Air Defense Command (CINCNORAD) to employ nuclear armed Untied States and Canadian forces under his operational control

(A) upon declaration of Defense Condition I or Air Defense Emergency; or
(B) in the emergency circumstances described in paragraph 8(e) of the agreement concluded today.

The use of such forces will be in accordance with approved NORAD rules of interception and engagement and nuclear weapons employment procedures.
It is understood that the declaration of Defense Condition I or Air Defense Emergency by CINCNORAD is subject to prior consultation except under the emergency circumstances referred to in paragraph (b) above.

In his autobiography, Secretary of State Paul Martin wrote about the consultation and authorization agreement and credited it with bringing about a steadier defence relationship with the United States. What he did not write about was the central question of prior authorization. Martin had total knowledge of the subject, as he provided Prime Minister Pearson with the written prior permission note for signature and delivery to the U.S. ambassador in Canada. The Canadian government, in order to gain access to nuclear weapons and to keep the United States happy, had made a pact with the devil. The agreement guaranteed consultation, but it also spelled out the circumstances in which consultation would not precede use. It even required both parties to give CINC NORAD prior (written) permission. The United States was hardly likely to take into account the voice of Canada as they geared up for a thermonuclear exchange. Full details of the Goose Bay and Harmon agreement and arrangements are provided in Chapters 5 and 7.

It was not only air defence forces which benefited from the prior authorization. With the signing of the Argentia agreement in 1967 which allowed the U.S. Navy to base nuclear anti-submarine weapons at Argentia, Newfoundland, there was a need for a similar arrangement for the USN. It is known that Pearson gave prior approval for their operational use. On 27 July 1967, Paul Martin gave Pearson the text of the "timely authorization for the employment of the weapons" which Pearson signed and forwarded to the U.S. ambassador. Martin wrote that the single-page authorization had originally been given to the prime minister on 26 May 1967 and approved by Pearson at that time.[154] There is no public copy of this page; however, the recent release of the Johnson prior permission should ease the path of declassification in Canada. Full details of the Argentia agreement and arrangements are provided in Chapter 8.

In this chapter I have discussed the ways and means for the consultation and authorization for the use of nuclear weapons in and over Canada. It is a dual-edged topic as it includes both U.S. nuclear weapons used by the Canadian forces, and US. nuclear forces deployed to Canada for the use of both the U.S. Air Force and U.S. Navy. These two sides are so deeply intertwined that it is not possible to talk about just the U.S. forces: any treatment had to delineate the controls for Canadian systems in order to understand the controls on the U.S. forces. The first significant area of consultation and authorization which was not covered here was that necessary for the use of the MB-1 (later Genie) which is covered in its own chapter (Chapter 2). The MB-1 Agreement for carriage of the Genie rocket is essentially an early consultation and authorization agreement, but one which was completely unsuitable for handling actual deployments in Canada as far as Ottawa was concerned. The second area is that of permissions for overflights by U.S. bombers and cargo aircraft carrying nuclear weapons. Since overflights began well before basing, and since they continued long after basing in Canada ended and included thousands of carriages over a period of several decades, they are treated in their own chapter (Chapter 3).

Chapter Two

GENIES OVER CANADA

In 1957 the United States Air Force, through the U.S. State Department, sought and finally received the permission of the Canadian government to carry out nuclear air defence flight operations over Canadian territory. The USAF Air Defense Command (ADC) had received its first nuclear air-to-air weapon, the Genie rocket (MB-1) in May-June 1957. With this qualitatively new weapon in hand, the USAF felt that it had no choice but to seek Canadian permission for operational interception overflights.

Nuclear weapons for air defence rockets and missiles had their birth in an ADC request to the USAF for such items on 31 January 1952. Nobody thought it possible at the time, as atomic weapons generally weighed several tonnes. However, by mid-1953 it was concluded that it would soon be possible to make a warhead small enough for an air defence rocket. The Joint Chiefs of Staff approved the development of the MB-1 Ding Dong, later mercifully re-named the AIR-2A Genie, on 2 April 1954.[155]

MB-1 GENIE ROCKETS

The Genie AIR-2A unguided short-range nuclear-capable rocket was designed for strategic interception of Soviet bombers entering North American airspace. The Genie was originally known as High Card, Ding Dong, Thunderbird and the official MB-1 designation. Although the

Genie was developed for Strategic Air Command, responsibility was moved to Air Defense Command (ADC). The Genie was designed for automatic firing by the fire control system on a lead collision type of attack. This Douglas Corporation weapon is made up of the warhead, the fuze assembly, the motor complete with tail assembly, and the nose assembly.

MB-1 GENIE AIR-2A ROCKET	
Length:	2.92m
Diameter (max.):	0.441m
Weight (total):	377.8kg
Throw-weight:	approx. 68kg
Warhead:	W25

The weapons system had to proceed without the knowledge which would have been gained from a full system test. This meant that the major components would be tested separately in three ground launches in 1955. Then, on 8 March 1956, a modified F-89D fired the first Genie rocket at Holloman AFB in New Mexico, not far from the Trinity atomic bomb test site. Douglas, through testing and prodding, had discovered that the timer fuze was not sufficient. ADC was not impressed with the MB-1's "slavish dependence on the interceptor's fire control system for a firing signal." ADC was aware that although the rocket could not be stopped, electronic countermeasures could interfere with the fire control system, making the system useless.[156] This situation continued until at least 1960 when a modification was developed, called the MMB-1, with timer and proximity fuzing, but it was installed in only a handful of test units as of 1963. The Genie would remain vulnerable until an infrared sighting system became operational on the interceptor aircraft.

Thousands of Genies were produced prior to 1962. F-101B and F-106 fighter-interceptor bomb bays could hold the live Genie, or the training rocket called ATR-2N, or the simulator called ATR-2A, or the conventional trainer called ATR-2L. Having no guidance system and fixed stabilizers, the rocket was considered very inaccurate. Flight times varied between 4 and 12 seconds at ranges of 2.5 to 9.5 km at Mach 3. The rocket was designed to be fired automatically and detonated by the fire control system in the F-89, F-101 or F-106. A full war load of the W-25/Genie was two rockets, generally carried inside the aircraft. The Scorpion carried the Genie on an under-wing pylon.

A SMALL WARHEAD[157]

The Genie rocket carried the W-25 nuclear warhead which had an explosive yield near 1.5 kt. Despite its small yield, the weapon was not to be employed against targets less than 1500 m above the ground. The core of the warhead, or physics package, was designed by Los Alamos Laboratory, and production warheads were assembled between 1956 and 1962. W-25 warheads had been designed and built exclusively as an air defence warhead for the Genie rocket. It was a combination plutonium-oralloy (Oak Ridge Alloy) fission weapon, probably containing Cyclotol (75% RDX) as the primary high explosive component.

Safeguarding features are still classified 15 years after its retirement, but the early date of the warhead excluded it from having permissive action link (PAL) safety locks. As one of the earliest of the new "sealed pit" and pressurized pit weapons, it did not have automatic in-flight insertion of nuclear materials. Since it was not PAL-equipped, once the weapon was loaded into the aircraft and the safety pins were removed, it could be fired without further input safety commands. After 1958 the safety features included an early environmental sensing device (ESD) for barometric pressure and an accelerometer. Only after readings consistent with high altitude flight had been registered by the ESD would it allow the arming of the warhead. The W-25 would also have to sense acceleration and then deceleration and continue on a flight path for a finite time before detonation was possible. Declassified records now show that the two ESDs would have to record an acceleration of 28 Gs, followed by a deceleration down to 15 Gs. The warhead was transported in its H-490A shipping container, the bottom of which could be used as a transporter base without the top attached. The W-25 could be assembled into the Genie rocket and checked for use in 30 minutes.

The W-25 warhead was built at the U.S. Department of Energy's Burlington, Iowa, nuclear weapons assembly plant, which was contractor operated by General Mills and where some 3150 units of both the Mod 0 and Mod 1 were produced. Deployment of the W-25 on the Genie began after the USAF initiated the combination in 1956.

Although the W-25 was development-tested during the Operation Teapot nuclear test series, the W-25/Genie combination would never be operationally tested prior to full deployment with ADC and yet would come into service on 1 January 1957 as mandated by the National Security Council. The USAF hoped to include a test of the small sealed-pit war warhead in the Dixie test series of late 1955, but this was not to be. The first handful of W-25/Genie units were classified as "emergency capability" EC-25 items and sent to two sites to arm six F-89J interceptors at Wurtsmith AFB, and nine interceptors at Hamilton AFB. The emergency deployments would last until the regular units were ready as of 1 July 1957.[158] The EC units lacked any safety features and were never loaded on the aircraft.

All combat crews were instructed as to the reconfiguration of the weapons from "ferry" mode to armed mode. This was considered necessary, as it was thought that the crews might have to disperse to various locations in the United States and into Canada with all of the weapons and no technicians, but would have to carry them in an unarmed state. Each pilot and navigator was trained to perform the delicate task of converting the W-25 from the ferry to the armed condition.

A properly cared-for W-25 had a reliability of 0.992 (high), and a properly fired W-25/Genie had a kill probability of 92%. This meant that with two W-25/Genies per aircraft, the USAF/ADC was virtually assured of a hit and kill with a single interceptor, provided that the aircraft was well piloted.

The W-25/Genie was a difficult weapon to use correctly. Only a very small envelope for the correct use of the weapon existed. Testing had revealed that an air defence nuclear weapon with a yield of less than 1 kt would not have a high enough yield to allow for a large enough kill radius, and therefore a larger allowable miss distance, to allow the interceptor aircraft to escape after firing. The fighter would have to be so close to the bomber to ensure a near hit that the warhead could destroy the interceptor as well. The other end of the spectrum showed that yields above 2 kt would be lethal to the interceptor pilots at great distances and therefore also prohibitive. This all meant that the yield would have to be somewhere between 1.5 and 2 kt, and that the time of flight would have to be between 4 and 5 seconds. This envelope would allow the interceptor pilot to escape but still ensure a reasonable chance of killing the bomber, crew and bomb.

A Genie with a live W-25 war reserve warhead was eventually launched and detonated at the Nevada test site at Indian Springs, Nevada, on 19 June 1957. Test "John" of Operation "Plumbbob" saw a Genie fired from a USAF F-89J aircraft to a mid-air target 4.3 km away. The rocket covered the distance in 4.5 seconds, and the W-25 warhead produced a nuclear yield of approximately 2 kt when it exploded at an altitude of 4500 m.

At the time of the first live test, no one was sure how to accomplish an interception and live. Nuclear blast was not the big problem for the air defence pilots: nuclear radiation was. Testing had shown that a pilot would have to be at least 6.4 km away from the blast if a 2 kt device was detonated at 16,000 m to escape the lethal radiation. This distance dropped to only 3 km near sea level, but the corollary was that below 1000 m there was significant risk of residential damage from such a burst. However, environmental sensing devices were supposed to preclude such low-level detonations.

THE REQUEST

The USAF Air Member had approached the Canadian staff on the Permanent Joint Board on Defence (PJBD) in August 1950 and broached the subject of U.S. interceptors flying into Canada.[159] The USAF wanted permission to conduct interceptions of unidentified aircraft flying in Canadian airspace that looked as though they might cross into the United States.[160] The Cabinet Defence Committee and the full Cabinetagreed with the proposal for an interim arrangement in December, only bothering to add that Canada would have reciprocal rights of interception over the United States in similar circumstances.[161]

What the USAF had actually sought was hidden under the language used at the Cabinet level. Air Defense Command wanted the authority to intercept aircraft and "be allowed unrestricted authority to destroy them." The Canadian government was not happy about this and responded at the 10 January 1951 PJBD meeting with a modification stating that destruction could only be over the national territory of the intercepting air force. The United States accepted, but knew that this could only be an interim solution on the way to getting full air rights over Canada.

The new request for expanded air rights came in the form of a letter from the chief of Continental Air Defense (CONAD) to the chief of the air force in Washington. On 26 April 1951, CONAD asked for "free and unrestricted employment of fighter-interceptors aircraft, regardless of the International boundaries."[162] This was not forthcoming, and even the original MB-1 Agreement on nuclear weapons would not allow such freedoms. What CONAD did get was a tacit agreement with the RCAF for day-to-day interceptions and routine training as well as scheduled air defence training exercises.

Actual permission for a form of overflight interceptions came on 31 May 1951. The RCAF/ADC informed the USAF/ADC that aircraft of both nations could now cross the border for training purposes. The USAF headquarters made formal notice of the arrangement to USAF units on 21 June.[163] It was not all the USAF/ADC had hoped, yet it laid the groundwork for later and more comprehensive arrangements and agreements. Given that there was not a bomber in the Soviet inventory which could make it such distances, there was little danger arising to the United States from lack of full air rights. This situation would remain fairly stable until the acquisition of nuclear air-to-air rockets by the USAF.

With only two weeks left before the airborne air defence entered the nuclear age on 1 January 1957, the minister of National Defence told the Cabinet Defence Committeethat the military and government scientists had been preparing for the advent of such weapons for several months. Canadian military officials and defence scientists had been invited by the USAF to see the development of the new MB-1 rocket and nuclear warhead, and the team reported on the operational characteristics and safety feature. Cabinet was now told that the United States wished to extend their overflight intercept rights to include nuclear weapon-armed aircraft.

In order to make the request seem more palatable, the USAF graciously offered to clean up any radioactive mess resulting from an accident such as a crash or inadvertent drop. The Canadians were told that at most 90 kg of high explosives would detonate, and that this might scatter a small amount of fissile material over a small area. As reported to Cabinet members "only a minor radiation hazard would exist,"[164] Canadian teams would be trained to deal with such radioactive incidents by USAF personnel. However, this training would have to wait until after Canada signed an agreement on the uses of atomic energy for mutual defence purposes. The problem, as Cabinet would later discover, was that the training could not proceed due to the restrictive nature of the "original sin": the McMahon Act on atomic energy. The nuclear incident response agreement is discussed in detail in Chapter 4.

Cabinet expected that eventually the United States would be willing to sell such weapons to the RCAF, at least once the U.S. laws were changed. The minutes note that "Canadians would probably be surprised if the request were refused." Against this positive background the minister told Cabinet that the Chiefs of Staff had recommended that a six-month interim arrangement be reached with the USAF. This arrangement would allow the MB-1 to be carried into Canada for the sole purpose of intercepting and destroying hostile aircraft after that aircraft had been positively identified by a conventionally armed interceptor. The military wanted the arrangement to include a provision for the United States to undertake decontamination after such a detonation. The chiefs felt that the matter would have to be further studied before a permanent arrangement could be initiated.[165]

After arguing about issues such as publicity and conventional forces in Europe, it was decided to allow the United States to use the new weapon over Canada for a six-month period. The only odd question is one of the state of alert which was necessary for the intercepts to be allowed. Cabinet was told that both yellow and red warnings could see the initiation of intercepts using the MB-1.[166] Yet the yellow alert only indicated that there may be a hostile aircraft in some adjoining territory. By this time, drafting of the agreement was well under way.

The vague terms of such an agreement had been presented to Canadian ambassador A.D.P. Heeney in Washington on 19 September 1956 during a meeting on the inclusion of nuclear weapons for air defence of the entire continent. A small handful of papers and a few meetings were enough to finish the first agreement by 19 February 1957. As negotiations quickly progressed, the Canadian embassy wanted to know what the future plans for the MB-1 and follow-on weapons over Canada were; what the USAF proposed to do if an aircraft carrying such a weapon were forced to land in Canada and therefore required special storage for the weapon; and how the United States intended to amend the interception and engagement rules to permit the use of nuclear weapons.[167] As to the last question, the United States felt that the agreement being then drafted would cover these needs, as the rules of engagement were not limited to conventional weapons.

At this time there were still only the emergency capability MB-1 units in service, and these could hardly be used. The USAF revealed that the weapons were stored at only two sites until the regular version came into the inventory on 1 July. As far as Canadian territory was concerned, the USAF did not have an actual plan yet for arming the Goose Bay and Harmon field forces.[168] Air Vice Marshal M.M. Hendrick noted in his diary on this question that General H.B. Loper, the military representative to the U.S. Atomic Energy Commission, suggested that the "circumstances wherein a weapon would require to be safetied and removed, and, at the same time, was not badly damaged, would be very unlikely. Therefore it was a problem more of fire-fighting and cleaning up after the normal high explosive discharge."[169]

Again secrecy came up from the Canadian side of the table. The USAF had prepared a press release about their new capability, but the Canadian government wanted to ensure that there was no mention of Canada. Saul Rae from the embassy said that the official position was that "it would not be necessary to mention the exchange of notes."[170] Questions and answers were being prepared for certain ministers in case questions were asked in the House of Commons, but the proposed answers would not mention the agreement and would not reveal that U.S. fighters so armed would be allowed over Canada. The USAF offered to share their Q&A package with the Canadian embassy.

THE MB-1 AGREEMENT

The United States then began, in the summer of 1957, to figure out how to broach the subject of the MB-1. The U.S. ambassador, Livingston Merchant, felt that

> the first question, it seems to me, is to reach a judgement on the desirability of informing the Canadian Government in advance that we intend to hold exploratory talks on a service level with respect to the further incorporation of nuclear weapons in our joint air defense. The talks with the Canadians at the service level could then proceed promptly, with respect to the SAC strategic requirement and to weapons for air defense. I believe, therefore, that we should first generally inform the Canadians at the diplomatic level of our intention to discuss frankly on a service-to-service basis all aspects of the atomic integration concept visualized in the MB-1 notes and that in those subsequent service discussions we should include the Argentia storage plans. I agree with you that we should avoid asking for "authorization" to talk at the service level. To do so might well result in Cabinet consideration of plans which on our part were still in a process of formulation.[171]

The negotiations proceeded quickly and smoothly, basically because no one in the Canadian government could see any reason why they should not allow the USAF to fly over Canada with nuclear weapons: this was a question beyond their comprehension.

The original agreement was signed in Washington on 18 February 1957 by U.S. Secretary of State John Foster Dulles and exchanged with the Canadian embassy in Washington on 19 February for Canadian Note number 91 signed by Ambassador A.D.P. Heeney. The document, entitled "Agreement on Carrying Air-to-Air Nuclear Rockets on US Fighters in

Canadian Airspace," was then updated by another exchange of notes on 30 June 1959. A primary point of the MB-1 Agreement was to give landing and take-off rights to USAF/ADC nuclear-armed interceptors within the parts of Canada around the Great Lakes up to about 50 degrees north latitude. This meant North Bay, Val d'Or, Ottawa, Montreal, Trenton, Toronto, and perhaps Bagotville. With the first MB-1 Agreement covering a period of only four months, extensions of the arrangement were signed on 28 June 1957, 12 May 1958, and 30 June 1958. The entire text of the agreement is reproduced in Annex A of this book.

The original agreement states that the MB-1 was issued to USAF units around 1 January 1957, but this was only partly true. The first 20 W-25 warheads for the Genie were considered "emergency capability" units and were withdrawn in favour of the established production run warheads available by 1 July. Emergency capability weapons were generally weapons with no safety features whatsoever, intended only as a stop-gap deployment until the regular product could be widely deployed. These never made it to Canada, never even making it off the ground for safety reasons. The reality was that "in NORAD, American aircraft carry the MB-1 on the aircraft but are not allowed to fly off the ground with the weapon without Presidential approval."[172]

The original agreement allowed that "the MB-1 be carried by USA military aircraft over Canada" for an interim period extending to 1 July 1957 as a sort of test period. As the life of the agreement progressed, both governments were committed to working out a more permanent arrangement to cover the post-July 1957 time frame. The only real rules in the agreement stipulated that

> USA air force planes so armed will enter Canadian air space only in the event an air defence warning Yellow or Red is declared. In such an event, the USA planes will confine their activities in the main to Canadian territory bordering on the Great Lakes and extending northward to about 50 degrees north latitude. USA planes armed with MB-1 weapons, under Air Defence Warning Yellow or Red, will be authorized by the Canadian Government to land at, or take off from, Canadian bases in the territory over which they have authority to operate.[173]

In addition, there was a section outlining precautions, salvage, and radioactive clean-up for the weapon. As requested by Canada, the United

States pledged to notify the Canadian government directly of any crash in addition to the usual service-to-service channel of information. This was a change from earlier practice when it had only been the RCAF which would be informed of any U.S. military crash inside Canada.[174] It was also this early permissive language that the United States would seek to replicate when negotiating the consultation and authorization agreement. See Chapter 1 for full details.

The test period progressed well since there was never a recorded occasion during which an MB-1 was carried into Canada. Since it is doubtful that the MB-1 in the emergency capability state was ever carried aloft at all, this is not a surprise. The governments therefore decided that instead of making a more permanent arrangement, the agreement would simply be extended. On 28 June 1957, just before it was due to expire, the MB-1 Agreement was extended for a full year until 1 July 1958. The renewal altered the geographic restrictions, but little else. The USAF could now fly north to 54 degrees latitude.

There was an odd incident during one of a series of regular Canada–United States meetings on the broad topic of nuclear weapons for continental air defence. These meetings usually dealt with the MB-1, but in the autumn of 1957 the deputy assistant secretary of state for European Affairs told Ambassador Norman Robertson that the United States was now willing to discuss bringing about a closer integration of atomic capabilities in air defence through the possible Canadian acquisition of "Nike-Hercules type weapons with atomic warheads."[175] The Nike-Hercules idea never went anywhere with Canada, but the United States did test the weapon under ultra-cold weather conditions at the Fort Churchill, Manitoba, rocket range in January 1959.

Although both sides went about it differently, each used the MB-1 Agreement to try to get nuclear weapons into Canada for Canadian and U.S. forces. The U.S. military representative was told that further Canadian action on a renewed MB-1 Agreement and the request for arming USAF forces at Goose Bay and Harmon with MB-1 weapons would probably not proceed until there was some movement towards Canadian acquisition of similar weapons for defensive purposes. "General [Charles] Foulkes made the point that there were outstanding agreements requested by the Americans for the flight of MB1s over Canada and for the storage of MB1s at Goose Bay and indicated that consideration of these requests would be linked with adequate resolution of Canada's desire to have atomic heads for its own defence."[176]

In the first year after the MB-1 Agreement was signed, there was no real intention of asking Canadian permission, much less seeking some sort of arrangement allowing the use of such weapons from Canada. The MB-1 would be introduced into Canada, and the United States would simply take the time and trouble to inform the Canadian government of the fact. Since they already had the MB-1 Agreement, the State Department did not at first see why they should have to seek any further agreement with Canada when it came to placing the Genies in Goose Bay and Harmon. In October 1957, the State Department told the Pentagon that Canada should be "informed" of such plans.[177]

The Canadian military could taste nuclear duty and therefore completely supported any U.S. activity or proposal. National Defence knew directly from the USAF that NORAD was going to request the storage of MB-1 rockets at Goose Bay for the use of the USAF F-89 squadron deployed there. The RCAF told the USAF to forward its proposal through normal diplomatic channels. The RCAF fully supported this requirement at Goose Bay and informally advised the USAF to this effect. However, at least the Air Staff had the good taste to state that all of this was without prejudging the eventual decision of the Canadian government.[178] It would take another five years to fulfill this requirement.

A TECHNICAL REVOLUTION

A substantial rewrite of the agreement was concluded on 30 June 1959, and the final notes exchanged in Washington between Ambassador Heeney and U.S. Secretary of State Christian Herter. However, as Herter was away, the document was actually signed by Robert Murphy, the under-secretary. The main reason for the rewriting was that the U.S. government considered that technological advances had altered the circumstances of air defence. The final agreement is a substantial revision of the original 1957 agreement based on four major changes.

First, the State Department and USAF wanted the agreement to become more than interim and wished it to become permanent with the possibility of amendments and annual renewals. To this end they proposed that the agreement become tied to the dates of the new NORAD agreement. The Chiefs of Staff wanted to keep the agreement annual as it would probably have to be dramatically altered or even scrapped when nuclear weapons came to arm Canadian military air defence systems. The Cabinet Defence Committee debated and decided that the renewed MB-1

Agreement should remain annual and not tied to the NORAD agreement.[179] They directed that the United States not be told why, but simply that Canada was not prepared to make it a 10-year agreement. The United States was therefore informed that the coverage of the revision could extend until such time as a new agreement entered into force. What nobody realized then was that the renewal would not happen until September 1965. However, the long-term never happened, and the agreement would continue to be renewed partly annually, but mostly haphazardly.

Second, the USAF wished to delete the reference to the MB-1 and replace it with "nuclear air defense weapons." This would take account of the Super Falcon (GAR-11) missile soon to come into the USAF inventory. The Falcon was then under development and testing, and some would be available in the very near future. While Cabinet was generally in favour of the proposal, they stipulated that it must be altered to read "nuclear air-to-air defence weapons" so that no one could think that it applied to the Bomarc missile under separate discussion.[180] Cabinet probably also did not want to restrict future access of the RCAF to older weapons types and may have felt that this could open the door to more modern nuclear weapons at Canadian bases.

Third, the USAF wished to extend the permissible flight areas beyond the 54th parallel. Faster aircraft with greater ranges had and were coming into the operational inventory, and the USAF wished to take full advantage of this applied technology. Therefore they desired that the old restriction holding USAF flights to below the 54th parallel be deleted, and that no mention be made of area restriction. The final wording would allow USAF interceptors during a condition of air defence readiness to use any Canadian military airfield. The Canadian Chiefs of Staff commented that "it would be advantageous to the defence of Canada to remove the limitations concerning the area of operations and allow full use of Canadian air space in the event of an attack"[181] and the minister had recommended this position to Cabinet. However, the secretary of state for External Affairs disagreed with this proposal, saying that it would be difficult to explain to Canadians why it was necessary for U.S. interceptors to overfly all of Canada when the last version of the agreement restricted flight to below 54 degrees. The MND replied that the last agreement was secret and that Canadians had no idea. He also said that since large parts of the country had little or no RCAF units assigned or available, this would increase the air defence potential across the country. Cabinet members liked the idea of the air battle being fought further north, and therefore away from population centres.

Members felt that it might be a selling point if the agreement became public. In the end, the CDC agreed that the USAF interceptors could go anywhere under NORAD command.[182]

Fourth, and last, the USAF and CINC NORAD (a USAF general) felt that the original limitations were too restrictive on air defence operation.

> The effect of restricting nuclear overflights to conditions of RED or YELLOW warnings precluded overflights during the critical period of first warning of approaching air attack and actual hostile penetration of the air defence combat zone. Because of the increased speed of bomber aircraft, the warning time was becoming shorter. There was, therefore, less time available to fit each aircraft with nuclear missiles, make the necessary adjustments and reach the hostile bomber to make an interception beyond the populated part of Canada. It was, therefore, considered prudent to allow the use of nuclear air-to-air weapons under conditions of Maximum Readiness — the highest state of readiness to which the air defence forces of NORAD could be called by CINC NORAD.

Both the minister and the Chiefs of Staff concurred in this USAF interpretation.

Under the old system, a condition yellow or red had to be declared, and this meant that hostile bombers were already flying in or beside the area of alert. The change would allow flights of nuclear interceptors at the warning of an approaching air attack. This would mean that the original wording of the agreement would be moot. Since the original called for conventional interceptors to first meet the hostile aircraft, and since the revision called for interceptors to be scrambled under a lower alert, it is unlikely that the old understanding would last.

The biggest problem Cabinet dealt with was one created by secrecy in the White House. Everyone was aware that the U.S. president had delegated some authority for the use of nuclear weapons to CINC NORAD, but nobody in the Cabinet room knew the details. It turns out that CINCONAD (commander-in-chief, Continental Air Defense) had such pre-delegated authority for the use of nuclear weapons, but not CINC NORAD. However, as both jobs were occupied by the same USAF general, it hardly made any difference. Cabinet wanted to know under what circumstances CINC NORAD could use nuclear weapons, especially if they were to agree to allow for MB-1 carriage under the conditions of maximum readiness. They would not be told the terms of the understanding; nonetheless, they agreed that "the authorization of nuclear overflights of Canadian territory be permitted under conditions of Maximum Readiness — Air Defence Readiness declared by the Commander-in-Chief, NORAD."[183]

The rest of the agreement, covering safety, notification of crashes, rules of engagement, and public release, were virtually identical to those of the original.[184] While the original agreement had opened the door to U.S. nuclear weapons in Canadian airspace, the renegotiated agreement dramatically altered the form and content of the conditions under which this could happen. It is reasonable to say that the whole point of the agreement was moot, in that the USAF/ADC interceptors would use Canadian airspace in times of war if they so chose regardless of a piece of paper.

BARGAINING CHIP

The agreement continued in force with little attention being paid until the Pearson government resumed negotiations with the United States over the process for consultation and authorization for the use of nuclear weapons in and over Canada. The negotiating record for the consultation and authorization agreement was discussed in full in Chapter 1; however, there are some points which specifically apply to the Genie and are discussed here.

Negotiations were not producing the outcome desired by External Affairs, and in the spring of 1964 they considered not telling the United States that the responsible ministers had already decided to renew the agreement for another year. Defence Liaison Division felt that this should not be communicated to the United States, as it could be used as a bargaining chip.[185] The United States government clearly felt that this was a real threat, and President Johnson, prior to his January 1965 meeting with Pearson, received some specific instructions. Dean Rusk, reminding Johnson that "the MB-1 expires in two weeks," told him he was to tell Pearson the draft consultation document was under urgent review.[186] The State Department finally broached the subject, asking that consideration be given to a one- or two-month extension.[187]

Canada was now ready to play rough in order to get slightly more out of the United States. Paul Martin recommended to MND that the agreement be extended by only two months. He pointed out that the previous extension had been for four months in order to keep up the momentum on the negotiations.[188] This worried the military in Canada, causing the chairman of the Chiefs of Staff to urge a quick signing before the agreement expired.[189]

When it came time for the end game to be played, Paul Martin kept quiet, both in Cabinet and with the United States. He told his Cabinet colleagues only that the MB-1 Agreement would be extended "from March 31 for a further period" pending the entry into force of the new agreement.[190] He then had his staff tell the Canadian embassy in Washington that the document should only be renewed for six months until 30 September 1965, pending the signing of the new (consultation) agreement.[191] With the signing of the new agreement, the important parts of the original and amended MB-1 Agreement gained new life as an appendix to the 1965 document.

Towards the end of its life, the MB-1 Agreement was being renewed on a rather spotty annual basis.[192] Sometimes it was for a couple of months, sometime four, and lastly for six until it finally expired at the end of September 1965. In the end it was simply superseded by the 17 September 1965 consultation and authorization agreement. This agreement, already discussed in Chapter 1, brought unity to the means for dealing with nuclear armed flights in and over Canada once the Canadian air defence forces had acquired nuclear weapons for their own use. Although it was eventually terminated, it served as a stepping stone for the USAF in their quest to station more armed fighter aircraft in Canada.

Chapter Three

OVERFLIGHTS AND DISPERSAL

World War II had brought a great degree of U.S. militarization to the far north, and once there, the United States had no intention of leaving. The U.S. Air Force was unprepared for Arctic flying, but determined to be successful. To this end, there was an ever increasing routine of transport flights being undertaken between Alaska and the continental United States, and between Alaska and Greenland under Exercise Polaris. By the end of 1946, the U.S. military high command had requested that the Canadian high command approach the government with a request to allow U.S. training flights over the Canadian archipelago. The Chiefs of Staff made the formal written request on 7 February 1948, and the Cabinet Defence Committee agreed to the flights during their meeting of 3 March 1948. The die was now cast.

The United States Air Force, although in fact a real organization, was not legally formed as distinct from the U.S. Army until the creation of the Department of the Air Force on 18 September 1947. Previous to this, the Strategic Air Command (SAC) had been established as part of the U.S. Army Air Forces on 21 March 1946. It was the mission of SAC to perform "long range offensive operations ... employing the latest and most advanced weapons."[193] The primary mission was negated by the lack of truly long-range bombers, thus SAC had to rely on unstable bases on the periphery of the USSR, and on overflights of and bases in Canada. Newfoundland, then still a part of the British empire but already administratively controlled by the federal government in Ottawa, is as close as it is possible to get to Europe without leaving North America, and SAC needed bases and overflight privileges.

At this time the fledgling SAC was a bomber force of 556 aircraft, including only 35 of the B-36 six-engined heavy bombers, and a medium force of 521 World War II-era B-29 and the derivative B-50 bombers.[194]

Through the mechanism of the Permanent Joint Board on Defence (PJBD), the USAF negotiated a short-duration agreed procedure governing various SAC flights in Canada. Entitled "Strategic Air Command Training Flights Over Canada - Agreement of 10 July 1950," and originally lasting only 18 months, this secret agreement provided simplified procedures for the authorization of SAC flights and allowed limited photography. Over the years the agreement was modified and renewed biannually on 1 January and 1 July by the minister of National Defence at the request of the United States.

Greatly increased military air traffic served to make the initial ad hoc system break down under the strain of the requests. Poor response times and a lack of coordination by Canada had become obvious to the U.S. government. The question of each overflight had to be dealt with on an individual basis, and by early-1951 the Canadian government was seriously looking at putting in place a new and streamlined system. Consultations between External Affairs and the U.S. State Department finally brought about an agreed procedural arrangement at the Meeting of Consultation on 14 June 1951. Both parties noted that

> requests of the Government of the United States for permission to make use of facilities in Canadian territory for the deployment of atomic weapons (both with and without their nuclear components) and for the conduct of operations involving the use of such weapons, or to overfly Canadian territory with such weapons, are to be addressed to the Canadian Government by the Department of State through the Canadian Embassy in Washington, and the reply of the Canadian Government is to be routed through the same channels. As much advance notification as possible is to be given by the Government of the United States, and on its part the Government of Canada will seek to answer such requests promptly.[195]

The only job now was to work out the actual route and make sure people were always on duty. Hume Wrong, the Canadian ambassador to the United States, promptly appointed three senior officials at the embassy as well as himself to be the contact points. The U.S. State Department was then provided with a list of names and home telephone numbers of the four Canadians who were designated as the conduits for such requests. The original group included Ambassador Wrong, Minister W.D. Matthews, Counsellor George Ignatieff and Second Secretary Peter Campbell. Any of these four men could then draft the request for Ottawa and send it on by means of encrypted teletype to External Affairs. The State Department was also told that in case of extreme emergency, the telephone could be used. Lastly, the embassy stated that it was the specific instruction of the prime minister that all such urgent requests be immediately brought to his attention.[196] The under-secretary of state for External Affairs, A.D.P. Heeney, told the U.S. ambassador that the prime minister had designated various people to receive information of such requests on his behalf. The small group included Norman Robertson, Gordon Robertson, Jack Pickersgill, and Ross Martin in the Privy Council.[197]

The problems were not, however, solved, and within months the need had grown for differentiating between the various types of requests, and for dealing with them in different ways. Early consideration was given to drawing a distinction between flights of political significance and non-significant flights. The Canadian government made the suggestion that it may have been possible to give a form of blanket permission for non-significant flights, while holding on to political permission for politically significant flights of SAC bombers engaged in preparation for an actual strike against the USSR. The Pentagon responded by delineating three categories of possible flights: (a) flights not involving strikes, whether stopping or overflying Canada; (b) deployment to bases in Canada in preparation for strikes; and (c) strikes from bases in Canada or involving overflights of Canada. The U.S. military then asked the State Department to request that the Canadian government give blanket permission for all flights in the first category. SAC, possibly under pressure from the State Department, granted that even under conditions of the blanket permission, there would be a notification procedure at the service-to-service level.[198]

The real long-term problem was identified by the Pentagon, and it would continue to be a thorn in the side of Canadian governments for decades. While it was clear that both sides felt that blanket permission would work for flights not engaged in strikes against the USSR, nobody felt that such was likely for any flight even preparing for offensive action. SAC hoped that further blanket permission would be forthcoming and even offered to institute a system of service-to-service prior notification.[199] As far as SAC and their commander, General Curtis LeMay, was concerned, authorization was not a word they were willing to let foreigners use:

foreigners were only going to be *told* when it was about to happen, and perhaps even after the fact. SAC now operated 669 bombers, mostly of the propeller-driven B-29 and B-50 variety, but was starting to build a force of the new jet B-47 bombers.[200]

B-50 SUPERFORTRESS

Span: 43.2m
Length: 30.3m
Height: 10.6m
Weight: 63 t
Armament: 4.5 tonnes of nuclear or conventional bombs
Nuclear Weapons: MkIII, MkIV, Mk5, Mk6
Engines: four Pratt & Witney R-4360-35 Wasp Major
Maximum speed: 600 km/h
Range: 10 000 km
Service Ceiling: 9000m
Number Built: 371

The information of U.S. intentions and desires did not sit long in Ottawa. Within a week instructions for Hume Wrong had been drafted, and the ambassador was instructed to tell the U.S. government that although blanket permission, with suitable notification at the service-to-service level, was acceptable, this was a new position for the government. Pearson wrote that such permission would not apply to assembled nuclear weapons as each such movement would require individual attention and permission. Pearson felt that the movement of containers or components was not a problem as these could be transported without fear of any detonation.[201] Hume Wrong promptly informed External Affairs that it was only one year ago that a SAC bomber had dropped an atomic bomb in Quebec, and that its high explosives had detonated, expressly for the purpose of destroying the bomb lest it fell into unfriendly hands.[202]

Despite the enormity of the changes going on in the nuclear world, Pearson and the prime minister were willing to agree to lessen the political control and hand some of it over to the chief of the air staff (CAS) in Ottawa. The CAS would be the Canadian end of the service-to-service channel for providing notification of flights. Wrong cautioned Pearson that the government should not go too far in relinquishing political control and that, at minimum, 48 hours' notice should always be provided. Pearson understood this and was adamant that the Canadian government was unwilling to even discuss blanket permission for bombers engaged in preparation for strikes. It was felt that these flights carried such political significance that any transiting of Canada would require consultation with and the authorization of the highest political leaders.[203]

All this discussion eventually grew to the point where formal Cabinet action had to be taken again. The PJBD had approved Recommendation 51/1 on 12 December 1951, and this document led to the approval by Cabinet of Privy Council order PC 2307 of 17 April 1952. These were the so-called XYZ procedures, and they divided flight types into three categories. Strangely, category X covered flights which were neither deployments nor dispersals nor exercises nor strikes, and this category quickly disappeared due to it being useless and non-descriptive.

Category Y referred to "flights carrying nuclear weapons or nuclear components thereof which are undertaken as part of routine deployments, stockpiling, increasing readiness, posture or emergency dispersal of nuclear weapons, using bases in Canada and/or overflying Canadian territory. This category includes bombers or transport aircraft carrying nuclear weapons." Flights in the Y category would require clearance at the governmental level for the series of flights, but only service-to-service notification for each individual flight. The CAS was expected to notify and gain the authorization of the minister of National Defence if there were any extra flights in this category.

Category Z referred to "flights carrying nuclear weapons or nuclear components thereof and engaged in strikes or deployment for strikes using bases in Canada or overflying Canadian territory. This category covers the case where an immediate strike is contemplated." Given the enormity of the situation should this type of flight be undertaken, Cabinet required that any contemplation of such flights immediately be communicated by the State Department to External Affairs and then on to the prime minister.

In operational terms, bomber flights could be broken into four categories: individual training sorties; unit simulated combat missions; large-scale exercises; and specialized operation. Approval for the first two routine types, individual flights and unit training, were requested by HQ USAF on a program basis annually. In these cases, USAF would state how many they thought would be flown in a year and how many per week, and where. The RCAF chief of the air staff had the authority to approve these flights.

The second, less routine, flights during large-scale exercises or special operation, had to be approved in a special way by the MND. Thirty days before each calendar quarter, HQ USAF would brief the CAS and Departments of Transport and External Affairs on all proposed flights for the following 90-day period. At that time a formal written request was made to the RCAF. If the CAS, External Affairs and Transport all agreed, the CAS recommended approval to the MND. The minister could either take it to Cabinet if the timing was sensitive or could sign it himself directly.

Control of the flights was vested in the RCAF on behalf of the MND. Each flight had to file a regular flight plan with Transport Canada, and the RCAF would ensure that the routes were approved and that the flight(s) did not interfere with civilian operations. Curiously, Canada Customs and Immigration rules still applied to the overflights, but generally special arrangements were made on behalf of SAC by the RCAF.

Most importantly, the USAF had requested that special arrangements be made for the clearance of flights carrying nuclear weapons or components. Schedule B of PC 2307 requires that government-to-government consultation take place for this approval to be given, and that there must be 48 hours' advance notice of the specific movement given to the Canadian government.

For all concerned this was a great improvement over the situation of the past six years. With statutory regulations in place, everybody seemed to know what to do and what kind of flights needed what kind of action. However, it did not take long for this system to break down under the ever-increasing demands of SAC. By 1953 SAC was complaining that PC 2307 of 1952 was too limiting and was causing aircraft to abort missions because the Canadians had restricted SAC from carrying practice bombs while overflying Canadian cities. SAC also complained that they were prevented from carrying so-called photo-flash bombs for use in photographic reconnaissance training in remote northern areas. With the complicity of the RCAF, SAC proposed that PC 2307 be amended to allow SAC training flights to carry practice bombs.[204] What is interesting is the wide latitude given to U.S. actions over Canada. SAC was allowed to give only 24 hours' notice of any flight, and flights were cleared annually in advance by the CAS. SAC was allowed to fly up to 25 aircraft on a single mission inside Canada; however, only one at a time could overfly a Canadian city, and even then only at a very high altitude.[205]

In less than two months, the issue had reached the Cabinet Defence Committee, where the minister of National Defence repeated the case as set out for him by the RCAF on behalf of SAC. The CDC approved the carriage of practice bombs over Canadian cities, and the carriage of photo-flash bombs as well as other ammunition. However, members of the committee made it clear that "the regulations did not cover the question of carrying nuclear weapons or components."[206]

In 1954 SAC recognized that the change from propeller-driven aircraft to jet-powered bombers meant that the Command could not attack Soviet targets directly from the continental United States rather than relying on possibly unstable overseas bases in Europe, Africa and Asia. This was also made possible by aerial refuelling of the bombers. This all meant that SAC was going to need a number of gas stations along the road to Moscow, and it was obvious that Goose Bay, Newfoundland, is the closest North American site to Soviet Europe. SAC needed to expand the facilities at both Goose Bay and Harmon to meet the need of the 1000-aircraft-strong B-47 force. Goose Bay and Harmon were about to change missions from being pre- and post-strike facilities for the B-36 bombers, to being pre-strike staging and refuelling areas for the B-47s, each holding a large number of KC-97 tankers. As an example of how important this concept was to SAC, it is sufficient to note that during 1954 the bombers accomplished some 142,000 in-flight refuellings and crossed the oceans over 3400 times.[207]

B-36 PEACEMAKER

Crew: 16
Span: 70.4m
Length: 49.6m
Height: 14.4m
Weight: 160 t
Armament: 37 tonnes of nuclear or conventional bombs
Nuclear Weapons: MkIII, MkIV, Mk5, Mk6, Mk17, Mk21,
                        B36, B-39
Engines: six Pratt & Witney R-4360-53 Wasp; and four
            J47-GE-19 turbojets.
Maximum speed: 700 km/h
Range: 17 000 km
Service Ceiling: 13 900m
Cost: $3,700,000.00 ($US)
Number Built: 385
Number Crashed: 22 (5.7%)

The rationale for forward airborne refuelling was quite clear. SAC had worked out that tankers could give more fuel to bombers if the tanker flew shorter distances; therefore, bases in Newfoundland and the north were required. At that time, the B-52 could reach from Ellsworth AFB in the central United States out to Arkangelsk in the Murmansk region and return without refuelling. A tanker at Churchill would allow the attacking bomber to reach Moscow and the industrial centre of Gorkii and still return. A B-47 from the Whiteman AFB in the central United States could reach the Murmansk region and then land at Lakenheath Air Base, U.K. The positioning of KC-97 tankers at Frobisher would allow strikes near Moscow before a post-strike landing in the U.K. The USAF planned to fly the tankers back and forth between the forward tanker sites and the refuelling areas in the north and Atlantic as many times as was required to supply the attacking and recovering bomber force.[208]

To this end, SAC originally envisaged single-squadron tanker operations at Frobisher, Coral Harbour, Fort Chimo, The Pas, Cold Lake, Great Whale River, Namao, Knob Lake, Winisk, Churchill, and Saglek Bay,[209] in addition to those already operational at Goose Bay and Harmon. In early 1955 Lester Pearson raised the subject with John Dulles, the U.S. secretary of state. Pearson had discovered the informal talks between SAC and the RCAF and stated that the possible stationing of 200 to 400 U.S. servicemen "raised some political and psychological problems in Canada." Pearson urged that Canada be allowed to provide as many of the troops as possible for the U.S. airstrips and said that he wanted Canadians to think of the polar region as a NATO sector.[210] The first formal proposal to the RCAF came on 3 February 1956, and A/V/M/C. Dunlap, the VCAS, urged caution in presenting this proposal to the Canadian government. Perhaps Dunlap did not know that a year earlier Pearson had already dealt with the matter. However, it was possible to ask for site surveys without getting into the thorny problem for SAC basing in Canada.

B-47 STRATOJET

Span: 35.4m
Length: 32.6m
Height: 8.53m
Max. Weight: 102 tonnes
Armament: 9 tonnes of nuclear or conventional bombs (max.)
Nuclear Weapons: Mk5, Mk6, Mk15, B28, B36, B42, B43, B53
Engines: six General Electric J47-GE-23 jets
Maximum speed: 980km/h
Cruising speed: 900 km/h
Range: 5500 km
Service Ceiling: 12800m
Number Built: 1260 bomber (total of 2041 airframes)
Number Crashed: 119 (6%)
Number of Known Nuclear Accidents: 8

The Cabinet Defence Committee examined the question and recommended that approval be given by Cabinet for site surveys.[211] One week later, on 21 June 1956, Cabinet gave approval for a joint RCAF-USAF survey of the listed sites, and the surveys took place between 17 and 28 July.[212] But Cabinet was bothered by the request. The extensive minutes of the CDC meeting show that members worried that if SAC was asking to base tankers today, bombers would be tomorrow. The vast number of U.S. personnel, estimated as "thousands" in committee, was of great concern, and in the future, Cabinet would try to steer the United States away from sites near population centres in order to avoid negative comment. The upside as the CDC saw it was that the B-47s were being replaced by the truly long-range B-52s, and once this was completed, the need for the refuelling bases would be diminished. The members noted that although SAC was not part of NATO, it had been presented publicly as a firm backing for NATO forces and policy, and to refuse the request for the surveys "would probably lead to considerable difficulties with the U.S. authorities."[213]

With the surveys completed, and the list of possible sites pared down, the final proposal was presented to the Cabinet Defence Committee, and approved, on 6 February 1957. The full Cabinet then approved that recommendation on 14 February. Again debate was extensive. Cabinet had approved the use of Frobisher, Churchill, Namao and Cold Lake. The CDC had no problem with Frobisher as it was already in use by the USAF. However, Cold Lake and Namao presented problems in that Cold Lake was already overtaxed and there was no U.S. presence yet. Namao was considered too close to Edmonton, and U.S. personnel were sure to be seen by the public. It was pointed out that moving everything away from Namao to Cold Lake would violate the principle of having only 40 tankers per dispersed forward tanker airfield. The biggest problem that day was not one of finances (as it would cost Canada nothing), or of land (it was all Crown land), but of politics with the Soviet Union. The minutes record that members worried the bases "would mean that Canada was becoming still more closely associated with what the Russians regarded as the greatest threat to their security."[214] In the end, CDC and the Cabinet gave approval, but not before specifying that construction work should be done by Canadian contractors.

Once Cabinet approved, the RCAF informed the USAF through the PJBD, and the State Department set to work formulating a formal note on the subject. The note came to Pearson from the U.S. ambassador on 9 August 1957 and merely formalized the refuelling base relationship as to how the USAF would establish, maintain and operate the facilities. Pearson did not immediately reply.

The political system in place for overflights was now fairly stable. The only problems arose from people not knowing exactly what their roles were or how those roles were to be executed. Just as the Canadians had put together a list of officials, the State Department designated the special assistant to the secretary of state and his deputy, the deputy under-secretary, and the deputy assistant secretary responsible for Canada as responsible for dealing with overflight requests from the Pentagon. The U.S. Air Force Headquarters had designated three generals and/or colonels from the Directorate of Operations as being authorized to contact the State Department with requests for overflights of Canada. In a particularly memorable letter to Gerard Smith, the special assistant to the secretary of state, the USAF informed him of the names, ranks, titles, office and home telephone numbers of the designated officers. The deputy director of the Directorate of Operations then told Smith that the code words for this emergency procedure remained in effect. Gerard Smith wrote in the margin, "So what are they!"[215] The primary code word for such an emergency, originally set out on 1 August 1952, was "Stargaze." Despite the remaining problems, requests from then on were handled on a more administrative basis. However, this was not always the case, and special circumstances would always lead to increased political interest.

It was also recognized in Canada that there would have to be people on call at all times. External Affairs therefore drew up a document outlining the action required in the event a "special message" was received from Washington during off-duty hours. If it was a weekend, the teletype operator in Washington would call the duty operator in Ottawa who would then call specially designated staff from Defence Liaison (1) Division at External Affairs. If it was a weekend, the senior duty officer would be called, and the teletype operators would open the line between Ottawa and Washington to send the message. This person was then supposed to rush to the East Block to receive the message. As soon as the message was in his hands, he was to telephone the under-secretary or deputy under-secretary of state for External Affairs, who would in turn telephone the External Affairs secretary of state and MND. Second, he would call the Cabinet secretary who would call the prime minister. Lastly, he would call the chairman of the Chiefs of Staff. If there was time, the senior duty officer would call the duty officer for the Joint Staff, and the duty officer for the Air Staff.[216] One is left with the almost inescapable image of a senior official in either Ottawa or Washington having to prod a corporal into shooting the lock off a soda pop machine in order to get the change needed to make the telephone call to launch the bomber force over Canada.

By this time SAC was operating a force of over 1500 bombers: some 1240 six-engined B-47 medium bombers, over 45 new B-52 eight-engined heavy bombers, and the soon-to-be-retired force of 205 ten-engined B/RB-36 heavy bombers.[217]

The year 1956 was to be a busy one for many SAC bombers over Canada. Open records show that on 28 September the USAF asked the State Department to contact the Canadian government for clearance of a flight of five B-47s which were flying from the United Kingdom across Newfoundland and Quebec, and refuelling mid-air over Sault Ste. Marie, Ontario, before entering the United States. Each of the aircraft would be carrying a nuclear weapon, and the USAF classified it as a "Y" mission. The State Department asked the Canadian embassy on 1 October, and a reply was received by cable from Ottawa on 3 October. The embassy staff then promptly telephoned the State Department, who informed the USAF well before lunchtime that same day.[218]

But the movement of five aircraft paled in comparison to what was moved only two months later. The Suez crisis caused SAC to greatly increase its readiness by sending part of the 750-strong tanker force of KC-97 aircraft to Goose Bay and Harmon AFB, and by sending huge numbers of aircraft out on long training missions with real nuclear weapons. Operation Roadblock and the closely related Operation Power House saw over 1000 B-47 bombers and KC-97 tankers flying gigantic simulated combat missions over North America and the Arctic region. The USAF again requested that Canada give permission for a flight of 72 B-47 bombers, 30 carrying full nuclear weapons and 5 carrying only the fissile material, to transit through Canada on 29 and 30 November. It was expected that these same aircraft would return on much the same route with much the same war load in the 3 to 5 December period. The USAF did not say if this was an X, Y or Z category request and would not supply the ultimate overseas base destination of the bombers. The route through Canada was in an area bounded by a line running from Ottawa out past Goose Bay, and a line running from Cape Sable Island in Nova Scotia to the southern tip of the Avalon Peninsula in Newfoundland.[219]

Ten days before the movements were due to begin, Gerard Smith met with the Canadian ambassador in Washington and proposed the flight clearance. Dr. Babbitt, the Canadian scientific attaché, asked the category of the flights, and Smith advised "Y." Smith could only say that the USAF was taking extreme precautions to avoid any provocation during the crisis and stated that the entire exercise might be cancelled. Five days later, on 23 November, a call from the embassy to Philip Farley (G/PM) at the State Department confirmed that approval had come from Ottawa for the nuclear overflights during the Suez crisis.[220] As the secretary of state for External Affairs, Lester Pearson had to know of the massive scale of the flights of U.S. bombers over Canada and that many were carrying nuclear weapons. The fact that Pearson knew some details of the U.S. nuclear preparations may be another factor helping to explain his push for a peaceful settlement of the crisis: an act which won him the Nobel Peace Prize.

With the end of the Suez crisis still warm, Brooke Claxton, the minister of National Defence, returned to the Cabinet Defence Committee with another proposal for expanded SAC flying and practice bombing in Canada. In a twist on the usual explanation to Cabinet that SAC was the greatest guarantor of freedom in the Western world, the minister stated that the RCAF wished to give SAC a new bombing range so that RCAF fighters could have more time in a convenient location to practise air interception of heavy bombers. A stretch of water in the James Bay area was chosen, and the CDC recommended that the bombing range be set up and that SAC be allowed to carry practice bombs to the range area and drop them.[221] Claxton pointed out that James Bay was a federal jurisdiction, so there would be no dealing with the provinces.

The nuclear weapon world was about to undergo a revolution in military technical affairs in 1957, and this fact had a direct impact on SAC flights over Canada. Ballistic missile research and testing in both the USSR and the United States was proceeding furiously, and on 3 August 1957 the Soviets tested the R-7: a real Intercontinental Ballistic Missile (ICBM). Later the USSR used the same launch vehicle to boost Sputnik and Yuri Gagarin into space. Although it would not be an operational weapon until the spring of 1960, and even then there would be only four of them, it was the dawn of the nuclear missile age, and this changed everything. With missiles able to cross the world in 30 minutes, each side knew that warning time for their forces was probably in the order of 15 minutes.

Strategic Air Command had already begun planning for the ICBM age by planning for one-third of the bomber force to be on ground alert, ready for launch. This meant that hundreds of bombers would be fuelled and loaded with nuclear weapons at all times, and that crews would be housed nearby for instant reaction. The first test of the concept, Operation Try Out, ran from November 1956 through March 1957. This and follow-on tests were successful, leading SAC to establish a full one-third ground alert for the bombers and tankers on 1 October 1957. In reality, the one-third ground alert posture was not fully achieved until May 1960. However, this new timing was in clear conflict with the XYZ procedures as laid out in PC 2307 of 1952.

The USAF recognized the problem and contacted Philip Farley at the State Department. Farley was asked to consult the Canadians over altering the XYZ procedures to make them more responsive to "middle of the night" actions by SAC. SAC wished to be able to launch the bomber force as a precautionary measure in times of increased international tension, and they wished to take their nuclear weapons with them. The Air Force pointed out that previous Y requests had taken from three to seven days to gain clearance from Ottawa, and that this was no longer acceptable. Farley responded that it was probably impossible to speed up the Y requests, and noted that although the Z requests would get an instant response, using the Z designation would make the Canadians think that SAC was actually setting out on an immediate strike rather than simply increasing the state of readiness in preparation for strikes. He felt that given the new situation, a whole new category would have to be devised, and he asked the USAF to forward written suggestions.[222] Nothing was done until after the 1957 election and the coming to power of the Conservative government.

Nineteen fifty-seven continued to be a busy year for SAC flights over Canada. More and more bombers were be stationed at overseas bases nearer the periphery of the USSR, and these "Reflex" action deployments regularly transitted Canada. Operation Pinegrove brought 180 B-47 bombers over Canada on a route which took them from just south of Regina to the Davis Strait northeast of Baffin Island. Seventy-two of the bombers carried nuclear weapons or components. The B-47s flew north from 13 to 16 January and came back via the same route 19 to 21 January.[223] A flight of nine B-47 bombers returning to the United States from bases in Morocco and/or Libya was to overfly Canada, armed with nuclear weapons, on 11 and 13 July. This was probably Operation Sharp Point. Operation Devil Tail called for the movement of a unit of B-47s across Canada from Thule, Greenland, back into the continental United States on 2 July. However, Devil Tail was later moved back to 1 August. The problem facing the USAF was that with the federal election under way in Canada, there were no ministers in Ottawa to clear requests. The Canadian embassy was able to respond to the 28 May request by 2 June, despite the electioneering of the doomed Liberal government.[224]

The launch of a Soviet ICBM, Sputnik, and later of Yuri Gagarin himself, posed problems for the tanker bases as well. Originally the bases were host to tankers sent in times of increased tensions, with only a cadre staff on a permanent basis. With the ICBM in the picture, SAC began to change operational procedures, and the need to enhance the forward refuelling sites increased. The RCAF was so informed in early 1958, and on 27 April SAC briefed A/V/M Dunlap. Dunlap and his staff were reported as being "very cool" to the changes and stated that it was not going to happen without a lot of negotiation. What the USAF now wanted was a massive increase in the number of tankers and personnel deployed to Canada. They also wanted to rebuild some of the sites to move the tankers to alert areas directly adjoining the ends of the runways.[225] The USAF gave details to the RCAF and the CAS gave those to the minister. The minister then presented them to a skeptical Cabinet Defence Committee on 26 May 1958.

Cabinet was being asked to allow the permanent siting of six tankers on the alert pads at the end of the runway at each airfield. In addition, SAC wanted rights to move another 20 tankers to each site when war appeared imminent, and to station on a permanent basis about 120 U.S. personnel at each site. SAC intended to rotate about 100 aircrew in and out of the sites on a weekly basis as the six tankers were rotated. In times of war, the strength would increase to 530 men.[226] The CDC would approve the change in posture in Canada, and Cabinet would give its approval on 19 June. The Diefenbaker government had made it contingent on the conclusion of the NORAD agreement, possibly hoping that such matters would go down better with the public if they could be presented as continental defence matters in which Canada had a voice. The CDC had recommended that any such agreement be presented to Parliament at the same time as the NORAD agreement even though the two might be confused.[227]

With the institution of one-third ground alert for the bomber force in 1957, the USAF now needed to act to bring the XYZ procedures into line with their new operational concepts. The Pentagon therefore requested that the State Department begin negotiations with Canada over a modified XYZ procedure and was even kind enough to prepare a draft acceptable to the USAF, which the USAF was going to discuss with the RCAF in informal talks. The assistant secretary of defense for international security affairs was anxious to move on this issue and even went so far as to try to invite himself and two others to an upcoming meeting the State Department had planned with the Canadian ambassador.[228] The military draft of Schedule B of the "Methods of Clearing Flights of USAF Aircraft over Canadian Territory Where the Movement of Atomic Weapons is Involved" simply called for the removal of the Z category, turning Y into a category for cases in which an immediate strike is contemplated and changing X into any non-strike movement of nuclear weapons by SAC. There is no evidence that the State Department broached the subject with the Canadian embassy immediately, and major revision of PC 2307 would have to wait until later in 1959.

In the meantime, the requests for more and more nuclear overflights poured in. It was not just bombers which carried nuclear weapons, as the USAF found it useful to transport nuclear devices in cheaper and more efficient cargo aircraft. To keep the arsenal fresh, as early weapons had a shorter shelf life than newer models, nuclear weapons would be rotated in and out of operational bases. In Operation Merry Mix, four flights of four C-124 cargo aircraft operated by SAC would be carrying one "Gas Pipe" nuclear weapon each to Brize Norton Air Base in the United Kingdom on 3, 4, 11 and 12 December 1957. They would return to the Kelly Air Force Base in the United States, carrying nuclear weapons for refurbishment, on 10, 11, 18 and 19 December. At no time would they land in Canada unless there was bad weather, in which case Ernest Harmon AFB would be a possible alternative landing site.[229] Even larger was Operation Mule Train in which 100 B-47 bombers, each carrying one "Board Fence" nuclear bomb, would be overflying Alberta, Saskatchewan, Newfoundland, New Brunswick, Quebec and the Canadian Arctic. Members of the 43rd, 301st and 303rd Bomb Wings were involved in this no-notice exercise which called for refuelling at Goose Bay and Harmon. The 26 November request by the USAF was immediately passed to the Canadian embassy, and a positive reply for Merry Mix was given the day before the first flight. However, permission for Mule Train was not forthcoming for another week.[230]

The rapid acquisition of new eight-engined intercontinental B-52 heavy bombers, combined with the new realities of the nuclear missile age, made SAC begin testing an airborne alert concept to back up their one-third ground alert operations. There were now 380 B-52 bombers in SAC, complementing the 1367 B-47s and 962 tankers.[231] The 42nd Bomb Wing at Loring AFB, Maine, newly equipped with the giant B-52, was to test the concept of keeping a portion of the bomber force airborne at all times under Operation Head Start I between 15 September and 15 December 1958. Accordingly, the State Department approached Saul Rae at the Canadian embassy on 29 August with a request for blanket permission for three months of four flights daily, each carrying nuclear weapons.[232] Rae replied on 11 September that it was the policy of the Canadian government not to grant blanket clearance over an extended period for the overflight of Canada by SAC aircraft. While the Canadian government was willing to allow the flights, provided that each one was cleared on a daily basis through the chief of the air staff, Ottawa reserved the right to cancel the permission should further consideration become necessary.[233]

B-52 STRATOFORTRESS

Span: 56.4 m
Length: 49 m
Height: 12.4 m (G & H version)
Weight: 83250 kg (empty)
Weight: 219600 kg (maximum take-off weight)
Armament: nuclear or conventional bomb load of up to
            31.5 tonnes
Nuclear Weapons: Mk5, Mk6, Mk15, Mk17, B28, B43, B53,
            B57, B61, B83.
Armament (missiles and cruise missiles): AGM-69A SRAM,
            AGM-28 Hound Dog, AGM-86B ALCM, and ACM-
129   stealth advanced cruise missile.
Engines: eight Pratt & Witney J57-P-43W, of 6187-7650 kg
            thrust each
Cost: $64 000 000.00
Cruising speed: mach 0.86
Range: 12000-14000 km (unrefuelled)
Service Ceiling: 15150m
Number Built: 744
Number Crashed: 67 (9%)
Number of Known Nuclear Accidents: 6

The most common SAC aircraft over Canada was the B-47 "Stratojet" bomber. The largest number of operational B-47s was achieved in December 1958 when SAC fielded 1367 of the aircraft, mostly the B-47E models.

The success of the airborne alert tests in 1958 brought more tests in 1959, and more requests to Canada for overflights. A small number of B-52 bombers were now being kept in the air, fully armed with a war load of nuclear weapons, 24 hours a day, and SAC needed a full-scale test in order to bring the entire force up to the new airborne alert standard. Deputy under-secretary of state Robert Murphy made a formal written request to A.D.P. Heeney, the Canadian ambassador. In the past it was not uncommon for clearance requests to be strictly verbal. However, Operation Airborne Alert was a massive undertaking. Murphy told

Heeney that the operation would last six months and involve 1436 aircraft launches from all over the United States, but that not all would overfly Canada. The flights would be of the Y category, and the RCAF would be informed of the exact route and nature 30 days in advance of the month of the flights. The proposed monthly flight schedule for the period was: January — zero; February — zero; March — 232; April — 330; May — 454; and June — 420. The State Department told Heeney that there would be no more than 14 launches per day.[234] The Pentagon had assumed that they could now get blanket permission for a multi-month exercise, as the previous November they had been told by the chairman of the Joint Staff in Ottawa that the XYZ procedures were cumbersome and that it was now acceptable to the Canadian government that clearances be done by the CAS for three- and six-month periods.[235]

Permission should never be taken for granted, and to make matters worse, another Berlin crisis was underway. Norman Robertson told the State Department that the Canadian government, specifically Cabinet, was particularly concerned with the large number of planes involved, and there was a question as to the relationship of this flying to the crisis in Berlin.[236] The State Department later informed Saul Rae that there was no relation between the exercise and Berlin as they were merely coincidental.[237] The reply from Ottawa came to the Canadian embassy on 6 March and was written up for the signature of the ambassador that day. The next day Livingston Merchant was called to Heeney's home and told in guarded tones that a reply was now in hand, and that it would be delivered to the State Department by Saul Rae later that morning. Heeney told Merchant that there had been a lot of discussion over this request and that Prime Minister Diefenbaker was directly involved in the debates.[238] As it turns out, there was more than a great deal of debate over the issue. The Diefenbaker government had actually asked the British foreign secretary to have the British prime minister speak with the U.S. government about the staggering number of planes, 1430, for which the United States had sought overflight permission. Foreign Secretary Lloyd noted that the Canadians were obviously very nervous about his action.[239]

The written permission was not quite as open-ended as the USAF had hoped. External Affairs wrote that the Canadian government "would not be justified in withholding its support" for the exercise, while at the same time writing extensively about the dangers posed by misinterpretation of the exercise by the Soviet Union. All the same, the government reserved the right to re-examine the issue and possibly withdraw permission anytime within the following four months of the flights. Heeney apologized for the long delay, but closed the letter by stating that his government believed it essential to prevent the press from learning of the exercise.[240] SAC would finally announce the airborne alert training to the world on 18 January 1961, over two years after it had started. The actual letter was handed to Acting Secretary of State Christian Herter by Heeney on 9 March during a courtesy call.[241] That the Canadians were nervous of possible press coverage was abundantly clear to the State Department, and on 3 April they delivered a note to Henney thanking him for the 6 March letter and assuring him that the U.S. government had no intention of publicizing the overflights of Canada. Herter even enclosed a copy of the statement made by the U.S. secretary of Defense one month earlier which disclosed that although the United States was testing the airborne alert concept, there was not at that time an airborne alert posture and the United States was still using the one-third ground alert system for ensuring force survivability.[242] The letter was handed to Gordon Ritchie at the embassy on 6 April. Curiously, this is not what the commander-in-chief of SAC, General Thomas Power, told Congress in February of that very year. Powers testified that SAC had already developed the system by which they maintained a fleet of bombers loaded with bombs and in the air 24 hours a day to guard against surprise attack.

Meanwhile, talks had begun on amending the XYZ procedures as originally requested by the Pentagon in 1957. The RCAF has been discussing the issue with the USAF in 1958, and in November staff from the Canadian embassy held exploratory talks with State Department officials. The U.S. military was proposing to amend the procedures by deleting reference to the X category; to make the procedures cover all military aircraft carrying nuclear weapons regardless of whether they belonged to SAC or to Air Material Command; and to permit clearance for six-month programs. The U.S. government was aware that the Canadians were uncomfortable with blanket permission, but SAC asked that the State Department once again try to gain the extra latitude of action.[243] Again, this would not be settled until the latter half of 1959, but the United States now acted as though the question of six-month permissions could be used as the standard.

The requests kept coming, and even before the first "Airborne Alert" exercise was over, the State Department approached the embassy on 18 June with a request for permission for another six months of flights. The expanded program called for the development of an emergency alert capability in every B-52 bomber unit, and therefore the July through December 1959 period would see 12 flights per day of B-52 bombers carrying nuclear weapons and accompanied by KC-135 tanker aircraft. A portion of each mission was to overfly Canada. This was the SAC "Steel Trap" Indoctrination Exercise. At the same time as the Canadian embassy was being informed of the request for the flights in the latter half of 1959, they were also informed that the USAF was already planning to hold a third series in the first half of 1960.[244] What they did not tell the Canadians was that President Eisenhower had not yet approved the exercises and was in fact awaiting the outcome of the Canadian deliberations before giving his permission to SAC.[245]

This time SAC did not get what it wanted. The Canadian government under Diefenbaker balked at the magnitude of the request and denied permission for the full six months. Feeling that they were perhaps being taken for granted, Cabinet had only allowed for four months of flights and reiterated that individual flights would be cleared on a service-to-service basis and stipulated that events in the future could cause the suspension of the flights over Canada. Lastly, there was the now standard call on the U.S. government to avoid any publicity of the flights.[246] In the United States there was a virtual ban on any but regular USAF personnel flying over Canada. The military liaison officer to President Johnson informed Secretary of Defense Robert McNamara that "in view of the sensitivity on the subject of publicity, that no personnel participate in any of these flights, except Air Force personnel, without the specific authority of the President." This prohibition extended to reservists, members of Congress, and USAF journalists.[247]

Since Ottawa had not granted permission for the full period of the exercise, Washington again approached the embassy. The deputy secretary of Defense, Thomas Gates, needed Canadian permission in order to complete the final two months of the six-month exercise.[248] The difference this time was that SAC already had presidential approval. Herter wrote to Heeney on 5 October and noted that the final two months would see 12 nuclear-armed B-52 bombers overflying Canada daily. Herter then asked that SAC be allowed to fly in Canada for the 1 November through 31 December 1959 period.[249] The Canadian government telephoned their permission to the State Department on 9 October and provided written confirmation on 14 October. The oral permission was immediately conveyed to the Pentagon. Their only stipulation was that there be no publicity given to the nuclear-armed flights over Canada.[250] SAC forces were up to 1366 B-47 and 488 B-52 bombers, and 1067 tankers.[251]

While the bombers flew daily, Cabinet finally grappled with the renewed XYZ problem. The minister of National Defence, George Pearkes, told the Cabinet Defence Committee that the United States was seeking revisions of the XYZ procedures, and that his department was agreeable to the U.S. proposals.[252] He stated that the X category be eliminated and the flights cleared through regular channels with all other service flights, and that flights now be cleared on a six-month basis rather than by individual program. The CDC accepted some of the argument and approved secret revision to PC 2307 of 17 April 1952. Thus was theoretically established the new method of clearing nuclear-armed flights over Canada. It was not enough.

The Canadian embassy handed the State Department an aide-memoire on the subjects on 10 July 1959 stating that the Canadian government was not willing to accept the U.S. wording extending schedule B of PC 2307 to all nuclear-carrying aircraft. Instead, Ottawa suggested that the wording be altered to refer to SAC bombers and SAC transport aircraft and that the title and appropriate section be so amended. Ottawa was willing to delete the X procedures, but was not willing to grant permissions for six-month periods. Instead they offered a new wording in which the United States would be allowed to seek and gain permission for entire series of exercises and operations at the political level, with details of individual flights handled at a service-to-service level and clearance of flights by the MND. Again, the document closed by reminding the United States that no publicity could be given, and that it was important that there be no mention that U.S. bombers carried nuclear weapons over Canada.[253] The Pentagon now had essentially what it wanted. After further talks on the subject, the wording was finalized and communicated in another aide-memoire from the embassy on 11 April 1960. The State Department was then informed through an aide-memoire from almost one year to the day after the 1959 aide-memoire was written, that the new regulations were now in effect.[254]

Around this time SAC began to actively lobby the RCAF in Ottawa by providing briefings of SAC activities to the RCAF high command every three months. At these briefings SAC requirements for overflight of Canadian airspace were presented for an upcoming six-month period, but only three months of flight permissions were specifically requested. To ensure coordination, RCAF, Transport Canada, NORAD and FAA officials attended these meetings if there were too many flights in the period.[255] This procedure was clearly used for the 1962 "Spring Thaw" exercise in which up to 430 SAC bombers and tankers flew over Canada in a 24-hour period between 22 and 28 April 1962. None of the aircraft were carrying nuclear weapons, but they were flying round-robin emergency war order profile missions. In this case the RCAF was an active participant as

NORAD aircraft were tasked with intercepting the bomber force on both sides of the border.

Twice the U.S. government came to the Canadian embassy in Washington seeking renewed permission of Ottawa for overflights and airborne alert training flights. The first request was due to the huge number of nuclear weapons logistics flights the USAF was making to NATO stockpile sites in Europe. The system was so backed up that the State Department asked for Canadian permission to fly 36 C-124 cargo aircraft through Harmon and possibly Goose Bay on their way from Europe. Dean Rusk assured Ottawa that the weapons would not be off-loaded in Canada and would always be under tight security. Flights would cross over Newfoundland from the Azores to Harmon, and then proceed south across New Brunswick to the United States.[256] The Canadian embassy in Washington replied with Note No. 143 of 7 March 1960 accepting the U.S. request. The only stipulation was that there be an absolute press blackout, and that the flights be cleared on an individual basis by the respective air forces.[257]

The other four requests both referred to the airborne alert program. Every three months in 1960 the State Department requested Canadian permission for the now-regular nuclear-armed airborne alert indoctrination flights. Canadian approval was often scribbled in the margin of the memo to the secretary of state for External Affairs.[258] However, this is not to say that permission was automatic, although it was usually just about that. Late in that year Norman Robertson wrote to Howard Green informing him that SAC had been negotiating with the RCAF for the use of low-level training routes in Canada. The USAF wanted a route to be used by at most eight single bombers per day, five days per week. Green wrote "NO" on the top of the page, and it had been decided by Cabinet that they would not grant permission for this facility.[259]

It was not only the regular and logistic flights which had to be cleared: the USAF was starting exploratory talks on a new system for getting SAC airborne over Canada. In 1960 SAC formulated a new emergency war plan "Operation Skip Out," which called for the grounding or diversion of all civilian air traffic while a significant portion (33%) of the bomber force flew over Canada on its way to destroy the USSR. SAC now sought to work out a plan with the RCAF and Department of Transport by which the ever-growing civilian air traffic could be moved out of pre-selected corridors to allow the bulk of the bomber force to move northeast across Canada towards the USSR. Air traffic controllers would have the plans in the facilities and upon receiving the proper message would begin to clear certain airspace. External Affairs officials simply told the SAC representatives who had come to Ottawa that they would have to inform the three ministers with primary responsibility in this field.[260]

The airborne alert grew from a set of massive training exercises into a massive operation. At the same time, the ground alert was being enhanced. President John Kennedy, on 28 March 1961, ordered that 50% of the bomber force be placed on 15-minute ground alert. While it had taken SAC three years to achieve the one-third ground alert, the Kennedy directive produced almost instant results. In July, only four months later, the bomber force had adopted the new posture. SAC now had 889 B-47, 66 B-58, and 571 B-52 bombers, as well as 1095 tankers.[261]

Requests from the United States were now far more regular and referred only to set periods. The new twist was that the State Department had begun to ask for permission to fly SAC missions which were not contemplated by the USAF. It turns out that on 5 December 1961 the State Department had approached Ambassador Heeney and asked permission for the "Chrome Dome" series of overflights in the period from 1 January through 31 March 1962. At that time Heeney was informed that such flights were not contemplated in the immediate future. The good little ally responded to the U.S. request with an affirmative answer on 15 December 1961, granting permission for no particular flights to overfly Canada.[262] A letter was handed to Jim Nutt at the embassy on 3 January 1962 informing Canada that SAC was about to resume the overflights on 15 January, and that all the details were being supplied to the RCAF as usual.[263] Intertwined with this initial non-request was a request from the Pentagon to the State Department to get the Canadians to agree to one of a few route changes which would allow the B-52s to overfly the Thule, Greenland, Ballistic Missile Early Warning System (BMEWS) site. The State Department responded by informing the Pentagon that it was better not to inform the Canadian government of the Thule flights, but rather that it should simply be done on a service-to-service basis. The general route changes were brought to the attention of the embassy.[264]

Chrome Dome became a standard operation for years, but it was discovered that the initial permission granted by Canada posed a small problem for SAC. External Affairs and the embassy had stipulated, quite innocently, in their note to the secretary of state on 18 January 1962 that any bomber experiencing an operational or mechanical emergency over Canada would be required to land at the nearest Canadian base. After receiving the suggestion of the USAF through the State Department, the embassy replied that they were perfectly willing to alter the original note to allow SAC bombers experiencing difficulties to overfly Canada "for the purpose of proceeding to a Canadian or United States airbase (sic))."[265] It is worth noting that this state of affairs existed for an entire year before it was quickly corrected.

The Cuban missile crisis saw the tanker program in Canada explode with activity. Goose Bay instantly became the largest and busiest tanker base in the world, as SAC moved in both KC-97 and KC-135 aerial refuellers. It also saw a potential for further strained relations over the tanker base program, and the USAF was anxious that this not occur. During the alerts, a U.S. commander at an unnamed refuelling base asked for extra security assistance from the local RCAF commander. After the Cuban crisis, HQ USAF requested that SAC base commanders in Canada "not seek any assistance other than [that] specifically covered by working agreements between our countries" as this could "inadvertently cause embarrassment to the USAF and US Government."[266] The USAF realized that the Canadian government was in a difficult position and did not wish to jeopardize its invitation to stay in Canada.

A realization of the sensitivity of the Canadian government to all the questions of nuclear weapons had pervaded all levels of the U.S. government. For that reason, although the USAF very much wanted to push their dispersal plan, the White House issued a National Security Action Memorandum (NSAM) on the subject, essentially banning discussions of the topic. Johnson believed "any proposal for the dispersal of US air defense aircraft and associated nuclear weapons to Canadian bases will be one which the new Government of Canada will not consider to be included in its pledge to honour 'existing commitments.'"[267] He therefore ordered that the United States did not wish to convey any idea that it was pressing the Canadian government with a new proposal. Accordingly, he further directed that the USAF and State Department should immediately desist from initiating any further discussions of the dispersal proposal with the Canadians.[268] The issue disappeared from the radar screen of political activity, at least for a while.

In the United States, the balance of power in strategic forces was changing rapidly. The ICBM force had grown to over 600 operational missiles, but the medium bomber force of B-47s was shrinking. The B-52 had become the "big stick" of SAC, and the Command began to realign the overseas Reflex force. In 1963 B-47s, now numbering 613 and dropping, were withdrawn from North Africa and concentrated in Europe. The reduction of the force meant that there was less need for the remaining 306 KC-97 tankers which had been a mainstay of the fleets found at various sites in Canada. SAC withdrew those tankers from Churchill Air Base in Manitoba, RCAF Station Cold Lake in Alberta, and the RCAF Station at Frobisher in the Northwest Territories. Reflex at Churchill and Frobisher ended on 1 July, with the last SAC aircraft leaving on 4 July, and the personnel reduced to 50 men by 5 July. Removal of staff and equipment would continue until the sites were finally abandoned to the Canadian government on 30 September 1963.[269] Tankers remained at RCAF Station Namao near Edmonton, Alberta, and at Goose Bay Air Base and Ernest Harmon Air Force Base in Newfoundland for the time being.

Another big change was coming, and one that would stand for years: Cabinet moved away from line item review and decided to grant overflight permissions for six-month periods. At the urging of the secretary of state for External Affairs, Paul Martin, and backed by the minister of National Defence, Paul Hellyer and the prime minister, Lester Pearson, the new Liberal Cabinet ordered that SAC would be given leave for operations for six months' duration.[270] In fact, the Liberal government was much more accommodating to the U.S. military than the Conservative Diefenbaker government had been since 1957. To this end, on 5 November 1963 at the Cabinet Defence Committee, Paul Hellyer proposed, and the CDC accepted, that SAC be allowed to build a radar bomb scoring facility on Canadian soil, as well as being allowed to undertake low-level flying and bombing training inside Canada. Increased Soviet air defence had made high-level bomber penetration extremely risky, and both the USAF and Royal Air Force (RAF) were moving to low-level penetration of enemy countries and target areas. Hellyer noted that to make this seem more palatable to the public, and to make it more NATO-like, the use of routes in Canada for low-level flying by SAC should be linked to the use of routes in Canada by the more acceptable RAF, and that any SAC personnel should be stationed away from population areas to avoid attracting adverse comment.[271] With all this happening, the Canadian government for some reason became more receptive to the dispersal proposal. The government had communicated that they were willing to talk about the issue at the upcoming 25 June 1964 Canada-USA Joint Ministerial Committee on Defence. With this in mind, the White House withdrew their earlier opposition to any agency trying to engage in such talks.[272]

Despite the change by Ottawa from a three- to a six-month schedule, the Pentagon continued to ask the State Department for permission every three months. By the middle of 1964 the flights were now regularly 12 per day over Canada on airborne alert.[273] Twelve was the maximum number permitted by agreement with the Canadians.

At this time, SAC had 626 B-52, 94 B-58 and 391 B-47 bombers, and 844 tankers.[274] In one fine example of a request, Dean Rusk told Ambassador Ritchie that the U.S. desired to continue the program of airborne alert overflights for the 1 October through 31 December 1964 period. "A maximum of twelve flights daily by Strategic Air Command aircraft carrying atomic weapons is envisaged on routes which would be determined by the Strategic Air Command and the Royal Canadian Air Force and the Canadian Department of Transport."[275] Oral approval came on 25 September, and Note No. 570 was received on 29 September. These notes were now often classified as merely secret instead of top secret. The Pentagon had insisted that if the notes contained information on routes or units or weapons the higher classification be used. However, the secret stamp was good enough if the note lacked details.

B-58 HUSTLER

Span: 17.3m
Length: 29.5m
Height: 9.6m
Max. Weight: 72.6 t
Armament: 9 tonnes of nuclear or conventional bombs
Nuclear Weapons: B28, Mk39, B43, Mk53, B61
Engines: four J79-GE-58, and/or P&W J58 jets
Maximum speed: 2100 km/h
Cruising speed: 800 km/h
Range: 6900 km
Service Ceiling: 15200m
Service dates: 01 August 1960 - 16 January 1970
Number Built: 116
Number Crashed: 23 (20%)

At the regular SAC briefing of Canadians on 19 November 1964, the United States asked for another change. Flights had been limited to 12 per day for years, but with a change in airborne alert routes, SAC now desired the leeway for up to 28 flights per day. SAC had developed a new pattern of holding areas for the bomber force, and under normal circumstances this would mean that there would usually only be four flights per day entering Canada. However, SAC needed prior permission for 14 to 28 flights under increased alert conditions without specific Canadian approval each time. The White House had ordered that this be kept very quiet, and that was why SAC chose to brief the friendly RCAF first in order to gain an idea of the reception such a change would likely receive. There is no record of the Canadian response, but it is interesting that for the State Department briefer, also at the talks, the trip was hardly a waste. Raymond Barrett was not going to miss the opportunity of picking up some cheaper and better Canadian rye, bourbon or scotch, or as he called it "Christmas cheer." He also intended to pick up Oka cheese to take back to Washington.[276] In the end, the State Department requested the regular 12 flights per day for the first half of 1965 in their note of 8 December 1964 from the secretary of state to the Canadian ambassador. SAC would therefore continue to put 12 bombers per day over Canada during the following year. For example, beginning on 1 July 1965 and lasting for 45 days, the 6th, 11th, 42nd, 92nd, 397th, and 410th B-52 bomber units were expected to each fly two sorties per day for a total of 12.

The B-47 bombers were breathing their last as the mighty B-52s took over all bomber duties. SAC had been slowly withdrawing the older force from the Reflex bases in Europe and North Africa for years, and by early 1965 there were only 90 of the old bombers left. As B-47s finished their final duty at overseas Reflex bases, Canada provided the way home. The State Department had asked permission for a specific flight of 29 aircraft which would be coming from Europe loaded with various atomic weapons between 2 and 6 April 1965.[277] Twelve bombers from the 380th Bomb Wing and 17 aircraft from the 509th Bomb Wing would fly over in two- and three-aircraft cells with one hour between each cell. A top secret, restricted data (TS-RD) document notes that "[blank] will be tactical ferry configuration."[278] This TS-RD annex does not give the locations. The Canadians were not told the location of the aircraft, but it turns out that SAC terminated the Reflex force at Moron and Torrejon Air Bases in Spain as of 31 March. It would have been a logical conclusion that the bombers came from Spain, except that a slip by the censors revealed that the aircraft were flying back from the United Kingdom.

Airborne refuelling of the B-47 fleet had become a dwindling activity. With fewer bombers and fewer overseas bases, the USAF closed tanker operations at RCAF Station Namao and converted the KC-97 fleet at Goose Air Base to the new jet KC-135 tankers in 1964. This left Harmon AFB as the only SAC overseas KC-97 base, and the life span of Harmon itself was only a couple of year more.

The USAF was still keenly interested in fighter dispersal in Canada. The tanker force would soon be withdrawn due to longer ranges of the aircraft, the fighters could still profitably be deployed to the north. At the February 1966 PJBD meeting, the Canadian team told the U.S. team that further discussion of the dispersal problem was not going to be entertained as long as the Argentia question remained outstanding. However, the U.S. embassy broached the subject in the early summer of 1966, saying that they would like to submit a note on the dispersal question. However, they were put off by External Affairs.[279] The United States wanted to build nuclear weapons storage facilities at both CFB Portage la Prairie, Manitoba; and at CFB Namao, Alberta.[280] The other site, at Val d'Or, already had storage bunkers used for the Genie weapons supplied to the RCAF 425th AW(F) interceptor squadron detachment deployed there. Clearly, it was going to be a problem presenting the idea of building nuclear weapons storage bunkers for USAF fighter squadrons less than one hour's drive west of Winnipeg in the former case, and right near Edmonton in the latter. As the government saw it, dispersal was problematic in that it was probably a short-term requirement which would cause the shedding of a lot of political blood. However, it was probably also a realistic NORAD requirement, and the government did not want to look like it was doing nothing for NORAD as it cut both planes and men. The idea was put forward that there would be "less hard feeling on the part of the USA if it [dispersal] withers on the vine than if we [the Government] administer the coup de grace."[281] So it did nothing.

The issue sat in abeyance at the request of the Pearson government, as they wished only to deal with it after the negotiations on Argentia had been successfully concluded. However, on 9 September 1966, the U.S. embassy delivered a note to External Affairs restating their interest in the dispersal program. They claimed that the tyranny of time, and the upcoming visit of the new CINC NORAD to Ottawa, made it more important that the issue at least be reviewed.[282] Nothing was done, and the government still hoped that the issue would quietly go away. Sending Robinson to Washington and telling him that he could talk about it was clearly a mistake as far as the leadership was concerned.

Events in 1966 and 1968 brought the bomber airborne alert program to a halt. On 17 January 1966, B-52G, No. 59-0256 from the 51st Bomb Squadron, collided with a KC-135 tanker over Palomares, Spain, during a Chrome Dome mission in the Mediterranean. The United States lost four Mk28RI thermonuclear weapons that day, and the program of airborne alert began to be called into question. Two bombs were recovered intact, but two had undergone a conventional explosion and scattered U.S. plutonium in a foreign country. (See Chapter 4 for a list of accidents in Canada and major accidents overseas.) The Joint Chiefs of Staff were willing to cut the program from 12 to 6 flights per day, and Secretary McNamara was willing to end it completely, relying on ground alert. The two sides agreed to four flights per day, and this compromise was presented to President Johnson in June 1966.[283] Chrome Dome flights over Spain were ended immediately. Then, on 21 January 1968, B-52G, No. 58-0188 crashed on the ice cap near Thule Air Base in Greenland. The United States lost all four Mk28RI thermonuclear weapons on board to fire that day. President Johnson and Secretary of Defense McNamara called an immediate halt to the airborne alerts. SAC responded by reviving the dispersal program and applying it to the B-52 and KC-135 force. It was not just the horrific accidents, but also the astronomical cost of keeping the aircraft airborne, and the demands for increased bombing of the South Vietnamese countryside which ended the airborne alert. In addition, the now massive ICBM force could be generated much more quickly. However, the U.S. government continued to ask for overflight permission on a regular basis from Canada. The request for the latter half of 1968 explicitly stated that the president had suspended his permission for the flights in January, and that the suspension was still ongoing.[284] SAC now had 579 B-52s and 632 KC-135s.[285]

Even during this turbulent period in SAC history, the Command continued to fly in Canada. Records show that a joint SAC and NORAD exercise was held every three months between the two major accidents. Each "Snow Time" exercise would see 30 B-52 bombers penetrate selected NORAD sectors and be intercepted by U.S. Air Defense Command and the RCAF. It is extremely likely that the bombers were unarmed by this time. Even more curious is that in December 1966 Cabinet considered the SAC low-level flight training program, and did nothing to stop it.[286] To help support both the overflight program and the training flight program, SAC stationed the new KC-135 tanker at Goose Bay AB starting on 2 October 1966 and running until 30 September 1976.

This is not to say that it was a quiet time in Canada. People were more and more up in arms against the idea of nuclear warfare. Although the protest movement of the 1950s in the United Kingdom had never really caught on in Canada, the horrific war crimes by the United States in Indo-China seen nightly on television had finally prompted Canadians to begin to voice contrary opinions. SAC was a prime target, being both the world's premier carrier of nuclear weapons and the operator of B-52 bombers symbolic of the destruction being wrought in South-east Asia. One record uncovered through the access to information[287] process shows that the secret police coordinated with the Department of National Defence to provide surveillance of anti-SAC protests. In one case, a prairie group planned a demonstration against the Strategic Air Command unit in Broadview, Saskatchewan, which monitored the low-level bombing runs flown by SAC bombers in that area.[288] The unit consisted of only four vans and 13 to 25 men, but it was symbolic of the penetration of Canada by foreign nuclear infrastructure. The government was not sure if this was going to expand into a greater level of anti-SAC activity, so the local RCMP assured that if it moved beyond the formative, more information "[would] be reported without delay".[289]

It was at the time of the Thule crash and the end of the nuclear airborne alert program that External Affairs came up with an interesting, although bizarre idea. They proposed to ask the Soviet Union to file international flight plans when they proposed to overfly the airspace adjacent to Canadian territory. External Affairs apparently planned to say that such flights were a hazard to commercial aviation and that commercial pilots should be made aware of Soviet bomber presence. They anticipated that the Soviets would respond by stating that the USAF operated freely in the area, but External Affairs would point out that under the Canada–United States arrangement, each bomber crew filed a flight plan with Transport Canada.[290] There is no record of the outcome of this plan, but since the Soviet Unions' Long-Range Air Force did not begin filing flight plans with the Canadian government, it can be safely concluded that the idea died a quiet death.

With the tankers gone and the airborne alert program winding down, dispersal became more important to the USAF. By the autumn of 1967, the Canadian government was now willing to discuss the matter directly, and sent Basil Robinson to Washington for talks. He was instructed[291] to tell the United States that they were now looking at the problem in a different light. The CAF had proposed that the USAF be allowed to use various sites as a way of compensating for reductions in equipment and manpower in their NORAD contributions. At the same time, it was not going to be possible for the USAF to use Val d'Or, as the government thought it would be closed in the near future. Lastly, Robinson informed the United States that no action would be taken until the matter of the future of NORAD had been cleared. Again, nothing was done.

Although the remaining tankers would be withdrawn from both Goose Bay and Harmon, tanker operations in Canada continued and would take numerous forms. Three years after giving back the refuelling bases to Canada, SAC once again requested permission to survey for refuelling sites. SAC explained that with fewer bombers than before, they were again interested in the bases.[292] As is shown below, future activities would be less of a government-to-government affair, and more of a service-to-service affair. The following four examples serve to illustrate SAC overflight and refuelling activities in Canada in the 1970s and 1980s.

- External Affairs and the State Department negotiated an umbrella agreement by which SAC would be allowed to undertake deployments and refuelling at Canadian Forces Bases in times of emergency.[293]
- CFB Edmonton had an agreement with SAC to provide support to the 22 Air Refueling Wing from March AFB in California. The 1 October 1983 memorandum of arrangement stated that Edmonton was designated as a Forward Located Alert Generation (FLAG)/Dispersal base, and that SAC would be able to send units other than just the 22 AREFW (Air Refueling Wing). Deployment of other forces, up to 31 aircraft and support teams, would be on short notice and only during periods of increased international tension.[294] Just before the memo was signed, the 22nd lost its two bomb squadrons, but retained one KC-135 tanker squadron and one KC-10 tanker squadron.
- The 42nd Bombardment Wing at Loring AFB in Maine had signed a letter of agreement with CFB North Bay "for the express purpose of Dispersal of 42 BMW aircraft as directed by SAC EWO 44-6."[295] The 42nd Bomb Wing had one squadron of B-52G bombers and two squadrons of KC-135 tankers.
- SAC Headquarters negotiated a 1979 letter of agreement with the Canadian Forces for SAC bombers and tankers to practise refuelling and for Canadian fighters to practise interception of SAC forces. The agreement allowed the use of airspace near the three Canadian nuclear weapons bases at Bagotville, Quebec, Chatham, New Brunswick, and Comox, British Columbia. The Bagotville Military Flying Area (BG-MFA) and the Chatham Intercept Training Area (CHITA) would normally be used by bombers and tankers of the 42nd, 380th, 416th, and 509[th][296] Bomb Wings. The Comox Military Flying area (QQ-MFA) would normally see use by aircraft from the 92nd, 93rd, 320th, and 456th Bomb Wings.[297]

Overflights of Canada would continue long after the end of the Cold War and the fall of the Soviet Union.

DISPERSAL OF NUCLEAR-ARMED FIGHTERS TO CANADA

The Liberal government of Lester Pearson had been elected partly on the promise to fulfill existing commitments between Canada and the United States. The USAF was hoping that this included dispersal of nuclear-armed interceptors to Canadian bases. Such dispersal, in the language of

NORAD, was called "ANTLER STAG." The White House, far more politically astute than the USAF, and recognizing that Pearson led a minority government, directed that for the moment, all U.S. overtures to Canada about dispersal be halted. The White House stated that this was not what Canada would consider a prior commitment. Any previous talks would from then on be characterized as merely explanatory rather than as proposals and negotiations.[298] However, this did not stop the USAF team from starting onto the question at the June 1963 meeting of the Permanent Joint Board on Defence.

This entire question arose because of the wording of the MB-1 Agreement and the 1965 consultation and authorization agreement. Both stipulated that nuclear-armed U.S. interceptors could only be deployed to Canadian bases in an emergency, defined as the declaration of DefCon 1. The United States now sought a way around this restriction they had in fact originally negotiated.

USAF/NORAD DISPERSAL PROPOSAL, 1964

To	Aircraft	From	USAF Personnel
Comox BC	6x F-101	Kingsley Field Oregon	117
Namao Alberta	6x F-106	McChord AFB Washington	165
Cold Lake Alberta	8x F-101	Glasgow AFB Malmstrom AFB Montana	164
Portage la Prairie (or Gimli) Manitoba	4x F-101	Grand Forks AFB North Dakota	122
Val d Or Quebec	6x F-101	Griffiss AFB New York	130
Bagotville Quebec	4x F-101	Dow AFB Maine	112
Chatham NB	4x F-106	Loring AFB Maine	117
Shearwater NS	4x F-101	Otis AFB	114

TOTAL AIRCRAFT: 42   TOTAL USAF PERSONNEL:1041

When the talks did begin, the initial USAF request was a non-starter. Both External Affairs and the U.S. Department of State recognized that the USAF proposal to disperse 50 fighters and 1163 personnel to nine Canadian bases was not going to be politically acceptable in Ottawa. First, the number of aircraft was said, incorrectly, to be greater than the number of interceptors Canada had operational; and second, far too many U.S. servicemen would be showing up in Canada. The biggest problem would probably be how to explain why Canada had aircraft in Europe if the Canadian territory was in such need of defence that the U.S. Air Force had to move in. Such questioning of the NATO need could not be allowed, and the USAF was going to have to accept less. The State Department recommended that the USAF reduce the number of requested dispersal bases to five or six and keep additional U.S. personnel down to around 100, and that the proposal be given to the RCAF and External Affairs on an informal basis.[299] It was hoped that this would produce a positive result at the upcoming 25 June 1964 joint Canada–United States ministerial committee meeting. It did not. In fact, External Affairs had already told the secretary of state for External Affairs on 22 June 1964 that any future U.S. request for dispersal "be turned down."

With increased CINC NORAD pressure brought to bear, the State Department presented the Canadian embassy in Washington with an aide-memoire on the topic on 9 September 1966. At this time they requested that negotiations be opened for the use of four unspecified bases in Canada. The U.S. team was told one month later that this request was being studied, but that it would have to be dealt with by Cabinet if it were to proceed past the exploratory stages. In October, Prime Minister Pearson gave his okay for exploratory talks, provided that they did not commit his government to any specific USAF deployments.

The request languished with the Canadian government and was again resurrected in 1967. The spring and summer meetings of the PJBD had dealt with the topic, and the USAF presented a revised list of bases. These were now limited to Val d'Or, Namao, Cold Lake and Gimli. The U.S. team said they would send another formal proposal through political channels but were discouraged when the Canadian team said that this presented "political difficulties for Canada."[300]

The U.S. embassy again broached the subject and External Affairs asked for formal comment from National Defence. Informal indications from DND were that the military supported the idea as a way of appeasing the U.S. military in light of proposed Canadian military force reductions and the closure of Val d'Or, a proposed dispersal base. The U.S. embassy was informally told that the proposal raised certain political difficulties for the government, and the minister of National Defence had decided that no action would be taken until the future of NORAD had been decided.[301] Both the minister of National Defence and secretary of state for External Affairs went to Cabinet with a formal proposal based on the U.S. request in May 1969,[302] but to no avail.

The Chiefs of Staff pushed, and even though the ministers did take it to Cabinet, and the proposal went nowhere. Fighter dispersal was never to happen on a formal and agreed intergovernmental basis and would happen only when arranged between bases and units in Canada and the United States. The proposal languished, only to be resurrected by the United States years later in 1984, again with little success.

Chapter Four

CRASHES AND NUCLEAR WEAPONS ACCIDENTS IN CANADA

Early in the nuclear age, the U.S. military developed a code language for speaking about incidents and accidents involving nuclear weapons. For quick reference the military would be able to use the following code words in describing an incident.

> **"Nucflash"** — This category of incident or accident signifies a situation in which a detonation or unauthorized incident could create the risk of nuclear war between the USA and USSR/Russia.
>
> **"Broken Arrow"** — The Broken Arrow code indicates that a nuclear weapon is in danger of exploding or that it has exploded or been lost. This does not refer to detonations which carry the risk of starting a war. It does cover the theft, seizure or intentional jettisoning of nuclear weapons or critical components.
>
> **"Bent Spear"** — This category covers incidents and accidents in which a nuclear weapon has been damaged and will need repair or the replacement of major components. There is no risk of detonation. It also covers incidents in which there is a political risk of adverse public reaction or the inadvertant release of information to the public.
>
> **"Dull Sword"** — This is the lowest level of nuclear incident involving a nuclear weapon or nuclear weapon system. These are non-significant incidents which could impair the operational capability of the weapon or weapon system, but are not capable of causing a detonation.

People in many countries had been worried about airborne nuclear weapons since the earliest days of the nuclear age. However, it was in Britain that the anti-nuclear movement got its start with the great philosophers and the Campaign for Nuclear Disarmament. The questions of overflights and the possibility of accidents had reached the House of Commons in London, and urgent news enquiries were made by the press. So strong was the demand for information that CINC SAC asked permission of the secretary of Defense to issue a statement on the hazards of nuclear weapons stored at and flown into bases in Britain. General Powers was proposing to say that USAF jet bombers had been flying over Britain for ten years (although it was not a normal state of affairs), and that sometimes alert aircraft loaded with nuclear weapons did fly over the United Kingdom. He would then stress that there was no hazard in living near a SAC base as the weapons were never fuzed until the bomber was aloft and a safe distance from the British public.[303] By this time, SAC had already crashed a B-47 bomber into a nuclear storage igloo at Lakenheath and nearly detonated three Mk6 atomic bombs.[304]

The concern over safety was real, especially given that the USAF and USN had already lost numerous aircraft and nuclear weapons systems to preventable accidents. In order to prepare for this grim eventuality, the Canadian government directed the Department of National Defence to negotiate an agreement with the U.S. military on responses to nuclear weapons accidents.

General Charles Foulkes, the Chief of Defence Staff, said he was aware there had been more than 700 SAC nuclear bomber flights over Canada in 1958 alone, and that the Diefenbaker government was now very concerned with the inadequacy of arrangements for dealing with nuclear weapons incidents. Foulkes pointed out that as it then stood, the USAF would send a team to the accident site. However, this would be difficult in the more remote areas of Canada and had no place for Canadian participation. The U.S. response to this real and legitimate concern was that they were prevented from divulging certain information, by various U.S. laws, which would be of great use to people involved in the mitigation and clean-up of a nuclear weapons accident. The bottom line for the United States was that there would have to be a mutual security agreement on nuclear co-operation before any additional information was given to the Canadian military for accident response purposes.[305]

With the signing of the agreement on co-operation on the uses of atomic energy for mutual defence purposes, and its technical arrangement on 22 May 1959, the bilateral relationship with regard to accidents entered a new phase. The United States was now allowed to provide the RCAF with the necessary technical information for dealing with any nuclear weapons which might have fallen from the sky, just as they had in 1950. Of course, there were security provisions: the secret security annex, still not officially released by either government, stipulated that anyone who had pleaded the fifth amendment to the U.S. constitution would be denied a security clearance by the Canadian government. Apparently, use of the "sacred" U.S. constitution in defence of freedom and personal liberty was seen as a threat to the security of the free world.

On 20 July 1961, well before nuclear weapons came to be permanently based in Canada, the two militaries signed the "Service to Service Agreement Between the United States Air Force and the Royal Canadian Air Force on the Responsibilities for Response to Nuclear Weapon Incidents Involving Canadian Territory."

The safety agreement stipulated that the command of the situation would fall to the Canadian base commander of the nearest Canadian military installation who would be required to take immediate actions to localize the effects of the incident until he was relieved by the designated nuclear incident control officer from Ottawa. The USAF would provide a chief advisor to the Canadian team who would be the chief U.S. representative during the incident, give technical advice and coordinate U.S. actions. Skilled U.S. disaster control personnel were expected to accompany the U.S. site commander. The United States was to be totally financially responsible for any assistance provided by Canada in response to a nuclear weapons incident. The agreement was renewed on 20 August 1968.

THE BOMBING OF SQUALLY CHANNEL, BRITISH COLUMBIA

In 1950, on a night-time, high-altitude, combat profile bombing mission of San Francisco from Eielson AFB in Alaska, to Carswell AFB in Texas, the new B-36B s/n 44-92075 experienced catastrophic engine failures and crashed. However, before the bomber crashed into the mountainside, the crew dropped the atomic bomb over the Pacific Ocean. It had been engaged in a developmental flight to perfect procedures for operating with atomic weapons from forward operating locations, especially in the far north.

The aircraft, one of the fleet of heavy bombers used by the 7th Bombardment Wing (Heavy) units stationed at Carswell Air Force Base near Fort Worth, Texas, was carrying a Mk4 (Fat Man-style) atomic bomb. The atomic bomb did not have the plutonium core installed, and it is unlikely that the core was even on board the aircraft at the time of the accident. The USAF official report to Congress states that "the airplane carried an atomic bomb, less nuclear component."[306]

The bomber was ferried to Eielson AFB in Alaska by a secondary crew. The primary bomb crew had been flown to Eielson AFB from Carswell AFB earlier that day in a C-54 transport aircraft. The Mk4 atomic bomb was flown to Carswell AFB on board an older B-50 bomber, and then transferred to the waiting B-36 for the flight to Alaska.[307] The bomb had to be sent to Carswell to begin with, as at this time the U.S. Air Force did not have full custody of nuclear weapons: they were held by the U.S. Atomic Energy Commission at six national stockpile sites. The bomb which was lost came either from site "Baker" at Fort Hood, Killeen, Texas, or from site "King" at Lackland AFB, Medina, Texas.[308]

```
INCIDENT:  Dropped Atomic Bomb/non-critical detonation
CLASS:  Broken Arrow
DATE:  14 February 1950 (c.07:50Z)
AIR FORCE:  8th Air Force, USAF
WING:  7th Bomb Wing (Heavy)
GROUP:  7th Bomb Group
SQUADRON:  436th Bombardment Squadron
BASE:  Carswell Air Force Base, Texas, USA
AIRCRAFT:  B-36 s/n 44-92075 (built 31 July 1949)
AIRCRAFT COMM:  Capt. Harold L. Barry
WEAPON:  Mk IV (derivative of Fat Man atomic bomb)
PLACE OF BOMBING:  over water, near 53.00N 129.49W
PLACE OF CRASH:  British Columbia, 56.08N 128.32W
NOTES:  DHist SAR reel #69, SAR Op BRIX.
```

INCIDENT

The crew and aircraft prepared for a 24-hour flight and carried 28 hours' worth of fuel. Their combat profile training mission called on the crew to fly the massive B-36 from Eielson AFB along the following flight plan: "120 R39 B26 A1 Cape Flattery 140 Drct Fort Peck 400 Solonsea Drct Frisco 400 Drct to destination Fort Worth."; essentially south down the west coast to San Francisco, then east to Fort Worth, Texas.

The weather in the area of the incident was not the most favourable, but it should have been manageable by the giant bomber. The cloud ceiling ranged from a high of 700 m to a low of 150 m, being broken or solid overcast throughout the area. Visibility ranged from 5 to 20 km, and there was a light rain. The winds were from the southeast and east-southeast, ranging from 30 km/h to as high as 80 km/h. Icing conditions were scattered throughout the flight path. However, this fact was unknown to the pilot, Captain H.L. Barry told the inquiry that "I hadn't flown in the Arctic and I didn't know when you are liable to get iced up there. I figured that as cold as it was all the moisture in the air should already be frozen."[309]

Lt. Colonel D.V. MacDonald, Captain Barry and the crew departed at 16:27 PST, and six hours into the flight icing caused backfiring which caused engines number 1, 2 and 5 to begin to burn. Standard operating procedure was to fuze and drop the bomb. The aircraft proceeded out over the Pacific and dropped the bomb. The bomb was fuzed for 1400 m. The crew observed the weapon's conventional high explosives detonate at about 1100 m. Some reports have noted that the bomb detonated on impact, but this is unlikely as it would have been fuzed to ensure destruction.

The Mk4 atomic bomb was an improved derivative of the Mk-III"Fat Man" atomic bomb which had been used on the Japanese city of Nagasaki on 9 August 1945. The casing was 3.25 m long, with a body diameter of 1.54 m. Its shape was based on an old U.S. Navy design for their World War I C-Class airship. Contained within this 4.9 tonne bomb was 2.2 tonnes of high explosives used to implode and detonate one of three different fissile cores: the 49-LTC-C levitated uranium-235 core; the 49-LCC-C levitated composite uranium-plutonium core; and the 50-LCC-C composite core. The choice of cores gave SAC explosive yield options of between 20 and 40 kilotons, or up to twice the bombs which destroyed Hiroshima and Nagasaki. With the final Mk IIIs removed in late 1950, and the first MkVI deployed in mid-1951, the Mk4 was the only atomic bomb in the U.S. arsenal at the time of the St. Lawrence incident. By the time the Mk4 had been retired in May 1953, 550 had been produced, five used in weapons tests, and five lost in accidents. The Mk4 bomb had been a complete redesign of the MkIII "Fat Man" bomb. The MkIII required a team of 40 to 50 men almost three days to assemble, and almost eight hours for a final check and core insertion. The Mk4 design had greatly reduced those times, and a small team could perform the final check of only seven removable components in half an hour. The in-flight insertion of the fissile core, a feature new to the Mk4, took only half an hour in testing, a substantial improvement over the earlier designs.

The core of the bomb was under the control of the U.S. Atomic Energy Commission and had not been released to the U.S. military. This action required an order from the president. Therefore, although there was a practice core aboard the aircraft, the real core remained in storage.

Captain Barry, who would parachute on to Ashdown Island, describes the final minutes of the flight:

> We were losing altitude quite rapidly in excess of 500 feet a minute and I asked the Radar Operator to give me a heading to take me out over water. We kept our rapid rate of descent and we got out over the water just about 9000 feet and the co-pilot ran the bomb bay doors and hit the salvo switch and at first nothing happened, so he hit it again and this time it opened. The Radar Operator gave me a heading to take me back over land, the engineer gave me emergency power to try to hold our altitude. We still descended quite rapidly and by the time we got over land we were at 5000 feet. So, I rang the alarm bell, and told them to leave. The Radar Operator told me that there was terrain which in a few places ran up to 3500 feet and that is one reason I wanted them out.

The bomb was dropped some 90 km at 330 degrees from Bella Bella on Princess Royal Island, British Columbia. This would place it in the Squally Channel or Estavan Sound. The aircraft then flew over Princess Royal Island where 16 crew and one passenger bailed out. Twelve were rescued and five were never found.

The last few minutes of manned flight of the crippled giant were recorded by the RCAF from survivor testimony and passed on to the USAF.

> Survivors of B-36 stated course was being plotted from radar screen steering 030 degrees magnetic as radioed when over Estevan Island 2345P. When in the vicinity of Whale Channel they altered course to 165 degrees magnetic. When three miles [5 km] inland the order to jump was given and all were out in ten seconds. The first six out are unaccounted for. The upper winds were from 188 degrees at 47 knots [90 km]. They jumped at 5000 feet [1700 m]. Possibility that six missing men are to the north of where survivors landed on Princess Royal Island, Gil Island, or Whale Channel.[310]

Further interviews of the crewmen by the USAF on 18 February revealed that the heading of the B-36 at the time of bail-out was 165 degrees true. It is probable that the heading during bail-out was constant. The first man jumped at point 53.12N by 128.57W. First 12 from the front section were out in ten seconds commencing at 0650Z. The five in the rear compartment were out in from five to three seconds. The aircraft was navigating by radar at the time of the jump and was obtaining a good clear picture. It is known that every man left the aircraft. It is believed that everyone left the aircraft over land. The pilot was able to see Mount Cardin before abandoning the aircraft. The last man out of the rear compartment landed at 53.05N by 129.07W.[311]

The first survivor, Sergeant V. Trippodi, was found at about 13:00 local time on 15 February by the *Cape Perry*, a fishing boat, on Princess Royal Island after the crew spotted smoke. Although the RCAF sent Cansos 11067 and 11015 to the scene, the survivors were picked up by a U.S. Coast Guard PBY aircraft for the flight to Port Hardy, B.C. Another man was picked up at the same time, and during the afternoon another nine survivors were found.[312]

The last survivor, Lt. C.G. Pooler, was rescued the next day. The last man reported seeing the searchlights displayed by HMCS *Cayuga*, and he said his morale was raised by the sighting.[313] The evacuation of Lt. Pooler from the island was no easy task. He was found at the edge of an uncharted lake by one of the HMCS *Cayuga* rescue teams led by Lt. D.E. Rosenroll. The 2 km trip to the edge of the island, carrying the stretcher through the snow, took seven hours.[314]

Those missing are presumed to have drowned in the icy waters of the north Pacific Ocean between Ashdown Island and Princess Royal Island. This is evidenced by the fact that a one-man dinghy was washed up on a shore in this area. Crew in the forward compartment did not wear or carry "Mae West" inflatable life jackets, and nobody wore exposure suite. Everyone was dressed in arctic clothing and mukluks.

SURVIVORS	MISSING
LCol. D.V. MacDonald	Capt. W.M. Phillips
(USAF observer)	Capt. T.F. Schreier
Capt. H.L. Barry	(weaponier/armer)
(aircraft commander)	Lt. H. Ascol
Lt. E.O. Cox	S/Sgt. E.W. Pollard
Lt. R.R. Darrah	S/Sgt. N.A. Straley

Lt. P.E. Gerhart
Lt. R.P. Whitfield
Lt. C.G. Pooler
    (last man rescued)
T/Sgt. M.B. Stephens
S/Sgt. J.R. Ford
S/Sgt. D. Thrasher
S/Sgt. V. Trippodi
    (first man rescued)
Cpl. R.J. Schuler

The bomber, without crew or weapon, proceeded on autopilot for another 330 km and crashed into the mountains 2000 m up the side of the Kispiox Valley near 56.03N 128.32W. Captain Barry had noticed the bomber circle and then disappear. If the ice had broken away from the wings, the bomber, less the weight of the Mk4 bomb, could easily have gained altitude and continued to fly in a somewhat erratic manner all the way into the B.C. interior.

The U.S. military, very concerned about the loss of 17 valuable crew members, one very expensive heavy bomber, and one of only a handful of precious atomic bombs, immediately launched a full-scale search operation. In conjunction with the RCAF, the USAF sent 10 long-range patrol aircraft and several B-29 bombers; the U.S. Navy sent 12 Neptune long-range patrol aircraft; and the U.S. Coast Guard sent another six aircraft. It would not be found until a search for another aircraft in 1953. The crash site can be located on the Bowser Lake maps of the Cassiar Land District of British Columbia, as produced by the Department of Energy, Mines and Resources Canada. The U.S. military successfully sent in a demolition party in August 1954 to ensure that no secret equipment could be retrieved.

But things were not so clear in Washington. It turned out that once the U.S. Atomic Energy Commission gave the weapon to the USAF, they (the AEC) lost track of it. It was only when the news of a B-36 crash made headlines in the Washington *Times Herald,* that the AEC became aware of the potential loss. Bill Sheehy of the AEC, who had seen the loading of this particular bomb, "became personally as well as officially alarmed" at the possibility that the first loss had occurred.[315] When he telephoned USAF Colonel Coiner to enquire whether this was the bomber in which the AEC had an interest, the colonel said that the USAF was not yet certain. The Air Force then began asking people at Fort Worth whether the aircraft had carried an atomic bomb. Within days it was clear that nobody knew anything, and the USAF was rather embarrassed. Finally, 11 days after the crash, AEC was advised that the bomb had been jettisoned, but not detonated to destruction. Three days later, the AEC was told that the bomb had been detonated at sea in a "live drop." On 28 February, two weeks after the incident, General Hall of the USAF Legislative and Liaison Section refused to tell the AEC the status of the bomb without a written request.[316] The final word was that the AEC was not happy with the attitude of the USAF, which was summed up as the Air Force saying nothing until they were "damn good and ready to tell us what the hell they did with one of our atomic weapons."[317]

The Department of National Defence, Directorate of Nuclear Safety, sent a radiological survey team into the site on 11 August 1997. DNS reported that the only radiation at the site came from the instrument panel which had been painted with radium so that it glowed in the dark. There had never been a nuclear core or even the remnants of the Mk4 at the crash site.

THE BOMBING OF RIVIERE DU LOUP

In late July and early August 1950, special arrangements were made for the temporary stationing of a United States Air Force's Strategic Air Command Bombardment Group at Royal Canadian Air Force Station Goose Bay, Newfoundland, for a six-week period of training. Given that the Korean War had begun, and that the USAF had deployed a wing of B-50 bombers to Europe due to the tensions there, this was clearly more than an exercise. SAC Headquarters picked the 43rd Bombardment Group/43rd Bombardment Wing for the assignment.

The 43rd Bombardment Group was one of only four equipped with the new Boeing B-50 "Superfortress" bomber. They had been the first unit to receive the bomber, when on 20 February 1948, No. 46-017 arrived at Davis-Monthan AFB, Tucson, Arizona.[318] A year later the B-50 would make world headlines for being the first aircraft to fly around the globe, nonstop. The *Lucky Lady II* circled the planet in 94 hours and one minute. Despite these impressive public relations exercises, the primary mission of the B-50 was to carry the first generation of atomic bombs being built by the United States.

Back in August 1950, USAF/SAC also sought high-level secret permission to bring 11 "special weapons" (atomic bombs) to the Goose Bay deployment site.[319] This was described as an action brought about by the current period of emergency, which also saw atomic bombs deployed to Great Britain. In 1950 the United States nuclear arsenal consisted of only 299 atomic bombs,[320] of which 264 were new MkIV bombs, and the remaining 35 were the old MkIII "Fat Man" bombs. The problem with mating the MkIII and MkIV atomic bombs to the B-50 bomber was that the bombs were both too large to fit under the airplane. In order to get the MkIV on its trailer under the B-50 and into the bomb bay, the bomber had to be jacked up under the nose, thus permitting the bomb to be slipped in from the front.[321]

Prime Minister Louis St. Laurent had been informed of the United States's request by RCAF Air Marshal Curtis. Strategic Air Command had chosen Curtis as the contact man in Canada and relied on him to deal with the prime minister and military staff. The prime minister limited his permission to the six-week deployment period.[322]

In Ottawa, the prime minister and Air Marshal Curtis were in the know; at External Affairs, the secretary of state and under-secretary of state as well as a select few men had this knowledge.[323] Only three people at the Canadian embassy in Washington knew of the plans, and the chairman of the Joint Staff was not one of them. The full Cabinet heard nothing of the deployment at all until 18 August 1950,[324] when the chief of the Air Staff told them, "It seemed probable that a request would be forthcoming for permission to move a group of medium bombers and two squadrons of tankers to Goose Bay. It is not clear exactly what purpose the units were to serve." In reply, Brooke Claxton stated, "In connection with the U.S. request, it might be desirable to get further information, although there should be no hesitation about granting any reasonable request." The Cabinet then agreed to instruct DND to seek clarification of the request. Goose Bay was then not discussed again until 25 October 1950 when the Cabinet briefly talked about the possible expansion of facilities at the station. No mention is ever made of atomic weapons or of the accident.

Before the wing moved, intricate preparations took place. The secret history of the 64th Bombardment Squadron states that on 23 August 1950, "Lieutenant Hawke departed for the maneuver area via a devious route. All Special Weapons personnel were briefed by Captain Ferko,[325] Group Special Weapons Officer. Second Lieutenants Richard C. Henry, Robert A. Wilke, and Stewart V. Spragins, all reported for duty." These Special Weapons personnel, all pilots, then prepared for the deployment.

The 43rd Bomb Group acted in compliance with Fifteenth Air Force Operations Order 18-50 of 3 August 1950 and prepared to move three bomber squadrons of 15 B-50 aircraft each to Goose Bay and two refuelling squadrons[326] of 19 KB-29 aircraft each to Harmon Air Base. Originally, five bombers were to fly to Goose Bay from Davis-Monthan AFB each day. Along the way, a number of the bombers would pick up conventional weapons at Gray Air Force Base for carriage to Goose Bay.

The 43rd Bombardment Wing began its move to Goose Bay on 26 August and was in place by 30 August 1950. Goose Bay Station records show that on the day of 27 August, 43 bombers arrived there. However, engine failures caused some aircraft to be delayed, and the final bomber arrived on 11 September. At the beginning of September 1950 the wing had 44 B-50 bombers on inventory, with 43 deployed to Goose Bay. Counting the tankers as well, they had deployed more than 75 aircraft.[327] The wing also had 616 officers and 3560 men living in tents scattered about the grounds at "The Goose." And deep in the forest they had 11 atomic bombs.

> INCIDENT: Dropped Atomic Bomb/non-critical detonation
> CLASS: Broken Arrow
> DATE: 10 November 1950
> COMMAND: USAF Strategic Air Command, SAC
> AIR FORCE: 15th Air Force, USAF
> GROUP: 43rd Bombardment Group
> WING: 43rd Bombardment Wing (Medium)
> DEPUTY COMMANDER: Lt. Colonel Moore
> SQUADRON: 64th Bombardment Squadron
> BASE: Davis-Monthan Air Force Base, Arizona, USA
> AIRCRAFT: B-50A (derivative of Boeing B-29)
> PILOT: Major Charles Gove
> WEAPON: Mk IV (derivative of Fat Man atomic bomb)
> PLACE: in the St. Lawrence River near Riviere du Loup, Quebec.

INCIDENT

A number of aircraft had clearly brought atomic bombs to Goose Bay. The secret history of the Security Section of the 43rd Bombardment Wing notes the following:

- "Upon arrival at destination, bomb carriers were met by cleared Air Police security guards. After classified units were unloaded from bomb carriers guards accompanied units from aircraft to Restricted Storage Area and aircraft were declassified. Units were stored in a forest, on gravel roads, approximately four miles from the base proper. Units were stored 300 feet apart and 1500 feet from nearest well-traveled road. Each unit was guarded 24 hours a day....A Corporal of the Guard was posted at the barricaded entrance to the Storage Area."

• "The Assembly Area was approximately two and one-half miles from Storage Area. Two roving foot patrols were utilized around the Assembly Building to double check SAC Identification Passes and for radiological safety enforcement."

The personnel caring for the precious few atomic bombs had brought 61 different types of handling equipment with them, and their assembly and technical buildings contained another 141 pieces of electrical testing equipment. The MkIV bomb was difficult to maintain.

Within days of their arrival at Goose Bay, the 43rd Bomb Wing was already in operation. On 6 September they flew six "Big Stick" practice strategic bombing missions,[328] probably in the direction of Europe.[329] During one exercise, a B-50 crashed off the end of the runway at Goose Bay. Fortunately, it was unarmed.

On 28 September USAF/SAC requested permission from the Canadian government[330] for the urgent construction of atomic bomb storage bunkers at Goose Bay, as there are absolutely no facilities of any kind at "the Goose." At that time SAC was already storing 11 atomic bombs out in the bush a short drive from the base. The Canadian ambassador to the United States commented to the under-secretary of state for External Affairs that the USAF did "not envisage the storage of special weapons at Goose Bay until the additional construction there is available."[331] In fact, the 43rd already had the atomic weapons with them, storage bunkers or no storage bunkers.

As this was only a temporary deployment, and as winter was beginning to set in to the region, the wing prepared to return all its men and equipment to the warmth of the southwest United States. It was also time to return the special weapons to their home in the United States. The secret history of the 43rd Bombardment Wing notes that on 9 November 1950 a "Classified mission [was] flown to Goose Bay, Labrador." It also noted that it happened the day before: on 8 November 1950, "18 B-50 aircraft departed for Harmon Air Force Base and Goose Bay, Labrador, to participate in a classified maneuver ordered by Headquarters Strategic Air Command." They flew under Wing Operation Order 20-50, and returned to Davis-Monthan AFB on 11 and 12 November. The Goose Bay records note that 17 B-50s arrived on 10 November for a western flight to the United States.

"It was during transportation of these weapons to the United States that the incident occurred over the St. Lawrence River in which one of the bombs had to be jettisoned and detonated owing to engine trouble in one of the transporting aircraft."[332] On 10 November 1950, a Strategic Air Command 43rd Bomb Group B-50 bomber on its way from Goose Bay to Davis-Monthan AFB, dropped a MkIV atomic bomb in the middle of the St. Lawrence River.

On the return trip of this classified mission, four bombers experienced engine troubles: one from the 63rd Bombardment Squadron, and three from the 64th Bombardment Squadron. Details of the incidents show that only one aircraft had a failure in two of its four engines. B-50 No. 46-038 had valve problems, possibly due to icing, on its way from Goose Bay to Davis-Monthan, and landed in Maine on 10 November. The aircraft had been flying at an altitude of between 10,000 and 15,000 feet. The engines failed, whether from icing alone, or from valve failures brought about by icing. It was, however, able to fly on to Limestone Air Force Base in Maine for repairs. This bomber, and the three others, returned to Davis-Monthan AFB by mid-November.

The other bombers from the 64th Bombardment Squadron to experience problems were No. 46-031, which blew out an intake manifold on one engine, and bomber No. 46-026, which developed a bad cylinder on one engine. All three stopped at Limestone Air Force Base in Maine for repairs. The trio returned to Davis-Monthan AFB by mid-November. B-50 No. 46-047A of the 63rd Bombardment Squadron had an oil leak due to a faulty oil seal on the propeller shaft of engine No. 2 on its way from Goose Bay to Davis-Monthan AFB, and also landed at Limestone AFB that day. It flew on to Davis-Monthan AFB on 13 November. Less than a week later, on 16 November, this twice-unlucky aircraft would crash and burn.

This was no ordinary bomber crew: they were what SAC Commander Curtis LeMay called a "Lead Select Crew" and were appropriately high ranked. Crew S-020 of 1 men flew No. 46-038 that cold, icy day. The aircraft commander, Major Charles F. Gove, acted as pilot that day; and the all-important position of the bombardier was filled by Major Newton Brown. Major Donald Barret was the navigator, and Major Bruce Knutson the radar observer. In addition, there was the pilot, flight engineer, radio operator, and four gunners. Wing Deputy Commander Lt. Colonel Moore was also present, acting as aircraft commander, as this bomber was the lead aircraft on the mission to return the special weapons to the United States.

As they approached the St. Lawrence River, their first engine failed. Soon a second engine, on the other wing, began to backfire and was throttled back. Fully loaded with fuel and the atomic bomb, the aircraft had little hope of making it to a U.S. base, and USAF/SAC Standard Operating Procedure called for the bomb to be dropped. The fuzes were to be set to detonate the bomb at 1200 m above the water. After checking the river for shipping both visually and with radar, and on consultation with the aircraft commander and pilot, Major Brown released the bomb from the bomb bay when B-50 No. 46-038 had made its way out over the centre of the St. Lawrence River, not far from Riviere du Loup, Quebec.

The 2200 kg of high explosive used to implode the fissile material in the 5000-kg bomb detonated at 775 m above the surface of the river, causing great alarm to the people of St. Andre de Kamouraska, St. Simeon, and Pointe au Persil[333] on both sides of the river. The fission package was not in the bomb casing, so there was no chance of a nuclear detonation. It was this in-flight insertion (IFI) feature which saved the middle of the St. Lawrence from being irradiated. The plutonium or uranium core was always carried separately from the bomb, and only inserted prior to approaching the target. It was not on board the aircraft that day.

The bomber would proceed to Limestone Air Force Base at Limestone, Maine, not far south of the Canadian border. Although not in the best condition for flight, the aircraft was serviceable and should have recovered safely. However, the pilot for the landing dropped the aircraft on to the runway with such force that the main landing gear was almost driven up through the wings. Nobody was injured, and the crew were immediately debriefed on the classified aspects of the incident.

The news would spread quickly of a massive explosion in the St. Lawrence, and the USAF promptly issued a cover story. As it was told in the *Montreal Gazette*[334] on 11 November, a SAC four-engined B-50 bomber on a routine training flight from Goose Bay to Tuscon, Arizona, jettisoned a load of 500-pound (220 kg) practice bombs into the St. Lawrence River after experiencing engine trouble. The article noted that the explosion had taken place between the Quebec river communities of Port-au-Persil and St-Simon to the north, and Kamouraska and St. Andre to the south. Residents reported thinking that in this time of international tensions, this was a bombing attack. The cover story did not fool External Affairs, and talks quickly began as the United States sought to mollify the Canadians.

I enclose a Memorandum prepared by Mr. Ignatieff of a conversation which took place in my office yesterday with Mr. Gordon Arneson of the State Department, at his request. From this conversation I was able to get a coherent account of various developments of which I had previously only had fragmentary knowledge. It was explained to me for the first time why the concern felt in Canada over the explosion of a bomb jettisoned by a U.S.A.F. bomber a few weeks ago while on a flight from Goose Bay to Maine had not resulted in the receipt of instructions to seek a full explanation from the U.S. Government.

After talking to Mr. Arneson I only know with certainty that Air Marshal Curtis and the Prime Minister are informed of the nature of the arrangements made for the temporary storage of special weapons at Goose Bay last August. I assume, however, from your instructions given in the last paragraph of your letter No. D-3376 that you are also aware of these arrangements. It would be helpful if in your reply you could indicate to me what others in Ottawa have knowledge of this very secret matter. At the Embassy it is only known to Mr. Ignatieff, myself, and my secretary, and I shall not mention it to the Chairman of the Joint Staff unless I learn definitely that he has already been informed.

You will note that Mr. Arneson's particular purpose was to establish the best channel to employ for further communications on this subject. The alternatives are a Service channel from the U.S. Air Force to the Chief of the Air Staff or a civilian channel from the State Department to me to you. The State Department would prefer not to use the United States embassy in Ottawa in this connection. I told Mr. Arneson that on the whole I thought the Prime Minister would prefer the employment of the civilian channel, especially since the decision to seek our concurrence is made personally by the President on the recommendation of the Secretaries of State and Defence and the Chairman of the Atomic Energy Commission.

In view of the gravity of the present international situation, I think it desirable that the procedure should be established within the next two or three weeks, although the present plans do not envisage the storage of special weapons at Goose Bay until the additional construction there is available.[335]

OTHER USAF CRASHES IN CANADA

What follows is a list of other SAC bomber accidents involving Canadian territory. There is little information on most of the items, and it is doubtful that some happened. Some may be duplicates of other entries with slightly altered details. I have included this fairly extensive list in the hopes that others will go on to do more in-depth analysis of the incidents. Details are provided where any are known at the time of publication. In some cases it is not even known what type of aircraft crashed, or even if it happened on the reported date. I have included all the reported accidents in the hope that researchers specializing in aircraft crashes will someday piece the entire puzzle together. In addition, various other significant SAC accidents worldwide are included as reference points and to provide context.

When news of the crash in B.C. and the loss of the atomic bomb in Quebec gained front-page coverage on 27 January 1997, the Department of Foreign Affairs responded by confirming the accidents, but stating that "Cabinet would have to examine a request for overflight of any aircraft carrying nuclear components, on a case-by-case basis." Further, Foreign Affairs wrote that "a request to overfly nuclear material would be examined by the Canadian Government very closely indeed. Such flights are no longer the norm - This Government has not received such an application for over two years."[336]

The last confirmed USAF bomber crash in Canada happened on 7 February 1969.

THE GOOSE BAY CRASH
INCIDENT: crash of flight from Goose Bay to Tucson; three engines on
        fire, possibly due to carburetor icing. All bailed out.
CLASS: Dull Sword (unarmed)
DATE: 23 September 1950
GROUP: 43rd Bombardment Group
WING: 43rd Bombardment Wing (Medium)
BASE: Davis-Monthan Air Force Base
AIRCRAFT: B-50 "Superfortress", s/n 47105
CREW: 16 survivors found by RCAF; crew evacuated by USAF
PLACE: beyond Goose Bay runway, 5257N 6257W

THE VANCOUVER ISLAND CRASH
INCIDENT: dropped atomic bomb/non-critical detonation
CLASS: Broken Arrow
DATE: 14 February 1950, 07:50z
AIR FORCE: 8th Air Force, USAF
WING: 7th Bomb Wing (Heavy)

GROUP: 7th Bomb Group
SQUADRON: 436th Bombardment Squadron
BASE: Carswell Air Force Base, Texas, USA
AIRCRAFT: B-36 "Peacemaker," s/n 44-92075 (built 31 July 1949)
A/C COMM: Lt.Colonel D.V. MacDonald
PILOT: Capt. Harold L. Barry
WEAPON: MkIV (derivative of Fat Man atomic bomb)
PLACE OF BOMBING: over water, near 53.00N 129.49W
PLACE OF CRASH: British Columbia, 56.08N 128.32W
NOTES: DHist SAR reel No. 69, SAR Op BRIX

THE RIVIERE DU LOUP INCIDENT
INCIDENT: Dropped atomic bomb/non-critical detonation
CLASS: Broken Arrow
DATE: 10 November 1950
COMMAND: USAF Strategic Air Command, SAC
AIR FORCE: 15th Air Force, USAF
GROUP: 43rd Bombardment Group
WING: 43rd Bombardment Wing (Medium)
DEPUTY COMMANDER: Lt. Colonel Moore
SQUADRON: 64th Bombardment Squadron
BASE: Davis-Monthan Air Force Base, Arizona, USA
AIRCRAFT: B-50A "Superfortress" (derivative of Boeing B-29)
PILOT: Major Charles Gove
WEAPON: MkIV (derivative of Fat Man atomic bomb)
PLACE: in the St. Lawrence River near Riviere du Loup, Quebec

THE GOOSE BAY CRASH
INCIDENT: crash
DATE: 4 or 14 August 1951
AIRCRAFT: RB-45C, s/n 8698, "Tornado" tactical bomber
WEAPONS: This was the first all-jet tactical bomber in the USAF. It
could carry the Mk5 and Mk7 atomic bombs, and dropped
two during live atomic tests in 1951-52.
PLACE: on hill, several kilometres north of Goose Bay, 5314N 6029W

THE GOOSE BAY CRASH
INCIDENT: crash
CLASS: probable Dull Sword
DATE: 12 or 13 February 1953

AIRCRAFT: B-36 "Peacemaker," s/n 3318
PLACE: at Goose Bay, 5306N 6041W
NOTES: This crash has never been written about and further details are
unavailable.

THE NUT COVE CRASH

INCIDENT: crash
CLASS: possible Dull Sword
DATE: 18 March 1953, 07:40z
WING: 28th Strategic Reconnaissance Wing (Heavy)
SQUADRON: 718th Strategic Reconnaissance Squadron
BASE: Rapid City AFB
AIRCRAFT: RB-36H "Peacemaker," s/n 51-13721
PILOT: Major Frank C. Wright
AIRCRAFT COMMANDER: Major General R.E. Ellsworth
PLACE: Random Island, across from Burgoyne Cove, Newfoundland,
48.10N 53.44W

The massive reconnaissance RB-36 had come from the Azores Islands
after finishing numerous sorties with a task force of 11 other RB-36
bombers during five days of intercontinental combat training. It was
returning to Rapid City AFB when it crashed into hills on Random
Island, Newfoundland. Being mainly a reconnaissance aircraft in this
case, and just returning to base from an overseas exercise, it is unlikely
that an atomic bomb was on board.

"Radio operators in St. John's, Newfoundland, intercepted an
emergency declaration that two engines had failed. Residents of the tiny
fishing village of Burgoyne, Newfoundland, watched helplessly as the
giant plane rumbled low overhead, then crashed into a hillside in the
nearly trackless forest, beyond. Exactly seven hours 40 minutes after
liftoff from Lajes Field—with Captain Pruitt still flying straight and level
— RB-36H No. 721 crashed into the frigid wilderness of Random
Island, near Burgoyne Cove, approximately 100 km east of Gander,
Newfoundland."[337] There were no survivors.

PERSONNEL KILLED IN NUT COVE CRASH

RANK	NAME	POSITION
SSgt.	I.V. Beard	Gunner
1Lt.	C.W. Bransdor	Observer, ECM

Capt.	O.F. Clark	Pilot
Gen.	R.E. Ellsworth	Aircraft Commander
Capt.	S.G. Fauhl	Observer, Navigator
A2C	K.E. Hoppens	Gunner
A1C	T. Kuzik	Gunner
Capt.	W.P. Maher	Observer, Radar Operator
TSgt.	J.H. Maltsberger	Crew Chief
A2C	P. Mancos, Jr.	Gunner
1Lt.	E.J. Meader	Aircraft Performance Engineer
Maj.	J.T. Murray	Observer, ECM
A2C	R.H. Nall	Observer, ECM
1Lt.	J.E. Pace	Aircraft Performance Engineer
TSgt.	W.A. Plonski	Radio Operator
1Lt.	J.A. Powell, Jr.	Observer, ECM
Capt.	J.H. Pruett, Jr.	Aircraft Commander
A2C	M.H. Rogers	Photographer
Capt.	H.G. Smith	Observer, Photo Navigator
SSgt.	R.E. Ullom	Gunner
A1C	B.J. Vaughn	Radio Operator
MSgt.	J.S. Winegardner	Photographer
Maj.	F.C. Wright	Pilot

On 13 June 1953, the USAF re-named Rapid City AFB in South Dakota after General Richard E. Ellsworth, who died in the crash.

THE BIG SANDY LAKE CRASH

INCIDENT: mid-air explosion during flight from Thule AFB to Riverside, California. No indication of problem given to other 10 aircraft in formation.

CLASS: possible Broken Arrow, probable Dull Sword

DATE: 12 February 1955, 13:50z, 07:50cst.

AIR FORCE: 15th Air Force, USAF

WING: 22nd Bombardment Wing

SQUADRON: 19th Bomb Squadron

BASE: March Air Force Base

AIRCRAFT: B-47E-65BW "Stratojet," s/n 51-7033A

AIRFRAME TIME: new, 602 hours

PILOT: LCol. K.G. McGrew

OPERATION: "Bob Sled" SAC training mission

CREW: 3 survivors, 1 fatality

PLACE: 65 km north of Squaw Rapids, Saskatchewan, or Big Sandy Lake, Saskatchewan 54.20N 103.50W. Wreck scattered for 15 km

LCol. McGrew took his new B-47 and crew aloft from March AFB in California at 01:01 zulu, and took on fuel over Canada at 04:40 and 09:30 zulu on a flight to and from Thule. The bomber was flying at about 10,000 m when the No. 4 engine, closest to the fuselage on the starboard side, exploded at 13:50 zulu. Engine No. 5, in the same pod, was seriously damaged. All three starboard engines were shut down, seriously unbalancing the flight characteristics of the bomber, especially when engine No. 2 quit due to a manifold problem caused by the cut-off of engine No. 6. The fire in No. 4 and 5 was extinguished by the airflow and careful management by the flight crew. The explosion had thrown flaming hot parts of the turbine wheels against the aircraft, resulting in a fuselage fire which could not be extinguished with diving airspeed. This was noticed by the pilot or co-pilot who saw a flickering reflection against the No. 4/5 engine pod. The fire in and around the bomb bay resulted in a massive explosion which tore the aircraft into three main parts: the forward crew compartment, the wing and main fuselage, and the empenage or tail section at about 7000 m.

LCol McGrew best described the accident:

> At the time of the emergency, the first abnormal indication was when number four engine blew up.... The aircraft had slowed considerably while operating on 2 or 3 engines, so I decided to take a few seconds to try to blow out the flames by diving to increase airspeed.... When the aircraft had accelerated the flames persisted and I was going to give the word to leave the aircraft when a violent explosion was felt which threw me forward and to the left in my seat.... I was held forward and left in my seat by what seemed to be G forces.... That was my last conscious moment. I don't remember ejecting or opening my chute. The next thing I knew I was free of the aircraft, drifting down in my opened chute. I saw one chute below me and called once but received no answer.... I couldn't see the other chute again, but saw a flaming part of the aircraft on the ground.[338]

Major Robert Dowdy died in the explosion. LCol Kenneth McGrew, Captain Lester Epton, and Captain Thomas Pittman survived with major injuries.

THE NORTH ATLANTIC DROP
INCIDENT: jettisoned one or more nuclear weapons during transit
CLASS: Broken Arrow
DATE: 24 February 1956
AIRCRAFT: USAF C-124 cargo
CREW: all survived
OPERATION: transport of nuclear weapon(s) from USA to Upper
Heyford, UK
WEAPONS: unknown type(s) of nuclear weapon(s)
PLACE: North Atlantic after leaving Goose Bay
NOTES: Numerous cargo shipments of nuclear weapons went to and from
Europe via both Goose Bay and Harmon AFB at this time.

THE LAKENHEATH IGLOO CRASH
INCIDENT: SAC bomber crashed on top of nuclear weapon storage igloos.
DATE: 27 July 1956
AIRCRAFT: B-47 "Stratojet"
CREW: three crew died in crash
WEAPONS: three Mk6 nuclear weapons were in the storage igloo and
damaged. "A miracle that one Mark Six with exposed
detonators sheared didn't go."
PLACE: Lakenheath Air Base, Cambridge, United Kingdom

THE NIPIGON CRASH
INCIDENT: crash after mechanical failure during training mission in
formation
CLASS: Dull Sword
DATE: 1 December 1956 00:05z
BASE: Barksdale Air Force Base
AIRCRAFT: B-47 "Stratojet," s/n 2025
PILOT: Maj. R.M. Slane ejected at 12,000 m and survived
CREW: all three crew died in crash
OPERATION: "Nurse Maid"
WEAPONS: none likely carried at this early date
PLACE: near Nipigon, Ontario. 49.01N 88.48W

THE CAPE SABLE ISLAND CRASH
INCIDENT: possible ditching
CLASS: probable Dull Sword
DATE: 27 April 1957

AIRCRAFT: B-57 "Intruder"
WEAPON: capable of carrying Mk7 and Mk43 nuclear weapons
LOCATION: southwest of Cape Sable Island, Nova Scotia
NOTES: no records found of this crash

THE GRAND BRUIT CRASH

INCIDENT: crew bailed out during flight from Plattsburg AFB to Gander,
Newfoundland
CLASS: probable Dull Sword
DATE: 17 September 1957
AIRCRAFT: B-47 "Stratojet," s/n 15811
PILOT: (Maj?) Garfield
CREW: 1 survivor, 2 missing
WEAPON: nuclear weapon(s) could have been carried
LOCATION: 47.15N 58.10W (at sea) 85 km south of Grand Bruit,
Newfoundland

THE GOOSE BAY CRASH

INCIDENT: crash in bush after engine flame-out
DATE: 30 November 1957
SQUADRON: 59th FIS
AIRCRAFT: F-94B
WEAPONS: the unit was not yet nuclear-armed
LOCATION: Goose Bay
NOTES: Cat "A" accident

THE MOROCCO CRASH

INCIDENT: bomber crashed and burned
DATE: 31 January 1958
AIRCRAFT: B-47 "Stratojet" on Reflex alert
WEAPON: single thermonuclear weapon
LOCATION: 150 km northeast of Rabat, Morocco
NOTES: USAF evacuated area as fire raged for seven hours. Severe
radioactive contamination of site.

THE LOST BOMB OF SAVANNAH RIVER

INCIDENT: bomber jettisoned weapon after collision with fighter
DATE: 5 February 1958
BASE: Homestead AFB

AIRCRAFT: B-47 "Stratojet"
WEAPONS: single high-yield thermonuclear weapon: never recovered
LOCATION: Wassaw Sound, Savannah River, Georgia

THE GREGG INCIDENT
INCIDENT: bomber on flight to Europe dropped single unarmed nuclear
weapon
DATE: 11 March 1958
BASE: Hunter AFB, Georgia
AIRCRAFT: A B-47 "Stratojet"
WEAPON: single thermonuclear weapon
LOCATION: garden of Walter Gregg in Mars Bluff, South Carolina
NOTES: Detonation of conventional explosives destroyed house and
injured six of the Gregg family. It also damaged five other
houses and a church.

THE GOOSE BAY CRASH
INCIDENT: crash
CLASS: probable Dull Sword
DATE: 24 April 1958
AIRCRAFT: B-47 "Stratojet," s/n ?
LOCATION: 13 km east from the end of runway 9 after takeoff from
Goose Bay at 5322N 6022W.

THE GOOSE BAY CRASH
INCIDENT: crash
CLASS: probable Dull Sword
DATE: 2 October 1959
BASE: Schilling AFB, Kansas
AIRCRAFT: B-47 "Stratojet"
LOCATION: Goose Bay

THE KENTUCKY CRASH
INCIDENT: bomber collided with tanker during airborne alert
DATE: 15 October 1959
UNIT: 4228th Strategic Wing
BASE: Columbus AFB
AIRCRAFT: B-52G "Stratofortress" s/n 57-0036
CREW: four crew died in crash
WEAPONS: two thermonuclear weapons, recovered; one burned.

LOCATION: Hardinsberg, Kentucky

THE PAGWA CRASH

INCIDENT: mid-air collision between B-47 and F-102; both went down
    in flames
CLASS: probable Dull Sword
DATE: 17 December 1959. 18:22z
AIRCRAFT: B-47 "Stratojet"
PILOT: Capt. Minor (co-pilot Lt. Adams)
CREW: 2 survived, 2 died
AIRCRAFT: F-102 "Delta Dagger"
PILOT: Lt. Treu (F-102) died
WEAPONS: nuclear weapons could be carried
LOCATION: 130 km north of Calstock, Ontario, or, 65 km northeast
    of Pagwa, Ontario50.30N 84.18W

THE PORT AUX BASQUE CRASH

INCIDENT: possible crash
CLASS: probable Dull Sword
DATE: 21 September 1960 (?)
AIRCRAFT: B-52 "Stratofortress"
WEAPONS: Mk28 most common
LOCATION: southeast of Port Aux Basques, Newfoundland

There is one crash of a B-52 in 1960 for which there is no public account. B-52D s/n 55-0114 crashed at an undisclosed location on 21 September 1960 during a low-level flight. The pilot concluded that the aircraft was breaking up and ordered the crew to eject. This may be the crash rumoured to have happened off Port Aux Basques, Newfoundland. At this time SAC was preparing for low-level penetration of Soviet air defence systems, and the carriage of nuclear weapons was common.

THE SECRET BRITISH CRASH

INCIDENT: alert aircraft crashed on take-off and burned
DATE: 16 January 1961, 09:15z
AIRCRAFT: probably B-47 "Stratojet" on Reflex duty
LOCATION : unknown USAF base in Britain
WEAPON: single thermonuclear weapon was "scorched and blistered,"
    according to secret correspondence dated 23/1/61 between the
    chairman of the U.S. Joint Commission on Atomic Energy and the

secretary of Defense's office. The U.S. government has never acknowledged the accident or its precise location. It could be Greenham Common, as there is a radiation signature held in the trees around the base which probably came from a nuclear accident.

THE GOLDSBORO CRASH

INCIDENT: bomber crashed when starboard wing fell off
DATE: 24 January 1961
BASE: Seymour Johnson AFB
UNIT: 4241st Strategic Wing
AIRCRAFT: B-52G "Stratofortress" s/n 58-0187
CREW: three crew died in crash
WEAPONS: two Mk41 weapons: one parachuted, one impacted and broke open. A portion of one weapon, containing uranium, was never recovered. Five of six safety locks failed, and a single switch prevented full detonation.
LOCATION: Goldsboro, North Carolina

THE NEWFOUNDLAND CRASH

INCIDENT: crash in water
CLASS: probable Dull Sword
DATE: 15 October 1961
WING: 4241 Strategic Wing
SQUADRON: 73 Bombardment Squadron
BASE: Seymour Johnson Air Force Base
AIRCRAFT: B-52G "Stratofortress," s/n 58-0196, call sign "Pogo 22"
PILOT: Capt. R.C. Starke, Jr.
OPERATION: Sky Shield II
WEAPONS: probably none carried
LOCATION: off Newfoundland coast

In this case, the aircraft was flying in exercise Sky Shield II, and as it was an air defence exercise, it is highly unlikely that nuclear weapons were carried. The weight and balance clearance form for the flight that day shows no "bombs, rockets, etc." in the forward, aft or external armament areas. The aircraft was unarmed.[339]

All eight people on board were lost. The dead were Roland Starke, Kenneth Payne, Dean Upp, Paul Fellows, Richard Wiksell, Gary Sprague, Helmut Christ and Francis Jones. The cause of the accident is unknown as no aircraft or crew were ever found.

THE YUBA CITY CRASH
INCIDENT: bomber ran out of fuel and was ditched
DATE: 14 March 1961
AIRCRAFT: B-52F "Stratofortress" s/n 57-0166
CREW: ejected prior to crash
WEAPONS: two high-yield thermonuclear weapons recovered from
wreckage
LOCATION: Yuba City, California

THE GOOSE BAY CRASH
INCIDENT: crash
DATE: 13 December 1962
AIRCRAFT: F-102A "Delta Dagger," s/n 61477
LOCATION: 5412N 6042W, near Goose Bay
NOTES: The 59th FIS at Goose Bay would eventually be armed with
nuclear missiles for air defence purposes.

THE CUMBERLAND CRASH
INCIDENT: bomber crashed after falling apart due to turbulence
DATE: 13 January 1964
AIRCRAFT: B-52D "Stratofortress" s/n 55-0060
CREW: three died, two survived
WEAPONS: two thermonuclear weapons recovered from crash site
LOCATION: Cumberland, Maryland

THE 4 WING CRASH
INCIDENT: aircraft crashed and burned
DATE: 26 October 1964
AIRCRAFT: F-106 "Delta Dart"
LOCATION: at or near RCAF 4 Wing airfield, Baden, Germany

THE ST. JOHN'S COLLISION
INCIDENT: collision and explosion during refuelling while bomber was
returning from Reflex duty in Spain
CLASS: possible Broken Arrow
DATE: 26 February 1965. c.12:30z
BASE: Pease Air Force Base
AIRCRAFT: B-47 "Stratojet"
BASE: Dow Air Force Base
AIRCRAFT: KC-135 tanker trainer

CREW: 4 persons in each aircraft died in the collision and explosion
WEAPONS: nuclear weapons could have been carried
LOCATION: 400 km south-southeast of St. John's, Newfoundland
NOTES: a massive search was launched by the USAF, USN, and U.S. Coast Guard

THE RICHELIEU DROP

INCIDENT: accidental dropping of two nuclear weapons training shapes
CLASS: possible Dull Sword
DATE: February-March, 1967, 1968 or 1969
SQUADRON: 528th or 529th Bomb Squadron
BASE: Plattsburg Air Force Base
AIRCRAFT: B-52 "Stratofortress"
WEAPONS: possibly B28RI nuclear training shapes
LOCATION: Richelieu River, Quebec, at U.S. border, 45.02N 73.17W

The nuclear weapon training shapes were said to have been found by the University of Quebec at Montreal archeology diving team using the pontoon boat *Explorateur*, in Richelieu River immediately north of the Canada-United States border during summer of 1972 or 1973. One person reports seeing the Canadian Forces float the objects and then airlift them by helicopter to the U.S. border under heavy guard less than 2 km south. A B-52 pilot from the base, famous for having been on the B-52 which crashed at Thule, does not recall the event and stated that all crews would have known as there would have been a safety briefing.

THE PALOMARES CRASH

INCIDENT: bomber crashed into tanker, dropped four nuclear weapons
DATE: 17 January 1966
UNIT 68th Bomb Wing
AIRCRAFT: B-52G "Stratofortress" s/n 58-0256
CREW: ten crew: seven died, three survived the collision and explosion
WEAPONS: four Mk28RI weapons; two sank, two wrecked on ground
LOCATION: Palomares, Spain

THE THULE CRASH

INCIDENT: bomber crashed into ice with four nuclear weapons
DATE: 22 January 1968
UNIT: 380th SAW
AIRCRAFT: B-52G "Stratofortress" s/n 58-0188

WEAPONS: four Mk28RI thermonuclear weapons burned on ice cap
LOCATION: North Star Bay, near Thule, Greenland
NOTES: crashed 12 km south of Thule Air Base in Greenland while
   carrying four war reserve nuclear weapons. The United States
   dug up the ice cap, put it in barrels, and shipped them all back
   to the United States for disposal.

THE TORONTO CRASH
INCIDENT: possible crash
DATE: 12 February 1968
AIRCRAFT: B-52 "Stratofortress"
WEAPONS: airborne alert with nuclear weapons had been ended in
   January
LOCATION: north of Toronto, Ontario
NOTES: This crash was reported by M. de Durand, "L'Epopee des B-52"
   in *La Tribune des Nations.* On 23 February 1968. There is no
   other record of a B-52 loss for this date.

THE GOOSE BAY CRASH
INCIDENT: aircraft overshot runway on landing, crashed in bush
DATE: 10 or 17 or 18 December 1968, 21:15z
WING: 95th Strategic Log (?), Goose Bay AB
BASE: Goose Bay AB
AIRCRAFT: a/c? USAF s/n 10065
LOCATION: off end of Goose Bay runway

THE PORTAGE LA PRAIRIE CRASH
INCIDENT: bomber hit ground in explosive fireball
DATE: 07 February 1969
BASE: Stewart Air Force Base
AIRCRAFT: B-57 "Intruder," s/n 0-54286
CREW: Cat A (fatal), two crew died in crash
WEAPONS: the B-57 was a conventional bomber by 1969
LOCATION: Portage la Prairie, Manitoba

Chapter Five

THE USAF AT GOOSE BAY

"In Limine - Ad Exemplum"
(On the Threshold - As a Warning)

During World War II the United Kingdom, desperate for war materials from the United States, offered the colony of Newfoundland, both in whole and in parts, to the United States. This would be a trade: land for weapons. Goose Bay, already a military site, was leased in part to the United States, and the airfield at Stephenville was leased in whole, thereby becoming Harmon Field or Ernest Harmon Air Force Base. Although Newfoundland came under complete Canadian control in 1949, the leased areas continued under U.S. domination, much like the U.S. presence at Guantanamo Naval Base in Cuba after 1959.

At the end of World War II, the U.S. military, with the concurrence of Newfoundland authorities, had been granted the right to temporarily station military and civilian personnel around Newfoundland. What the Cabinet understood was that this arrangement was good only until the peace treaty with Germany was signed. However, they were aware that on several occasions in 1946 the United States had indicated their interest in securing long-term rights at Goose Bay. Cabinet felt that this question should not be pressed by U.S. authorities.[340]

The very first U.S. interest in Goose Bay as a site for supporting the new superpower expansion in the post-war world and into the new Cold War came in 1946, with World War II only one year past. Major General Guy Henry, the senior U.S. Army member of the Permanent Joint Board on Defence, issued a memorandum in which he called for the use of Goose Bay as an important strategic asset.[341] His words are worth quoting.

Strategically, the United States Air Forces wish to push out on the perimeter as far as practicable. U.S. Air Forces would therefore like to station tactical groups at Goose Bay Air Base, Labrador. The tactical groups presently contemplated would consist of one (1) very heavy bombardment group and one (1) fighter group, together with the necessary supporting troops, leaving at Harmon Field one (1) very heavy bombardment group, one (1) fighter group and one (1) all weather fighter squadron, plus one (1) very long-range reconnaissance squadron, together with the necessary supporting troops.

The first known consideration of the question of more permanent U.S. forces at Goose Bay by Cabinet came very quickly, but nothing would be done. On 9 January 1947, the Cabinet Defence Committee simply noted that the U.S. government had formally asked a granting of military rights for the peacetime use of Goose Bay airport which they regarded as the most strategically important airbase on the continent. Cabinet deferred.[342]

Half a year later, the secretary of the committee issued a memorandum pointing out that the United States was expressing increased interest in Goose Bay. The memo noted that there were now over 500 personnel on site, and that married quarters had been provided.[343] The United States viewed Goose Bay as one of the most strategically important military sites in the world, and they were determined to acquire increased rights. The only response of Cabinet was to further discourage the United States from making such requests. They felt that the question should still not be pressed, and that in any case, there was no suitable government in Newfoundland with which to carry on negotiations.[344]

The USAF then requested Canadian authorization to build storage facilities for at least 6.7 million litres of aviation fuel. The amount was very large at the time, but the USAF felt that as Goose Bay was inaccessible during the winter, all the fuel had to be in place at all times.[345]

On 23 July 1948 the Chiefs of Staff recommended that the minister of National Defence and the Cabinet Defence Committee approve extensive modification to Goose Bay airfield. These changes would be made by the U.S. Air Force and would include extensions of the main runways with the addition of steel planking at either end; the lengthening of the main runways with concrete; the building of new taxiways; and the installation of runway and approach lights. The Chiefs of Staff pointed out that this work would be done in 1948 and

1949 by 759 "white" men. The stated reason was that "the current Berlin situation and the necessity for reinforcing the US Air Force in Europe has necessitated the dispatch of an unusually high number of transport and heavy bomb aircraft through Goose Bay".[346]

The Cabinet Committee considered the proposal a few days later, and after noting that the U.S. government would be responsible for the expense involved but would retain no vested rights in the facilities, decided to "recommend to the Cabinet that the United States request ... be approved on the basis proposed."[347] At the same meeting, they approved a shadow organization responsible for the implementation of the decisions of the Censorship Committee which would plan in detail the functions and duties in peacetime Canada.

In the meantime, the USAF had already formed the 1227th Air Base Group at Goose Bay. The 1227th was tasked with providing support to strategic air operations, transport, weather services, and joint defence of the base.[348] Cabinet may have been hoping that further U.S. requests would not be forthcoming, but the USAF was already well ensconced in the northern base.

The United States Air Force's Strategic Air Command was the first U.S. military organization to bring an atomic bomb to Canada. During the summer and autumn of 1950 a large force of SAC B-50A bombers were deployed to Goose Bay with 11 Fat Man style atomic bombs. (See Chapter 4 on accidents for full details of this early deployment.) Although the bombs stayed only until 10 November 1950, their presence prompted the construction of storage bunkers for SAC nuclear weapons at Goose Bay. From that time on, nuclear weapons could be stored at Goose Bay anytime on a transient storage basis.

In August 1950, Prime Minister Louis St. Laurent agreed to the temporary storage of 11 atomic bombs at Goose Bay. This short deployment had shown both SAC and the USAF the usefulness of Goose Bay as the closest North American nuclear storage site to Europe. By 13 November 1950 they had paid approximately $250,000 for the construction of eight storage buildings[349] at the Goose Bay airfield. The area set aside for the ammunition bunkers and the storage of special weapons covered 2.34 square kilometres in a space measuring 1.28 km on each side.

The first large movement of Strategic Air Command forces to Newfoundland came as a result of a request to the Canadian government by the U.S. embassy on 18 August 1950. They asked if there would be any objection to moving 65 B-29 and B-50 bombers of the 43rd Medium Bomb Group into Goose Bay for a six-week training exercise. The main impression in Ottawa was that the group was being deployed against a possible general emergency in Europe, possibly over the Berlin situation.[350]

What SAC really wanted was the total and unfettered use of Goose Bay as the principal advance assault base for attacks against the USSR. In the early years, when bomber aircraft did not have the range they now do, SAC wanted to be able to station large numbers of bombers and support aircraft and supplies there in peacetime. During war they planned to stage further large numbers of bombers through the base and use it as a "final" refuelling and supply point. External Affairs was given the impression that some 250 bombers would pass through during the first attack.[351]

The Canadian government had granted to the USAF the right to build extensive structures at Goose Air Base. SAC wanted permanent storage facilities and were allowed to build eight storage buildings and associated facilities. In addition, they built 20 troop accommodation structures, and warehousing. This was all done on the understanding that no atomic weapons would be brought in and stored without the express authorization of the Canadian government.[352] By this time, the Goose Bay munitions storage area could provide for several hundred warheads.[353] During this time, the United States reorganized things, and the 6603rd Air Base Wing was activated at Goose Air Base by SAC.

It was during this time that the subject of a fighter-interceptor squadron was raised. During the PJBD meetings, and in informal conversations between the RCAF and USAF, it was learned that anti-aircraft defence, both on the ground and in the air, would be useful as the bases expanded in Newfoundland.[354] This would eventually lead to the stationing of the 59th Fighter-Interceptor Squadron at Goose Bay. Already the question of what to tell Canadians was coming up. Cabinet wondered how the government was going to explain why Canada was off defending Europe with men and weapons when Canada had to be protected by the United States.[355] This question would never go away.

The Canadian government worked away on the understanding that the United States would not bring nuclear weapons into Canada without the express permission of the government. What most did not understand, and this reached almost to the very top, was that permission had already been granted by the prime minister, who did not act through the normal chain of command. It was an inauspicious start as far as real government control in Canada over U.S. actions was concerned. Without the knowledge or consent of government, the prime minister had made a secret deal, and this would bring the first batch of 11 atomic bombs to Canada. This would become clear only to those at the top after one bomb exploded over the St.

Lawrence River in Quebec later that year. (For a full explanation of one of the world's first nuclear weapons accidents, see Chapter 4.)

Having already dropped an atomic bomb in Canada, but still desiring the use of much of Newfoundland for military purposes, Gordon Arneson, special assistant to the U.S. secretary of state on atomic energy questions, visited the Canadian ambassador in Washington on 1 December 1950 to discuss the ways and means by which any further approach on the storage of special weapons at Goose Bay should be made.[356]

The Arneson visit prompted immediate reaction in Ottawa. Hume Wrong at External Affairs first took up the matter the following day, cautioning that the situation in Europe and Asia was particularly grave, and stating that procedures should be put in place within the next 20 days to allow more formal U.S. access to Goose Bay. The most interesting part of the Wrong memo was his admission that "present plans do not envisage the storage of special weapons at Goose Bay until the additional construction there is available."[357] The USAF had begun construction of high-security weapons magazines some months earlier. Within days Lester Pearson had written that all future requests for nuclear storage at Goose Bay should come through the civilian channel of the government.[358] That would become the standard from then on, even though the USAF would continue to keep the RCAF informed of all actions. In fact, the RCAF was usually informed well before the civilian chain of command, but from then on, the channel of permission was civilian.

Around this time the 7th Aviation Field Depot Squadron showed up at Goose Bay AB. The 7th had been formed at Sandia Base in New Mexico on 20 October 1950 with a staff of 212. It was their job to look after and assemble the few precious MkIII, Mk4, and Mk5 atomic bombs. The unit was moved to an overseas base only identified as being assigned to SAC 8th Air Force and attached to Northeast Air Command.[359] This refers to Goose Bay. It is not known how long the unit remained at Goose Bay AB, but they would be reassigned there in 1957. It is therefore not a coincidence that in July 1952 Goose Bay AB was pre-stocked with supplies under "Project Seaweed" necessary for SAC to fight a nuclear war.[360] With this done, the United States reorganized things again, and the 6603rd Air Base Wing was changed to the 6603rd Air Base Group. The Canadian government was all the time aware that nuclear activities were expanding at Goose Bay. Hume Wrong told Arnold Heeney that the United States was then engaged in a massive build-up of forces worldwide, and that Goose Bay was to be turned in to a year-round facility. There would be an expansion in the number of SAC bombers, as well as the "expansion of the number of special weapons to be used in these operation".[361] It may have seemed that there was nothing which could be done to stop this, and there may have been no reason in 1950 for the Canadian government to wish to do so.

Pearson reported to the Cabinet Defence Committee in October 1952 that the Canadian government was being kept in the dark about U.S. military activities. He had advised that the Canadian team on the PJBD ask the U.S. government to provide a timely note on any unit or function changes which the USAF might contemplate at Goose Bay. The other problem was not that the Canadian government had little idea of what was going on at Goose Bay, but that they had no idea what the U.S. government was planning for the site. Pearson had therefore directed that inquiries be made through the PJBD as to the future plans and requirements of the USAF.[362]

While all this was going on, the USAF moved the 95th FIS into Goose Bay on 3 November 1952. They flew the F-94B Scorpion air defence fighter. The 95th was soon replaced by the 59th. F-94B interceptor jets of the USAF 59th Fighter-Interceptor Squadron quickly arrived to take up permanent duty providing air defence for the Goose Bay region.[363] The only problem, as far as Canada was concerned, was how to make the U.S. government understand that the Canadian government did not think that the Goose Bay lease gave the United States unconditional rights to the use of the airfield. The government was reserving all those rights for itself, and the stationing of the unit posed a problem.[364] Within a day, the CDC had decided that the government should sign a new lease for Goose Bay, but that it would be accompanied by a note stating that the lease did "not apply to any arrangements for the defence of Goose Bay or any other new developments which would continue to be dealt with by the appropriate agencies of the two governments."[365] The Chiefs of Staff discussed the matter with the MND and concluded that they were unable to provide the required air support, and therefore recommended that the USAF be allowed to station, as opposed to deploy, interceptors to the region. The United States planned to station fighters at Goose Bay, Harmon, and at the U.S. naval station in Argentia. To help make their case, the chiefs and the MND pointed out that the units would fall under the operational control of a joint RCAF-USAF integrated air defence commander.[366] The proposal was presented to the Cabinet committee, but no decision was reached.[367] The stationing of the 59th is discussed in detail in Chapter 6.

What the Canadian government actually did was sign a new lease for Goose Bay with the U.S. government. On 5 December 1952, Brooke Claxton, the acting secretary of state for External Affairs, and Stanley Woodward, the U.S. ambassador in Canada, signed the new lease. The most important part was the attached letter from Woodward stating that "the Canadian Government is to be consulted with regard to any proposal substantially to increase the numbers of United States personnel at Goose Bay."[368] The United States planned to increase the numbers, and to increase them substantially.

When U.S. servicemen arrived at Goose Bay, they found few of the amenities associated with service in the more southerly United States. In the early years there was little support for the troops, and early arrivals were dependent upon the RCAF. In fact, they were fed by the RCAF in the local mess. The USAF history of the period reflects that "although the diet was probably nutritious, the type of food was unusual and often unpleasant to the Americans."[369] The World War II expression from Britain, referring to the U.S. military servicemen, now applied to Newfoundland: "Overpaid, oversexed (overfed) and over here."

The JCS established the North-East Air Command (NEAC), with headquarters at Pepperell Air Force Base, Newfoundland, and gave it a two-fold responsibility: to defend, in cooperation with ADC, the northeast approaches to the United States, and to develop bases and related facilities to support SAC units deployed through or staging out of them.

The U.S. commitment to make some arrangements for joint control was immediately seized upon by the Canadians. The government directed the PJBD and the joint Military Co-operation Committee (MCC) to draft plans to ensure at least some Canadian control over the United States in Newfoundland. The new arrangement stated that any forces would be under the control of a commander from the country in which the forces were operating. Immediate command would still be exercised by the commander from the nation owning the unit. Most importantly for the government, it stipulated that U.S. air defence forces operating from Goose Bay would fall under the operational control of a Canadian commander.[370] The issue had been settled. However, until the RCAF provided a competent commander on site, the arrangement would remain only meaningless words.

But fighters were not the big issue in the 1950s. It was a remote possibility that Soviet bombers would be appearing over Newfoundland en masse, but it was more likely that SAC would be using the region as a springboard for an attack on the Soviet Union. With this requirement in mind, the USAF chief of staff asked the chief of the air staff to pass on the requirement for the rotation of various SAC units through Goose Bay. The purpose of this was to provide SAC with familiarization and simulated combat operational training. The MND told Cabinet[371] that the U.S. requirement would

(a) Locate an Aerial Refuelling (Tanker) Squadron at Goose Bay on a continuing basis. The squadron wouldl be rotated every 90 days and would consist of 20 aircraft and 400 personnel. This squadron was actually at Goose Bay at the time on a temporary basis.

(b) Rotate occasionally four additional refuelling squadrons for periods not exceeding 30 days, consisting of 80 aircraft and 1600 personnel.

(c) Rotate occasionally one medium bomber wing for 90-day training periods; the wing to consist of 45 aircraft and 2000 personnel.

At that time there were 418 RCAF and 3634 U.S. military personnel permanently stationed at Goose Bay. The new SAC requirements would see 400 additional U.S. personnel. The new units were for the sole purpose of supporting SAC activities and had no connection with the defence of Goose Bay. There was a rash of construction, and in 1954 SAC had another nine hangars, a steam plant, four more warehouses, two fire stations, and various general base support structures built.[372] Administratively, SAC deactivated the 6603rd Air Base Group and activated the 6606th Air Base Wing on 1 June 1954. Everything was appearing but the weapons, and this eventuality worried the government.

By early 1955 the inner Cabinet was already considering the possibility that the United States would soon request permission to utilize the Newfoundland bases for atomic weaponry. While there had been no request for stockpiling, the secretary of state for External Affairs and MND felt that it was only a matter of time before such a request arrived in Ottawa. The only hopeful sign they saw, and this was wishful thinking, was that the provision of refuelling facilities could mean that such requests would not be made because aircraft carrying these weapons would be refuelled in the air and not have to land.[373] Therefore the CDC recommended that "permission be given for the location on a continuing basis of an Aerial Refueling (Tanker) Squadron at Goose Bay; the rotation for periods not exceeding 30 days of a further four refueling squadrons; and the rotation occasionally for 90-day training periods of one medium bomber wing consisting of 45 aircraft and 2000 personnel."[374]

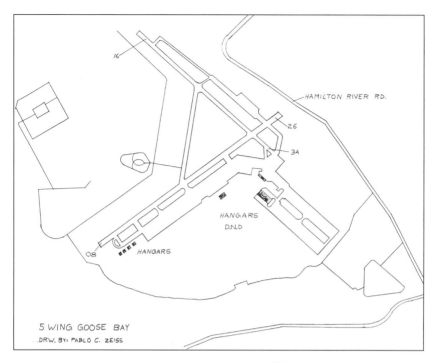

Goose Bay Air Base, Nfld.

Although the importance of Canada to the U.S. actions over the Suez crisis were discussed in Chapter 3 on overflights, there is some detail on the role of Goose Bay which bears mention here. In the gigantic simulated combat missions associated with the Suez crisis in late 1956, Goose Bay and Harmon supported large tanker task forces.[375] This was due to the number of bomber wings which were being forward deployed to Europe and North Africa, and due to the increased readiness of SAC forces in the continental United States for first strikes on the Soviet Union.

On 1 April 1957, the 6606th Air Base Wing was deactivated by SAC and the 4082nd Strategic Wing was activated. Concurrently, North-East Air Command (NEAC) was deactivated, and its resources assigned to ADC and SAC. It was at this time that Goose Bay Air Base received as a new unit the 7th Aviation Depot Squadron. The 7th Aviation Depot, later Munitions, Squadron was again located at Goose Bay AB from 1 April 1957 until 1 February 1961 for the purpose of storing any nuclear weapons on Goose Bay AB. It was originally thought by the USAF that the MB-1, or "Genie," nuclear air defence rocket would be stored at Goose Bay and Harmon Field. This was the first air-to-air nuclear air defence weapon in the U.S. arsenal, and if deployment had been allowed immediately, this would have been the weapon used. While it does not seem at first that the mission of a SAC munitions unit and an air defence weapon are related now, they certainly were in 1957. The MB-1 had been developed for SAC, because in the early days, SAC had its own fighter forces. It is very possible that the 7th was moved to Goose Bay a second time in the hope that it would care for the MB-1 which would soon be deployed throughout the USAF.

It was time to push out on all fronts. The State Department decided to move in all directions at once with Canada, provided that the Canadians would go along, and that was doubtful if the proposals were not put forward in the correct manner. It was therefore decided to tell the Canadian government that the Pentagon wished to introduce and store weapons at Goose Bay and other bases for air defence use, to introduce and store nuclear weapons at Goose Bay for possible employment by SAC, and to introduce and store ASW weapons at Argentia.[376] The State Department had a firm belief that the Canadian government should be consulted and informed of U.S. plans before nuclear weapons were introduced at any base in Canada, and the department was ready to do that now at a diplomatic level by aide-memoire. The State Department called in the Canadian ambassador and told him that, regarding Goose Bay, the USAF had plans for storage of MB-1 rockets for employment by USAF interceptors at Goose Bay and that the USAF had an immediate need to deploy heavy offensive nuclear weapons to existing storage facilities at Goose Bay in order to improve the operational effectiveness of SAC.

The State Department decided that the direct approach was desirable, since there was no question of Canadian use of these weapons and long-standing procedures had been in effect with the Canadians covering the clearance of SAC bombers carrying atomic weapons.

The MB-1 Agreement had been concluded, and the United States now sought to store the MB-1 (Genie) at Goose Bay.[377] But this was of passing importance, as what the State Department really wanted Canada to do was allow the storage of heavy offensive nuclear weapons at Goose Bay AB. Norman Robertson, the Canadian ambassador, was called in and told by the State Department that there was an immediate need to deploy nuclear components to existing storage facilities at Goose Bay in order to improve the operational effectiveness of SAC. Robertson was given an aide-memoire outlining the U.S. proposal in this connection. The ambassador asked whether the United States had arrangements with the United Kingdom for the use of bases there by

SAC, and how the civilian chain of command exercised authority over SAC's use of nuclear weapons.[378]

Perhaps it was Christmas cheer, but General Loper, responsible for nuclear weapons internationally, told Robertson that the White House had extensive arrangements with the United Kingdom governing the use of bases there by SAC.

> With regard to the extent of civilian control over SAC's use of nuclear weapons, he pointed out that the Atomic Energy Act gave the President sole authority over the use of nuclear weapons and that the extent of the consultation he might wish to make before authorizing their used was a matter for him to decide. However, the degree of prior consultation possible would, to a large extent, be dictated by the amount of time available. Since SAC would not come into operation against an enemy except in retaliation against an attack, the President would in all likelihood be afforded little, if any, opportunity to consult before authorizing a nuclear strike.[379]

Accompanying Robertson was Air Commodore Cameron who asked whether the United States contemplated the use of Goose Bay for initial strikes. Loper told both men that only follow-on strikes were contemplated, and that this might provide time for consultation with the Canadian government before it would become necessary for SAC to make a nuclear strike from Goose Bay.[380] The 12 December 1957 aide-memoire bluntly stated that

> in order to improve the general operational effectiveness of the United States Strategic Air Command, the United States Government desires to deploy nuclear weapons to existing storage facilities at Goose Bay. This proposed deployment is intended to implement long-range planning for the maintenance of the operational effectiveness and readiness of Strategic Air Command.[381]
>
> It is envisaged that, upon receipt of the general clearance of the Canadian Government for the proposed deployment program, subsequent notification of aircraft movements would be made by filing of flight plans 48 hours in advance, as specified in procedure "Y" of schedule B to Order-in-Council (PC 2307) dated 17 April 1952. Government-to-

Government clearance under established "Y" procedures will of course be required in any case where an immediate strike is contemplated.[382]

Cabinet finally dealt with the matter in the New Year, or at least selected members did. The minister of National Defence, George Pearkes, submitted a memorandum which informed his colleagues that the USAF wished to increase the effectiveness of their nuclear air defence activities at Goose Bay and to bring heavy offensive nuclear weapons to Goose Bay AB. The minister and Chiefs of Staff recommended that Cabinet agree to allow negotiations.[383] Cabinet immediately agreed, and the military promptly began to organize for service-to-service talks with the USAF on their plans for Goose Bay AB.[384] Talks between the Chiefs of Staff and the CINC SAC began on 5 February.

Finally, two months later, the minister of National Defence briefed the Cabinet with a February submission. He promptly recommended that "the Canadian Government approve the request by the US for the deployment

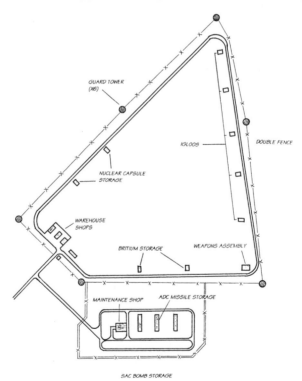

Weapon storage area #3, Goose Bay Air Base, Nfld. c. 1963

of nuclear weapons to the existing storage facilities at Goose Bay." The justification was that SAC forces were widely dispersed in the United States with forward bases in the United Kingdom, Spain, North Africa, Alaska and the Pacific and nuclear weapons were dispersed at these overseas bases so that aircraft could be rearmed for a second attack without making the long flight to their home bases. Because of its favourable location, Goose Bay would be a valuable forward base for SAC. The minister assured Cabinet that Goose Bay would not become a permanent bomber base, and that no initial strikes would be launched from there. The Chiefs of Staff had told him that the storage of nuclear weapons at Goose Bay would add to the flexibility, capability and effectiveness of SAC and would not create any additional risk. He mercifully informed his colleagues that SAC would not be requesting other facilities for this purpose.

The minister's last comment to Cabinet had no basis in reality and would seem curious to his colleagues in a very short time. He stated that the USAF had no plans for increases to the air defences of Goose AB.[385] Given that the United States already planned for MB-1 (Genie) deployment to Goose Bay, this was an interesting assertion. The December 1957 request by the U.S. government would be dealt with by the new Diefenbaker government. John Diefenbaker had been elected, and one of the first questions facing his new Cabinet was what to do with the request from the USAF, backed by the U.S. Joint Chiefs, for storage rights. There was no question of defence here, as the United States wanted to store strategic heavy thermonuclear gravity bombs for use against Soviet urban-industrial and fixed military targets.

The chairman of the Chiefs of Staff reported that although construction of nuclear weapon storage bunkers had been authorized in 1951, he was not aware or was at least unwilling to tell Cabinet that any bombs had been stored at Goose Bay.[386] Cabinet ministers groped their way through the information, which up until then, had been held exclusively by the institutionally ruling Liberal Party. Ministers discovered that they had no real veto over SAC use of the base for launching attacks. They discovered that the Atomic Energy Control Board was empowered to issue authorization for the import of nuclear weapons under the Atomic Energy Control regulations. They discovered that the importation of nuclear weapons was of interest to the National Revenue Department, which required import and export certificates for each movement, although the items would come and go duty free. What really worried ministers was the possible division of the country as atomic weapons were to be stored in Canada. The secretary of state for External

Affairs pointed to the example of the problems in Britain caused by U.S. nuclear deployments.[387] Deep divisions had occurred in the U.K., and the Diefenbaker government wanted to avoid that at all costs.

After Diefenbaker announced on 20 February, 1959, in the House of Commons that his government was starting negotiations with the United States for the acquisition of nuclear weapons for Canada, and for the storage of nuclear weapons in Canada, something had to be done. When the issue re-appeared at Cabinet a year later, it got just a passing reference. The minister of National Defence, George Pearkes, said that it was not proposed at that time to seek a decision on the request to store nuclear weapons for the use of SAC.[388] In a typically Canadian fashion, nothing would be done, and the issue of offensive weapons would begin to fade over time. Also at this time, the government had cancelled the CF-105 Avro Arrow program, throwing Canadian air defence squarely into the arms of the United States' military contractors.

During the Lebanon crisis, in which the United States invaded Lebanon, CINC NORAD increased the state of alert to DefCon 4, and Goose Bay Air Base was prepared for more tankers and possible bomber movement. In the meantime, NORAD had firmly established a requirement for the storage of MB-1 rockets at Goose Bay for the use of the USAF F-89 squadron deployed there. This subject was discussed by the two air forces, and it was agreed that the USAF would allow the State Department to pass the request to Canada through the embassy.[389] The 59th FIS was one of only a couple of air defence units which were deployed to Goose Bay AB. The other was the 323rd FIS which flew the F-102A between 6 June 1960 and 1 July 1960.

More information about what would be stored at Goose Bay was now coming in. Pearkes was finally told, and was able to pass on to his colleagues, that the MB-1 rocket was purely an air-to-air defensive weapon and was used by the F-89J Scorpion. The Rules of Engagement for this weapon were already covered in the exchange of notes on 30 June 1959 (the MB-1 Agreement), and under normal conditions, the interceptors would be on 30-minute alert. "During abnormal circumstances such as might result in declaration of a state of air defence readiness they may be put on 15-minute alert. They will not be put on a higher state of alert until an air defence emergency has been declared by CINC NORAD or higher authority."[390] A week later Cabinet, with fairly full knowledge of the system, approved the Canadian draft text on storage of nuclear weapons at Goose Bay and Harmon Field for U.S. forces.[391]

The United States now saw definite movement on the part of the

Canadians and decided to press their seeming advantage. They encouraged George Pearkes to again approach Cabinet on the question of heavy weapons at Goose Bay AB. Pearkes went in with a detailed proposal. He reminded his colleagues that the United States had been allowed to build massive storage bunkers at Goose Bay during the Korean War, but that their use had been limited to the temporary storage of nuclear weapons and components in transit on authorized flights, when the aircraft carrying these weapons or components had become temporarily unserviceable on landing at Goose Bay. No permanent storage had taken place at Goose Bay. He therefore recommended, having been pressed by the Chiefs of Staff and USAF, "that the Canadian Government approve in principle the request by the US for the deployment of nuclear weapons to the existing storage facilities at Goose Bay." He then submitted the following proposal.[392]

1. The weapons under consideration are Strategic Air Force weapons as may from time to time be made available to the US Strategic Air Force under the command of C-in-C Strategic Air Force, United States Air Force.

2. These weapons would be stored at Goose Bay, Labrador. The cost of the establishment, maintenance and operation of the storage facility shall be the responsibility of the United States Government.

3. The arrangements for physical security of the storage sites will be the joint responsibility of the two Governments. Safeguards in the design and handling of these weapons to minimize the possibility of accidental explosion and to afford the maximum protection of lives and property will be the responsibility of the United States Government and will be subject to approval by the Canadian Government.

4. Ownership and custody of the nuclear warheads shall remain with the United States Government in accordance with United States law.

5. Transportation to or from storage facilities of these weapons and warheads through Canadian airspace will be governed by Canadian regulations. Import and export of these weapons will be subject to Canadian Government regulations, and detailed procedures will be negotiated between appropriate Government Departments.

6. It is understood that weapons stored at Goose Bay will

not be used for an initial strike.

7. The removal from storage for operational use will be subject to the concurrence of the Canadian Government.

8. Any test firing of these weapons which may be required will take place outside of Canada.

9. The terms of this Agreement will be reviewed annually by the two Governments and may be terminated by either Government upon six months' notice.

10. Supplementary arrangements or administrative agreements between authorized agencies of the two Governments may be made from time to time for the purpose of carrying out the intent of this agreement.[393]

The real problem was that the Canadian government was very uncomfortable with the concept of SAC heavy weapons being stored at Goose Bay. Although the government was on record as supporting the strategy of the nuclear deterrent, and although the RCAF argument for the use of storage facilities at Goose Bay was based on the premise that the use of such facilities would strengthen the deterrent, and even though there was no stated SAC intention that Goose Bay would become a permanent base or that initial strikes would be launched from there, the government was still uneasy.[394]

To help assuage its conscience, they considered that future negotiation for such use of Goose Bay would have to include a demand that the concurrence of the Canadian government would be required before use was made of strategic weapons which might be stored at Goose Bay. In a strangely open-minded way for the time, it was felt that "careful explanation, at the appropriate time, of the exact purpose of the storage" would make Canadians feel better about it. This was important because the Diefenbaker government was caught between a difficult Canada-United States relationship on one side, and a Canadian public who were never all that fond of nuclear weapons on the other.[395] Diefenbaker was fully aware that many voters were uncomfortable with nuclear weapons.

Two meetings at the end of 1959 dealt with the problem of Goose Bay. First, the Cabinet Defence Committee spent part of the day discussing a problem they all seemed to wish would just go away. George Pearkes summed up the history of the awkward situation by telling his colleagues that "during the Korean War the U.S. had requested authority to construct storage facilities for nuclear weapons in the U.S. leased portion of Goose Bay. The then Canadian Government had authorized this construction on the understanding that further authority would be required prior to the actual storage of such weapons at Goose Bay. The structure had been completed but its use had been limited to the temporary storage of nuclear weapons and components in transit on authorized flights when the aircraft or the weapon had become temporarily unserviceable. No permanent storage had been undertaken."[396] He then pushed for an agreement.

Members of Cabinet wondered what the public would think of storing offensive weapons in Canada. The year 1959 was seen as a time of diminishing tensions, and Canadians were likely to call this move provocative. They were leery, but since the issue was not likely to go away, they wanted any agreement to reflect that removal of the heavy weapons from storage in times of war for a follow-on attack would require the prime minister's authorization, as was the case in the United Kingdom.[397]

Only days later at the Joint Ministers meeting, the U.S. secretary of Defense, Niel McElroy, told the minister of National Defence and the secretary of state for External Affairs that the United States was seeking two things at Goose Bay: atomic storage for the air defence forces, and for SAC re-strike use. He pointed out that both questions had been under consideration in Ottawa since 1957 and the USAF would like an answer very soon. Sidney Green, secretary of state for External Affairs, agreed in principle to defensive weapons for Harmon and Goose Bay and said that this had already been agreed, but only in principle.

Canada drew a sharp line of distinction between defensive and offensive nuclear weapons. The Canadian government had agreed in principle to the storage of air defence weapons, but would not yet agree to store SAC heavy weapons. The Canadian team pointed out that it was important to the present government whether the weapons were used in a first strike or only in follow-on attacks, and they were assured by Secretary of Defense McElroy that only re-strikes were contemplated.[398]

When attention turned to SAC heavy offensive weapons, Sidney Green stated that the removal from storage at Goose Bay would require Canadian government approval. The United States was surprised by this opinion, and it became clear that they had not read the latest Canadian draft agreement.[399] Green was told that the authority for use can extend from the president through a command commander if necessary, and that if this were restricted by a special authority for removal from storage there might be no time for them to be put into use. Canadian ministers reiterated that this was a matter of sovereignty and very vital to the Diefenbaker government. Green and McElroy agreed that storage of air defence weapons was possible, but that storage of SAC weapons in Canada was a separate and more difficult problem. Green told of how very difficult it was for the Cabinet to agree to the storage for defensive purposes, and that it was even harder to agree to storage for offensive purposes. He stated that although the St. Laurent government had allowed SAC to build storage bunkers, they had never gone so far as to agree to heavy offensive nuclear weapons being stored on a permanent basis.[400]

The U.S. secretary of Defense audaciously announced that he felt that "the Canadian public could easily be made to accept the storage of these weapons on Canadian soil." Green responded by disagreeing and said that it was difficult to explain to the Canadian people, especially as the U.S. arguments about the deterrent would justify the storage of anything in Canada. George Pearkes told the assembled ministers that DND agreed with the stated SAC requirement, but that "it was politically awkward in view of the present relaxation of tension which appeared to be in the air."[401]

By early 1960 the United States had 3505 military personnel stationed at Goose Bay. They employed a further 37 U.S. civilians and 905 local Newfoundland civilians: this was the whole economy of the region. All these people supported a massive base structure consisting of the following USAF units:

4082nd Strategic Wing Headquarters, including an Air Refueling
    Squadron and supporting units;
4732nd Air Defense Group, including a Headquarters, and,
    59th Fighter-Interceptor Squadron
1623rd Support (Transport) Squadron
1932nd ACS, detachment of Communications and Relay
    Squadrons
1876th RAR, Global Communication Station
 639th Airborne Control & Warning Squadron
  54th Air Rescue Squadron
   5th Weather Group, detachment
   6th Air Postal Squadron, detachment
1005th Special Investigation Group, detachment
1031st Auditor General Squadron, detachment
   7th Aviation Depot
 868th Medical Group, detachment

The base was also hosting a storage team servicing the bunkers, and any agreed storage policy could be implemented immediately.[402] It is now known that the 7th Aviation Depot was the unit responsible for the SAC storage bunkers. By 1950 the USAF had set up a small handful of special units known as aviation depots, which were solely responsible for the storage of nuclear weapons. The 7th was known to be one such unit in the early 1950s. The 7th Munitions Squadron was located at Goose Bay AB from 1 April 1957 until 1 February 1961 for the purpose of storing any nuclear weapons on Goose Bay AB should permission ever have been granted by the Canadian government to do so.[403] Sometime in 1960, the 7th Aviation Depot Squadron was renamed as the 7th Munitions Maintenance Squadron, the current name of USAF units caring for nuclear weapons.

During the May Day crisis, in which the Soviet *PVO-Strany* (air defence forces) shot down a CIA U-2 spy plane, CINC NORAD increased the state of alert to DefCon 4, and Goose Bay Air Base was prepared for more tankers and possible bomber movement. In the immediate aftermath of the May Day affair, the 323rd FIS and its complement of F102A interceptors was deployed to Goose Bay between 6 June and 1 July 1960.

More meetings between working-level officials seemed to bring progress. The U.S. team left one July meeting with the distinct feeling that an agreement was at hand because both parties were in complete agreement. The State Department even expected to see a draft agreement from External Affairs in the very near future.[404] The draft was not what they expected.

Again that summer the U.S. ambassador asked the Diefenbaker government when the United States could expect some action on storage. Merchant said that they had all already agreed to a draft, but the Canadians had again changed it. Merchant noted that the United States could accept the changes if two small points were added.[405] When the chief ministers of both governments met at the Seigniory Club that July[406], the U.S. team requested an additional simple paragraph in the agreement to permit warhead repatriation to the United States. The U.S. side also wanted a written explanation of how approval for such movements would be made by the Canadian government. The secretary of state for External Affairs and minister of National Defence said that they would check into these matters. When the ambassador asked Diefenbaker of the status of the work, he was brushed off by being told that nothing more would be accomplished for U.S. forces until the question of weapons for the Canadian forces was settled.[407] That would be another four years.

This was more than Diefenbaker snubbing Kennedy. The full Cabinet had decided that an agreement on Goose Bay had to wait until after the question of nuclear weapons for Canadian forces was dealt with.[408] It was clear to the United States that nothing was being done. With few bombers ever showing up at Goose Bay, and with tankers as the primary occupant, there was no need for munitions staff. HQ USAF therefore redeployed the 7th Munitions Maintenance Squadron back to the United States on 1 February 1961.[409] At this rather chilly point in Canada-United States relations, the only talks going on were military to military.[410]

By the spring Diefenbaker was ready to allow negotiations to proceed, and so informed the U.S. government. Nevertheless, he was still adamant that U.S. forces would only be so supplied after Canadian forces. The problem as the United States saw it for arming the Goose was that any arrangements for the storage of nuclear weapons must provide for "joint control" and "joint custody." Of the two, joint control presented the simpler problem, as a form of joint control over use was already provided in the MB-1 Agreement. Comparable control procedures could doubtless be devised to meet different operational requirements. The joint custody concept posed a more serious problem due to the U.S. Atomic Energy Act. The White House had little desire to try for an amendment to the act and therefore hoped that something else could be negotiated on custody.[411] The State Department stressed to Ross Campbell, the chief Canadian negotiator, the importance they attached to storage at Goose Bay of nuclear weapons for use by SAC on "reflex-strike" missions. The military policy was, in the United States' view, becoming more valid as the Soviet missile forces grew in strength. Campbell told them that storage for SAC presented great difficulties politically, and he made it clear that no decision could be taken at that time.[412]

Campbell's remarks were a direct reflection of the feeling of the prime minister. Diefenbaker had met with U.S. ambassador Merchant and told him that there had been an upsurge of feeling against nuclear weapons generally, and that this "was not limited to communists and left-wingers, but also included professors and many others." Diefenbaker always read his mail, and it was not lost on him that his mail was very heavy with letters against nuclear weapons, "including a very high percentage from mothers and wives."[413] Merchant knew that there were strong elements in Cabinet, particularly Secretary of State for External Affairs Green, who opposed "dirtying Canadian hands and reputation with nuclear weapons under any circumstances."[414] Merchant was turned away after being told that storage of nuclear weapons in Canadian soil was politically impossible at the moment, but that some time in the future it might be possible under some form of joint control. Diefenbaker doubted he could carry his own Cabinet on the issue.

One of the proposals floated by Diefenbaker on the nuclear question was of warhead storage in the United States, with the warheads being airlifted to Canada in times of crisis. This idea was dismissed by critics then and continues to receive abuse. Interestingly enough, though, the U.S. Air Force not only considered it, they implemented it for Goose Bay. A secret USAF report, not releasable to foreign nationals, stated that "there were no W-54 warheads pre-positioned at Goose Air Base for the use of this [59th] squadron. The plans called for the storage of the nuclear warheads for the Goose Squadron at the nuclear storage area at Stonybrook, Massachusetts. In the event of hostilities, these nuclear warheads were scheduled for airlift to Goose Air Base."[415] Nevertheless, "there was one general difficulty. As of 30 June 1962, the storage depot at Stonybrook had no warheads for ... the 59th [which was] quite far down on the priority list."[416] Perhaps the Diefenbaker idea was not as laughable as critics make out.

There is also the possibility that air defence nuclear weapons had already been stored at Goose Bay. The same secret report, which could not be shown to Canadians, went on to note that "Goose Air Base had the storage facilities formerly used for the MB-1 rockets which were considered adequate for the GAR-11 W-54 warheads. The Goose storage area could provide for several hundred warheads."[417] It may simply be that Goose Bay only held the rocket bodies, but as the rockets are stored separately from the warheads, and the report specifically mentions space for warheads, it is very likely that warheads were at least briefly present in the massive SAC nuclear weapons storage facilities. Even then, we must balance this possibility against some evidence found in a secret SAC report which stated that "nuclear weapons had never been allowed on Canadian soil."[418] It is almost certain that this referred to permanent strategic deployments, as there had already been temporary deployments.

During the Cuban Missile crisis, Goose Bay Air Base assumed an increased alert posture in keeping with all other SAC and ADC sites. At 23:00z on 22 October 1962, CINC NORAD declared DefCon 3. Promptly, nothing happened at the Goose. Then, on 24 October, at 17:34z, Goose Bay made a smooth transition from DefCon 5 to DefCon 3. Operationally this meant that it was prepared for more tankers and possible bomber movement.

There were usually 28 KC-97 tankers, but an additional 40 were moved in to make 68 tankers on station. The 4082nd SW supported over 1100 SAC and non-SAC aircraft through Goose Bay AB during the Cuban Missile crisis.[419] To put this in perspective, the largest tanker force in history moved into Goose Bay during the Cuban crisis, and this was superimposed on top of the usual deployments which saw Goose Bay normally hosting the largest regular tanker reflex force in SAC. After the crisis, with the rapidly diminishing KC-97 force, fewer overseas support bases were required and SAC withdrew its tankers from Churchill, Cold Lake and Frobisher RCAF stations. Ground alert forces of KC-97s remained at RCAF Station Namao, Goose Bay, and Harmon.[420]

Not only the tankers went on higher alert. The 59th was notified that from that moment until further notice, 15 minute alert aircraft were not to be flown on training missions. The squadron commander was told that the unit would maintain this state of readiness until such time as the international situation permitted a stand-down.[421]

Two days before Pearson was to meet with Kennedy, the two Pauls presented a draft of the Goose/Harmon agreement to the CDC, asking that it be approved for passing to the U.S. negotiating team, and that External Affairs be allowed to resume negotiations on this U.S. requirement.[422] This was done in order to have some Canadian action taken before the May 1963 summit meeting between Pearson and Kennedy which was supposed to cover nuclear weapons policy. Pearson had been advised to tell Kennedy that the storage of defensive weapons at Goose Bay was a second stage after Canadian systems had been provided for, and that bombs for SAC at Goose Bay were going to be a major problem. Kennedy responded by telling Pearson that this SAC requirement had a much lower priority now. With this, the question of heavy weapons storage at Goose Bay essentially disappeared.[423]

This is not to say that SAC bombers never called at Goose Bay Air Base any more. Only a month later CINC SAC was reminding Goose Bay personnel of the importance of two-man rules. Although Goose Bay Air Base was not involved with bombardment aircraft on a daily basis, key personnel had to be familiar with the two officer/two man mode of operation required in the U.S. military.[424] It was, therefore, probably a good thing that the RCAF finally signed in April 1963 an arrangement with the USAF to govern the response to nuclear weapons accidents at Goose Bay.[425]

Back at Goose Bay, preparations were being made to facilitate the safe handling and storing of either strategic or air defence nuclear weapons. In preparing for the eventual storage, the USAF 8th Air Force sent a team to Goose to inspect the facilities and determine what renovations and new facilities might be necessary. Captain William K. Gobble and his team found the facilities of the 59th FIS adequate to meet the mission requirements. Even still, a list of suggestions on how to improve these

SAC B-36B ten-engined heavy bomber over Ottawa, escorted by two CF-100 Canucks, 26 September 1956. DND negative #PL105278.

SAC B-47 six-engined medium bomber over Ottawa, 24 September 1956. DND negative #PL105291.

SAC KC-135 refuels an eight-engined B-52 bomber, early 1960s. Official USAF photograph.

SAC Mk28RI thermonuclear weapons, in a four-weapon clip, as carried by B-52 bombers during airborne alerts over Canada. This type was lost in two crashes over foreign territory. Ellsworth AFB, July 1975. U.S. Archives negative #243-B-15-002-3, #342-KKE-64058.

Damaged SAC Mk28RI thermonuclear weapon recovered at Palomares after the 1966 crash of a B-52 and KC-135. Photo by author.

Goose Bay Air Base, 1960s. Close-up of nuclear weapons storage bunkers. Negative #A20597-20.

SAC 43rd Bomb Wing, B-50 bombers, on the ramp at Goose Air Base, October 1950. It was during this deployment that a bomber dropped an atomic bomb in the St. Lawrence River. SAC photo courtesy of author.

SAC 43rd Bomb Wing, B-50 bombers in maintenance area at Goose Air Base, October 1950. SAC photo courtesy of author.

B-36B SAC very heavy bomber partly in maintenance hangar at Goose Air Base.
c. late 1955. USAF negative #156161A.C. U.S. Archives negative #RG342-B, ND-010-17, #156161AC.

Ernest Harmon Air Force Base, 7 February 1965. Wide shot of Runway 28, with Quick Reaction Alert aircraft shelters diagonal off end of runway. Note the 21 KC-97 tankers on the apron. Negative #VVR2631-190.

Four F-102A interceptors of the 59th FIS on the ramp at Ernest Harmon AFB, October 1957. DND negative #PL108614

F-102A interceptor s/n 61301, of the 59th FIS on the ramp at Ernest Harmon AFB, October 1957. Colour. DND negative #PCN270.

F-102A interceptor s/n 61301 of the 59th FIS on the ramp at Ernest Harmon AFB, and four pilots (two RCAF and two USAF), October 1957. Colour. DND negative #PCN271.

SAC B-47 medium bomber pictured behind a KC-97 tanker, as used in Harmon, but pictured at Ottawa, 1956. DND negative #105258.

MB-1 Genie rocket without W25 nuclear warhead, about to be loaded on USAF F-89J Scorpion interceptor during 1957 flight tests. USAF negative #158545AC.

MB-1 Genie rocket without W25 nuclear warhead, pictured on port pylon of USAF F-89J Scorpion interceptor during 1957 flight tests. Note that the fins have been opened prior to flight. USAF negative #173695USAF.

GAR-11, or AIM-26F, Falcon with nuclear warhead, Engineering
test pilot Chris Smith from Hughes, and F-102A interceptor. 26
May 1960. B&W. USAF negative #S-30833. US Archives
negative #RG342-B, 08-004A-2, #163508AC.

AIM-26F nuclear Falcon (on left), and other Hughes Corporation conventional Falcon guided missiles. 4 April 1960. Colour. USAF negative #S-30233. U.S. Archives negative #RG342-B, 08-002-6 (AIM-4), #K-KE-13255.

Argentia Naval Station, 1970. Close-up of nuclear weapons storage bunkers. Negative #A21443-57

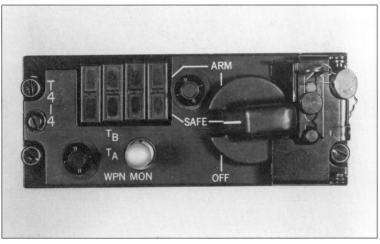

Nuclear weapons control panel from maritime patrol aircraft. This would be used by the pilot to arm the Mk-101 or Mk-57 prior to dropping on a submarine target. 27 August 1963. DND negative #RE21035-18.

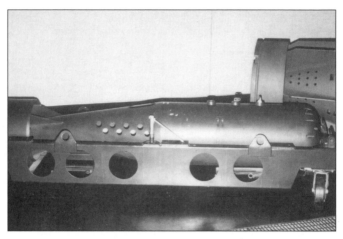

Mk-101 Lulu nuclear depth bomb. 1989. Photo by author.

Mk-57 nuclear depth bombs, as carried by the P-3A Orion at Argentia. The bomb pictured is actually the BDU-11A/E practice device.

P-3A Orion of VP-8 squadron on patrol during the Cuban missile crisis. VP-8 used the P-3A Orion extensively at Argentia. USN Historical Agency photo courtesy of author.

P-3A Orion of VP-8 squadron fly in formation. USN Historical Agency photo courtesy of author.

Sgt. Ernest Killen mans the Q7 computer at the NORAD underground SAGE site in North Bay, October 1965. Note the "No Lone Zone" signs indicative of an area which deals with nuclear weapons control. USAF Negative #176772. U.S. Archives Negative #RG342-B, ND-010-1, #176772.

U.S. Army Nike-Hercules cold-weather test launch facility at Fort Churchill, Manitoba, January 1959. The Nike-Hercules could carry a W-31 nuclear warhead for intercepting bombers. (Rear view) DND negative #PC6446.

U.S. Army Nike-Hercules cold weather test launch facility at Fort Churchill, Manitoba, January 1959. The Nike-Hercules could carry a W-31 nuclear warhead for intercepting bombers. (Side view) DND negative #PC6426.

facilities was supplied to the wing and the 59th.[426] One action they requested was that the 59th get training in the operation and maintenance of the American District Telegraph (ADT) intrusion alarm equipment.

Now that the agreement for Canadian forces was signed, Cabinet would work quickly on the U.S. agreement. On 12 September Cabinet agreed that it would expedite the agreement if the talks were restricted to just Goose Bay and Harmon, and to air defence weapons.[427] As Pearson said, "Canada could not logically refuse to permit the storage for USAF interceptor squadrons in Canada of warheads which this country had now arranged to have available for its own interceptor forces."[428] As he saw it, "In view of the status of the US leased base at Harmon, it is questionable whether, strictly speaking, there was any need for the US to obtain Canadian consent to the storage of nuclear warheads there." Four days later the Canadian draft was given to Walt Butterworth, the U.S. ambassador in Ottawa, by Paul Martin, and only eight days after this the United States replied that it was ready to accept the Canadian wording with only four minor textual changes.[429]

At the 26 September 1963 Cabinet meeting, Paul Martin recommended that the text be approved as negotiated and that he be authorized to sign the new agreement on nuclear weapons deployment to Goose Bay and Harmon Field.[430] The draft agreement provided for the storage of nuclear warheads for MB-1 air-to-air missiles used by U.S. interceptor squadrons stationed at those points. Strangely, these were not to be used, as the 59th was now equipped to carry the Falcon nuclear missile. The full Cabinet approved the draft agreement and agreed that Martin be authorized to sign on behalf of the Government of Canada.[431] An order in council was quickly drafted and signed by the prime minister[432], and two days later the final agreement was signed.

It would come to be known as the Goose-Harmon Agreement. Unlike other agreements, the original note and the reply bear different dates. The entire agreement is contained in the Canadian note, and the U.S. note of reply merely accepts the wording on behalf of the U.S. government. Paul Martin, secretary of state for External Affairs, handed the 28 September 1963 Canadian note No. 162 to Walt Butterworth. Two days later the U.S. embassy would deliver the reply of acceptance in note No. 112. The reply has never been declassified in Canada as it is considered the property of a foreign government. However, this makes little difference, as all the substantive text is in the Canadian note.

The operative paragraph of note No. 162 states that "the Canadian Government is prepared to permit the storage of nuclear air-to-air defensive weapons at Goose Bay and Harmon Air Force Base for United States forces." The rest of the short agreement simply notes that ownership and custody of the weapons shall remain with the United States; that the USAF will provide and be responsible for the security of the storage sites; that safety procedures for storage, maintenance, transport, loading, delivery and salvage of nuclear weapons will be at least equivalent to U.S. standards; and that authorization of transportation of the weapons in Canada will be subject to Canadian law.

Most importantly, at least from a historical perspective, and probably from the perspective of many of the Cabinet ministers in the Pearson government, was paragraph six. This was the control and authorization clause, and it stated that

> the release of nuclear warheads to meet operational requirements will be the subject, where practical, of prior inter-governmental consultation. They will be used, when authorized by both Governments, only in accordance with procedures established by CINCNORAD. The MB-1 Agreements, of June 30, 1959 and June 1, 1962, shall apply to the removal of these weapons for operational reasons from the areas utilized by U.S. forces at Harmon and Goose Bay under existing agreements between the two Governments.

Then the government did an odd thing in the nuclear age: Pearson proposed to stand up in the House of Commons, announce the agreement and name the storage sites at Goose Bay and Ernest Harmon field in Stephenville, Newfoundland. When the U.S. government got wind of this idea, they moved very quickly to ensure that the statement was never made. As far as the United States was concerned, such a statement by a respected world leader like Pearson could have serious repercussions in Europe and Asia. Other people might start to agitate for this information, and foreign governments might feel obliged to make similar statements in their parliaments about the location of U.S. nuclear weapons. This simply could not be allowed.

Norman Robertson advised Pearson that the Canadian draft statement to be made in the House of Commons was totally unacceptable to the U.S. authorities because it mentioned Goose Bay and Harmon, as this was information classified under the U.S. Atomic Energy Act. The State Department asked that the names be removed and that the phrase "stationed in Canada" be inserted. Pearson was provided with the short but firm U.S.

memo on the subject.[433] To follow the U.S. suggestion would raise problems in Canada, since "stationed in Canada" is so vague that Robertson and Pearson felt it might raise in the public mind an impression of a much more far-reaching set of U.S. activities. Robertson pointed out that the location of the bases was already public knowledge and would in any event soon come out under questioning in the House of Commons. The two men agreed that the names could be removed, but that a general reference to "the US leased bases in Newfoundland" would have to be made.[434]

The immediate question was how to provide for the legal framework to allow the weapons to be brought into and to become operational in Canada. What was needed was a supplementary service-to-service arrangement to spell out the procedures. Robertson told the military that this was absolutely necessary as the 28/30 September notes provided even less detail than did the agreement to arm Canadian forces with nuclear weapons the previous month.[435] He suggested that the military include items which may be inadequately covered in the notes. This included the following:

- Responsibility for and arrangements to ensure base security;
- Various forms of authorization required for movement of nuclear weapons;
- Authorization, and procedure for obtaining it, for flights transporting nuclear weapons;
- Safety regulations;
- Procedures relating to accidents involving, and emergency disposal of, nuclear weapons;
- RCAF access to leased areas;
- Responsibility of RCAF commanding officer at Goose Bay; and
- Operational use.[436]

National Defence immediately agreed, but pointed out that "the RCAF is not directly involved with the storage agreement for Goose and Harmon, except insofar as we are responsible for the exercise of Canadian sovereignty at Goose Bay, it is assumed that the Government would require the DND to exercise such Canadian authority over USA activities as may be necessary, and that the Minister would assigned this responsibility to the RCAF."[437] The military would assign the task to the RCAF[438] and ensure that negotiations began immediately in order to produce a supplementary arrangement similar to that done for the Bomarc and Genie rockets supplied to Canada.[439] However, there was not the rush associated with the arrangement to bring warheads into Canada for the Canadian forces. This was because the USAF had told the RCAF that it did not expect to be in a position to emplace weapons before the end of 1963. As the two countries entered 1964, the USAF indicated that storage was still some time away, as the facilities were built for SAC and required modification and extensive refurbishing and structural adaptation.[440]

What is odd about this is that the USAF seemed to be telling different stories to different offices. Only two weeks later they informed the vice-chief of the air staff that the bunkers which had been built for SAC had remained empty except for "occasional transient and small-scale storing" and that "no modifications are needed ... to accommodate nuclear weapons for ADC at Goose at any time on short notice."[441] What was likely happening was that the RCAF was being told everything was fine and things could proceed quickly. In fact, as is demonstrated by the Goose Bay and 59th FIS records, the USAF was feverishly working to make the bunkers and support facilities hospitable to the new nuclear weapons. During this period the concrete floors in the storage bays were sealed with Sonomar sealer. Plumbing was marked, and one man was certified qualified on nuclear Falcon AIM-26A's and B's at Goose Bay Air Base.[442]

It was not just the military in Canada which was preparing for the arrival of U.S. nuclear weapons. Cabinet had designated the MND as authorized by Cabinet to permit "dealings in" nuclear weapons and components on 12 September 1963, and the MND had designated Director of Air Force Movements (DAFM) and D/DAFM (Air Force Movements) as having authority on 9 November 1963.[443] However, now Revenue Canada and the Department of Trade and Commerce were involved. Nothing moved in or out of the country without being inspected and usually taxed. Government regulations made no exceptions for nuclear weapons, and therefore, the MND had to apply for permits. The weapons were to be met by customs inspectors, who were to then pass them without duty being applied. There were only two ways for the warheads to leave the country: in the first case they would simply be re-exported to the country of origin; and in the second case there would not be any customs inspectors left alive to notice what had happened.

Department of Trade and Commerce
In Reply refer to file No. 6731-2
        January 14, 1964
Attention: Mr. J.R. McKinney,
The Under-Secretary of State for External Affairs,
Ottawa, Ontario

> Application #486695 has been received from the Deputy Minister of National Defence, Department of National Defence, Ottawa, dated January 13, 1964 for permission to export to USA the following: Nuclear air-to- air defensive weapons brought into Canada under the Canada-US Agreement of 28 and 30 September 1963 and any amendments thereto, and exported in accordance with the provision of that Agreement. (see copies of letters attached) This equipment is valued at $__ and is consigned to United States of America.
>
> I should be grateful if you would let me know whether an Export Permit may be issued to cover the above shipment.
>
> (signed for the)
> Deputy Minister of
> Trade and Commerce

For some reason this system broke down. Although the MND had been authorized by the Atomic Energy Control Board on 18 December 1963 to designate someone who would be permitted to engage in "dealings in" nuclear weapons, it appears that Paul Hellyer had not done so.[444] The MND had indicated that the director of Air Force Movements would have some authority, but this was withdrawn, and it now seemed that the chief of Defence Staff or the director of Nuclear Weapons had some authority in this area. In the confusion, E.B. Armstrong, the deputy minister of National Defence, asked the deputy minister at Trade and Commerce for an export permit. Trade and Commerce promptly asked External Affairs if this was okay with them. External Affairs was confused at first, but then understood that the changes brought about by service integration made no difference to the permit process.[445] Permission was granted, and the process once again fell dormant.

By 18 March 1964 the arrangement had been accepted by the USAF, and the next step was preparation of the final document and the collection of authorizing signatures. The chief of air staff and vice chief of staff, USAF, would sign, rather than political staff. The only lingering problem, and a fairly insignificant one, was that because the association of the nuclear warheads with Goose Bay and Harmon Air Force Base had a restricted data connotation, USAF officers requested that the cover page not relate nuclear weapons specifically to these two bases. The RCAF was told that both Goose Bay and Harmon could be mentioned in the main body of the agreement.[446]

A week later the chief of air staff, Marshal Dunlap, told Hellyer that "the USAF expects to be able to introduce these weapons into service at Goose Bay by late May or early June."[447] Hellyer signed it almost two weeks later and handed it off to his Cabinet colleague, Paul Martin.[448] The legal division at External Affairs then got their hands on the document, and by the end of the month claimed that "the draft is considered satisfactory and there is no objection to its being concluded."[449] Therefore, on 15 May 1964, the "Service-to-Service Arrangement Between the United States Air Force and the Royal Canadian Air Force to Provide for Implementation of the Government-to-Government Agreement of 28 and 30 September 1963 Concerning Nuclear Weapons for United States Air Defense Forces at Goose Bay and Harmon Air Force Base" was signed by both air forces. The entire arrangement is reproduced in Annex B at the end of this book.

With the arrangement near, activities at Goose Bay reached the penultimate step: USAF Missile Maintenance Section personnel assigned to the ADC special storage site were moved to the nuclear weapon facility. This was supposed to provide an increased responsiveness to alerts and insure that the storage site was operational under any circumstances immediately.[450] Goose Bay was an oddity of all the nuclear storage sites in Canada which belonged to the United States. Because it was essentially a Canadian base, and because of the wording of the Goose Bay lease, a Canadian would have access to the weapons. The original wording of the lease allowed free access by the RCAF commanding officer at RCAF Station Goose Bay to all areas on the U.S. side of the facility. The service-to-service arrangement stated that the RCAF would have right of inspection at agreed times to ensure the adequacy of the safety and security systems. The problem was that U.S. law would prohibit any foreigners from being in a place where the actual war reserve nuclear weapon sat, other than on alert. So the RCAF had to agree to waive the right of free access and inspection once the weapons or other restricted data items were in place.[451]

SAC, possibly hoping that moving ahead on this front would help with their perpetual search for a heavy weapon storage agreement with the Canadians, told the office responsible for Goose Bay that the recent service-to-service agreement between the USAF and RCAF had permitted delivery of nuclear warheads to Goose Bay AB ahead of the programmed 1 October 1964 date. USAF ADC wanted to advance the importation of warheads to Goose Bay up to 15 July 1964, and SAC supported this.[452] The 8th Air Force HQ replied that there appeared to be no significant problems which would prevent meeting a 15 July 1964 support capability.[453] The 8th therefore told the 4082nd at Goose Bay

AB that "CINCONAD has expressed a desire to achieve a nuclear capacity at Goose AB at the earliest possible date, preferably by 15 July 1964. The nuclear alert aircraft requirement for Goose has been deleted. The present two aircraft on five-minute alert (conventional weapons) will be continued."[454] Goose Bay now had a deadline of one month to prepare for the arrival.

The official historian of Strategic Air Command, 4082nd Wing, told the story of the final preparations for the arrival of warheads:

> At the present time, the 4082d Strategic Wing has no nuclear weapons. The wing is expecting to receive AIM-26 type nuclear weapons around 15 July 1964. These weapons will be used by the Air Defense Command's F-102 fighter interceptor aircraft assigned to Goose AB. The wing, being the host organization on Goose AB, will be responsible to man and implement necessary security measures for storage and alert areas. The 4082d Combat Defense Squadron (CDS) received an approval of 28 more men to be transferred to Goose AB in September 1964 to support ADC in the storage of nuclear weapons. The Goose AB security manning indicated that 4082d CDS was manned to support 28 aircraft and only 18 aircraft were on alert. The original target date for the nuclear weapons was 1 October 1964. Higher headquarters requested verification in June to the effect that the 4082d CDS could support the operation of the munitions maintenance storage area out of the resources from 15 July until 1 October 1964 when projected inputs will be in place. No significant problems at Goose AB were foreseen to prevent meeting a 15 July 1964 support capability.[455]

The warheads did not promptly arrive.

With the Cuban missile crisis two years behind them, the refuelling squadrons on reflex duty at Goose Bay were switched from KC-97s to KC-135s. At the end of the year, Ernest Harmon Air Force Base, Newfoundland, was the only overseas base still supporting KC-97s.[456]

On 14 December 1964 the RCAF signed the joint RCAF-USAF Procedures for Restricted Data/Formerly Restricted Data Cargo. This allowed the actual physical movement of U.S. nuclear weapons into Goose Bay. No weapons arrived. At the June 1965 PJBD meeting, the U.S. team told Canada that "no nuclear weapons were stored at either Goose Bay or

Harmon." Discussions about the future of these two bases revealed that it was possible that no nuclear weapons would ever be stored there.[457]

The Initial Capability Inspection (ICI) of the 59th FIS at Goose Bay AB was conducted 19 through 23 June 1965.[458] The unit was rated "ready to receive warheads." The problem was that two limiting factors were noted. The first limiting factor prohibited the use of the alert facilities with nuclear armed aircraft during peacetime. This was not a big problem as the 59th and Goose Bay AB had only been assigned a five- and fifteen-minute alert commitment for identification purposes. This meant that there was no requirement to have nuclear weapons in the alert shelters. Loading of the nuclear Falcon would be allowed in the mass load area when DefCon 1 or higher was declared. The other limiting factor was that the unit did not have enough tools and general maintenance equipment for the proper care of the new nuclear weapons. The USAF/ADC inspector general declared that nuclear weapons at Goose Bay could not be stored for operational purposes, or even imported, until certification of rectification was obtained following a full review of the problem.[459] This was a Goose Bay problem, and both SAC and ADC would work together to fix it.

Not all was well at Goose Bay. The armament section had only nine qualified load crews with 18 qualified staff. A staff assistance visit by 26th Air Division Munitions Standardization Team was there from 8 to 10 September 1964, and the section performed in a satisfactory manner. All aspects of the "Weapons Release" Section functioned correctly.[460] While this situation was improving, the limiting factors would mean that Goose Bay was not going to be a fully operational nuclear base in the very near future.

The summer of 1965 was short in northern Newfoundland, and the 59th air defence squadron at Goose Bay flew 1656 operational sorties for a total of 2528 hours in the air. The warheads were delivered on schedule in July 1965.

The office of the deputy minister of National Defence told External Affairs that the warheads had been delivered to Goose Bay in the last week of June 1965. No one at External Affairs was aware of this fact. It seems that no one in the deputy minister's or office of the minister of National Defence knew either until External Affairs asked them the question on 15 July 1965.[461] It was later determined that "nuclear weapons are in Goose Bay on a storage only category and will remain in this category until such time as government procedures are adopted." Therefore, Paul Martin's office proposed to take no action on the preparation of interim procedures for U.S. weapons at the Goose.[462]

Goose Bay spent the summer and autumn of 1965 preparing for the inspection which, if passed, would allow the nuclear weapons to be loaded on the aircraft for alert duty. The November capability inspection (CI) saw the unit rated as satisfactory. However, the base did not pass. The inspector general wrote that the existing aircraft alert facilities did not meet the physical security standards for the protection of alert aircraft armed with warheads. Furthermore, they did not meet the explosive safety distance requirements. This limiting factor precluded use of alert facilities with nuclear armed aircraft, and HQ USAF adjusted the unit mission accordingly.[463] It is unlikely that Goose Bay and the 59th ever became fully operational with their W-54 nuclear weapons. It is most probable that the limiting factors stayed in place until the eventual removal of the warheads 12 months later.

On 31 December 1965, the U.S. embassy told External Affairs that the 59th FIS, constituting the entire U.S. fighter interceptor force at Goose Bay, was to be deactivated by 1 July 1967.[464] This had been agreed between HQ USAF and CINC NORAD. Given that the Canadian government knew that the only unit using nuclear weapons was being removed from Goose Bay, it is curious what they became concerned with. By mid-1966 the secretary of state for External Affairs was again concerned that "Canada has no physical control over the nuclear weapons at Goose Bay and Harmon, and cannot veto their use if there is no consultation." External Affairs recognized that the USAF could use nuclear weapons in Canada if it felt there was no time for intergovernmental consultations. Regarding air defence weapons, it had already been agreed that the prime minister would grant his authority to CINC NORAD, without consultation with the president, in the case of "emergency circumstances." A veto was only possible if there was time for consultation.[465] The reason this probably became an issue again was that negotiations for the U.S. naval weapons at Argentia were now under way, and this was a tough area for control to be exercised. It now applied little to Goose Bay. (This was discussed in detail in Chapter 1.)

Washington had made other plans for Goose Bay, and the plans were moving quickly. The State Department told the Canadian ambassador in a note dated 16 November 1966 that deactivation of the U.S. interceptor squadron at Goose Bay was now scheduled for completion by the final day of the year. By New Years Day, 1967, there would be no interceptors left at Goose Bay.[466] The Canadian government was assured, however, that the base would continue as a servicing and refuelling point for SAC. This meant that there would be no reduction of Canadian civilians employed at the base as it would still have to perform the SAC missions.[467] It was at this time that the prime minister found out that despite the removal of the nuclear weapons and the air defence squadron, the United States indicated that they "wish to retain the nuclear weapons storage rights at Goose Bay although the nuclear weapons stored there, which are exclusively designed for use by the interceptors, are also being withdrawn, beginning this week" (22 November 1966).[468]

Some of the more security fetishist U.S. military personnel wanted to ensure that no civilian aircraft could land at Goose Bay. They were especially worried as Czechoslovakia was seeking north Atlantic flights, Cubana Airlines already flew through Gander, and the USSR was about to sign the Chicago Convention on international air travel. This would mean that Aeroflot would be able to fly in and over Canada, and perhaps even try to land at Goose Bay. The State Department wanted the embassy to pressure the Canadian government to ensure that no "communist" or "other unfriendly" aircraft landed at Goose Bay AB.[469] This eventually produced the "Memorandum of Understanding Among DND, DoT and USAF on the Special Handling of Designated Aircraft at Goose Civil/Military Airport" of 19 June 1968, but by then there were no nuclear weapons remaining on site.

Discussions of U.S. activities at Goose Bay were now centred on the fighter-interceptors. The 59th had been gone for almost a year, but up to six USAF fighter aircraft of the 27th FIS deployed on continuous alert dispersal from Loring AFB, Maine. The Canadian Forces recognized in November that this detachment was to be withdrawn on 31 December 1967.[470] But, that too, moved fast, and by the beginning of December there were no more U.S. interceptor aircraft resident at Goose Bay. The CAF sent a detachment of CF-101 VooDoo interceptors on temporary duty to stand alert at Goose Bay during the month of March 1968, but these would be quickly pulled out. At this point Goose Bay, with no air defence nuclear weapons and no fighter-interceptors, returned to its usual undefended state. What the Canadian government did not realize was that in focusing on the air defence nuclear weapons, they had missed the politically-charged issue of heavy strategic weapons. SAC had deployed such heavy nuclear bombs to Goose Bay in the late summer of 1950, and these types of weapons were not withdrawn until June 1971.

Chapter Six

"FREICUDAN DU": THE 59TH IN NEWFOUNDLAND

The 59th Fighter-Interceptor Squadron was the only United States unit permanently stationed in Canada to be armed with nuclear weapons. Due to the unique nature of this unit, a full chapter has been devoted to what it was, how it got to Canada, its arming with nuclear missiles, its operations at Goose Bay Air Base and Ernest Harmon Air Force Base in Newfoundland, and how it eventually left.

Named after the Black Watch Highland regiment, Freicudan Du, or the 59th Fighter-Interceptor Squadron, began its service life as the 33rd Pursuit Squadron of the U.S. Army Air Corps at Mitchell Field, New York, in January 1941. It gained the designation 59 in 1942 and promptly moved to French Morocco. The 59th served 15 months in the European theatre of operations in World War II and was deactivated in February 1944. The unit was reactivated in India in August 1944 to fight against the Japanese, and at the end of the war returned to the United States and was again inactivated. The unit entered the jet age by being reactivated in November 1947 at Roswell, New Mexico. There is no evidence that they were involved in the space alien incidents at that location. The unit used the F-84, then the F-86 and then the F-94. The 59th moved to Otis AFB, Falmouth, Massachusetts, on 16 November 1948. Eventually the unit gained the century series fighter, the F-102 Delta Dagger, which would be used in Newfoundland. The designation "Fighter-Interceptor Squadron" was conferred on 20 January 1950.

Their first visit to Goose Bay came in 1948 when a group of 16 F-80 aircraft flew non-stop to London from Goose Bay AB. This was the second crossing of the Atlantic by jet, as the USAF had been beaten to the honour by the RAF flying the extremely tiny and short-ranged Vampire.

Proceeding on the basis of their understanding of the lease they had for the use of Goose Bay Air Base, the USAF intended to station a fighter-interceptor squadron there in 1952. During the 25 September 1952 Permanent Joint Board on Defence meeting, the USAF member informed the Canadian air member that a USAF unit was earmarked for Goose Bay and would be stationed there as of 1 October 1952. The USAF had already made shipping arrangements and had given notification of the posting to squadron members. Some members had already been in transit.[471] The U.S. member had taken the opportunity of informing his Canadian counterpart as a courtesy, because the United States felt there was no requirement to ask Canada's permission for such activities.

The problem from a tactical point of view was that there was no Canadian air defence squadron available to cover the Goose Bay air defence sector, and under Canadian rules and over Canadian territory, U.S. interceptors would come under Canadian command. Since there were no facilities at Goose Bay for the establishment of such a command, and since there was little guaranteed communication with Goose Bay, in practice command would have to fall to the USAF. External Affairs mused that they might try to get the USAF to act under Canadian rules.[472]

External Affairs, through the U.S. embassy in Ottawa, informed the United States that the immediate stationing of the USAF squadron would be inconsistent with the Canadian interpretation of the Goose Bay lease. The U.S. embassy did not contest the Canadians, and offered a collateral letter on the deployment. Since personnel at External Affairs and in the RCAF did not see how Canada could politically or legally object to the stationing, a face-saving measure would have to be found which both allowed the deployment and made it look as if Canada were exercising some sovereignty over the area and its own defence. Meanwhile, the RCAF was issuing orders of its own and telling the USAF that the USAF now had the delegated authority of the air officer commanding Air Defence Command to intercept foreign aircraft over Canada.[473] However, the RCAF at least did not tell the USAF that they were free to station whatever units they wished to Goose Bay.

The 59th never did show up in 1952, but was stood down until 1953. The unit was alerted to move in July 1953 and the entire squadron was in place at Goose Bay Air Base by October. For reasons not entirely understood, the USAF had just slightly earlier moved the 61st FIS into Goose Bay, and then left it there for four years at the same time as the 59th. After the 59th arrived, it proceeded to organize for alert duty. This was initially a temporary duty of indefinite duration, but it later became a permanent assignment for the squadron. There was a command staff flight called Hotel Lima Staff of the commanding officer and his section commanders. There was also a sub-command staff called Echo Papa Harmon with the same duties at Harmon AFB. The squadron was then divided into four operational flights, called Hotel Lima A Flight through D flight, of about nine pilots each. Flights would rotate in and out of Harmon on a regular basis so that no flight crew were permanently posted to Harmon.

The USAF originally thought that the MB-1, or Genie nuclear air defence rocket, would be stored at Goose Bay and Harmon Field for use by the 59th FIS on their F-89 Scorpions. This was the first air-to-air nuclear air defence weapon in the U.S. arsenal, and if deployment had been allowed immediately, this would have been the weapon used.[474] The MND was told that the new MB-1 was a long-range unguided rocket armed with an atomic warhead. The MB-1 rocket had no air-to-ground, ground-to-air or ground-to-ground applications; it was purely an air-to-air defensive weapon. It was then in squadron service with the F-89J USAF air defence aircraft. The rules of engagement affecting the use of atomic air-to-air weapons were concluded by an exchange of notes on 30 June 1959 whereby U.S. aircraft armed with air-to-air atomic weapons could operate in Canadian air space subsequent to the declaration of maximum air defence readiness.[475]

It was now time for the USAF to get the State Department to prod Canada into accepting nuclear permanent deployments in Newfoundland.[476] The eventual deployment to Goose Bay in 1964-65 may not have been the first time air defence rockets were at the Goose. There is evidence that the USAF did briefly store the Genie system at Goose Bay. The *History of the 64th Air Division, January - July 1962*, written by the USAF and classified as "Not Releaseable to Foreign Nationals," clearly states that "Goose Air Base had the storage facilities formerly used for the MB-1 rockets which were considered adequate for the GAR-11 W-54 warheads."[477] This remains a mystery. If it were true, the nuclear weapons could have armed the F-89 Scorpion fighter-interceptor aircraft which were operated by the 59th.

NORTHROP F-89 SCORPION[478]

The F-89 was a twin-engine, all-weather fighter-interceptor designed to locate, intercept and destroy enemy aircraft by day or night under all types of weather conditions. It carried a pilot and a radar/weapons operator who guided the pilot and fired the weapons. The first F-89 made its initial flight in August 1948 and deliveries to USAF began in July 1950. Northrop produced 1050 F-89s. On 19 July 1957, a Genie test rocket was fired from an F-89J: the first time in history that an air-to-air rocket with a nuclear warhead was launched and detonated. Three hundred and fifty F-89Ds were converted to "J" models which became the Air Defense Command's first fighter-interceptor to carry nuclear armament.

NORTHROP F-89 SCORPION

Wing Span: 17.9m
Length: 16.1m
Height: 5.25m
Max. Weight: 21.7 t
Engines: two Allison J35 turbojets
Maximum speed: 1000 km/h
Cruising speed: 700 km/h
Range: 2500 km
Service Ceiling: 13 500m
Armament: Two AIR-2A Genie plus four AIM-4C Falcon missiles
Crew: Two
Cost: $1,009,000.00

The issue of how to arm the squadron had again come up at the Cabinet level. The minister of National Defence had a submission for the Cabinet Defence Committee prepared on a broad range of nuclear issues; one of those issues was the 59th. Back in October 1958 Cabinet had agreed that senior officers should initiate negotiations with United States authorities regarding the acquisition and storage of defensive nuclear weapons for Canadian forces. At the same time, they had also "agreed to the storage by the United States of air defence nuclear missiles at Goose Bay and Harmon Air Force Base subject to the conclusion of a satisfactory exchange of notes."[479] When a draft of the notes was presented to Cabinet in July 1960, Cabinet undertook to further examine the issue. The CDC was therefore reminded that the USAF interceptor squadron at Goose Bay and Harmon, as part of NORAD, was already equipped to carry nuclear air defence missiles, and that these missiles were now in the general USAF inventory. The MND pointed out that use of the nuclear missiles "would greatly increase the air defence capability of these squadrons. [And that] immediate realization of this improved capability is now dependent solely upon completion of an international agreement covering their storage in Canada."[480] Despite the substance of the agreement already having been worked out, Cabinet did nothing, and the 59th would remain unarmed with nuclear weapons for another four years.

What was the place of the 59th in air defence in North America? In 1960 the USAF Air Defense Command fielded 798 interceptor aircraft in North America. Of these, 193 were the F-102 used by the 59th. To fly the aircraft USAF ADC had 308 air crews checked out and committed to the F-102A, a surplus of 96 air crews. ADC estimated that 91% of the crews were combat ready. The USAF ADC force of 41 manned squadrons was spread out over 37 bases in the United States, Goose Bay and Thule. SAC was the host base at 11 of the sites, including Goose Bay. For USAF ADC, the future was a nuclear one, and all units were to be equipped with nuclear air defence weapons. In the early years after 1957 this meant the Genie rocket with the W25 nuclear warhead, and after 1960 it meant a slow move to the more sophisticated GAR-11 nuclear Falcon missile. USAF ADC even intended to supply nuclear weapons to all USAF Air National Guard units doing air defence work, provided that adequate nuclear security could be assured. This was not always possible, as many were located at civilian airfields. Most squadrons had 18 aircraft, while a sizable number had 24 or 26 aircraft. The 59th converted from the older F-89 Scorpion to the newer F-102A in 1960, and Goose Bay was unique in having a programmed force of 33 F-102A interceptor aircraft, the highest in USAF ADC.[481] During the Cuban missile crisis, they had 28 combat-ready aircraft out of an actual fleet of 28.

THE CONVAIR F-102A DELTA DAGGER

The primary mission of the F-102 was to intercept and destroy Soviet heavy bombers coming over the northern region of North America. It was the world's first supersonic all-weather jet interceptor and the USAF's first operational delta-wing aircraft.[482] The Convair F-102 became operational with USAF Air Defense Command in 1956. At the peak of deployment in the late 1950s, F-102s equipped more than 25 ADC squadrons with some 975 single-seaters.[483]

This Convair design began life in 1951 in competition with other contenders for a new USAF jet interceptor needed to carry the new Falcon missile and associated fire control system above Mach 1. In March 1951 the

USAF picked Convair and two other companies to design and build the so-called 1954 Interceptor. The Convair proposal had not been highly rated in logistical support, and dead last in feasibility, but budget cuts in September 1951 made the aircraft the only one being built. Already there were doubts that the aircraft would be finished by 1956, let alone 1954.

The mock-up of the aircraft included all sorts of features which had not yet actually been built by other companies. The black boxes were representative of advanced systems which the F-102A would never have. The only marginally advanced system would be the original E-9 fire control system built into the first several hundred airframes. The aircraft was powered by the Pratt & Whitney J57-P-35 turbojet engine. The aircraft would be a delta-winged plane, but the first ten built had straight bodies. This produced great drag, and the aircraft never reached the speeds or the altitude promised. Convair had to be forcibly convinced that the aircraft needed to be reshaped to conform to the area rule, or "Coke-bottle" fuselage shape, whereby the middle is thinner and the front and back thicker then tapering. The body got thinner in the middle, longer, and the wings moved back starting with production aircraft No. 11.

Convair took the aircraft aloft for the first flight on 24 October 1953, and USAF Major General Albert Boyd became the first military test pilot of the F-102A on 28 April 1954. Flight testing did not go well, but the problems were often attributable to malfunctioning components from third suppliers. The chief Convair test pilot, R.L. Johnson, crashed one onto the runway when the gear failed to lower. He was seriously injured, but recovered in time to take part in more tests. In fact, he flew the first area rule version of the F-102 called the Hot Rod, and it was an immediate improvement over the straight fuselage version.

The USAF received their first operational F-102A at the 327th FIS at George AFB in California during April 1956. By the end of 1958 there were 627 Delta Daggers in USAF ADC service. Close to 1000 of these aircraft saw service with the U.S. Air Force. With the introduction of the better F-106, numbers dropped, and by 1961 there were only 221 serving in ADC. However, upgrades with the new MG-10 fire control system in 1958 and the nuclear Falcon missile meant that some squadrons would continue in service until 1967.

The first 458 of the production F-102A fighters lacked the MG-10 fire control system which was installed as a standard feature only beginning with the 459th production airframe. Backfitting the previous 458 aircraft took three to four months each in 1958. Even then, the system was not fully operational. Additional modifications in 1960 allowed the MG-10 to control the firing of the nuclear Falcon missile. This new Fig 7/GAR-11 modification of the F-102A of the 59th was completed on 1 November 1961.[484] The F-102, now seven years late, could carry and fire nuclear missiles.

CONVAIR F-102A DELTA DAGGER

In service: 1956.
Wing Span 11.62m
Length 20.81m
Gross weight 14.28t
Engine: Pratt & Whitney J57
max speed 1328km/h, Mach 1.25
Cruising speed: 1000 km/h
Service ceiling: 16 400m
Cost: $1,184,000.00

TYPE	Number built or Converted	Remarks
YF-102	10	Prototype
YF-102A	4	Area rule YF-102;
F-102A	875	Interceptor
TF-102A	111	Dual-cockpit trainer
F-102B	0	Became F-106

Primary armament consisted of six Hughes Corporation Falcon conventional warhead short-range air-to-air infra-red missiles. These were stored inside the missile bay on launching rails which extended outside the fuselage for firing. Special, nuclear armament consisted of two AIM-26A/B missiles with the W54 nuclear warhead which were fired in the same manner.

THE 59TH

The 59th, as the only USAF unit to be armed with nuclear weapons in Canada, received no small attention from the United States government. In the same month that the agreement for arming the air defence unit at Goose Bay was signed, U.S. ambassador Walt Butterworth showed up for a tour of the 59th facilities. Unit records show that he was especially interested in the missile maintenance section. Escorted by the 59th Squadron commander, the Goose Bay Air Base commander, and two colonels from Goose Sector, Butterworth was almost undoubtedly shown the GAR-11 Falcon nuclear weapon system he helped to arm.[485]

But it was not only the visit of the ambassador that made the 59th busy. They were now actively preparing for the GAR-11 Falcon to be used, and much had to be done. The missile maintenance section was modifying the WSEM weapons system Checkout Consoles to give them a GAR-11 checkout capability, and one console was placed in the missile checkout area of building S-45. The same activity was going on at Detachment No. 1 at Harmon, where they prepared to check out the GAR-11 and GAR-11A missiles.[486] Once it had finished rebuilding the storage areas, Harmon was given 36 additional AIM-26 missiles by Goose Bay.[487] The 38 primary air crews at Goose Bay and Harmon saw 2584 hours of flying time in the fourth quarter of the year. They were almost ready for the warheads.

The most important visitor to the 59th that month was not Walt Butterworth, it was the team lead by Captain William Gobble which conducted the staff visit. The primary finding of the team was that the "facilities support furnished to 59th FIS (ADC) for operations pertinent to munitions support were found generally adequate to meet mission requirements in the near future." The team was mostly concerned with security at the ADC munitions bunker facility which was part of the SAC nuclear weapons bomb dump at Goose Bay. The team recommended a new evaluation of the SAC manning of the bomb dump and a probable increase in space. However, it was noted that SAC was providing adequate support to the ADC unit at Goose.[488]

At the end of 1963 the 59th had 662 staff of 57 officers and 604 airmen and one civilian, a woman named Ivis K. Moore. The last big event of the year was the unit being invited to complete in the William Tell World-Wide Interceptor Weapons Meet in Florida. Given that the USSR and its allies were not invited, it was hardly a worldwide event. The team did very well in low-altitude intercepts, but had trouble at higher altitudes, and experienced some problems firing and guiding their AIM-4A/4C conventional Falcon missiles. Back home at Goose Bay, the unit was still preparing for the nuclear Falcon. The flight simulator was rebuilt to allow nuclear Falcon simulation, and the buildings were being re-floored and painted, and security systems were being updated.[489] Up to this point, maintenance of the nuclear Falcon system, minus the warheads, was being conducted at the nuclear storage site. The real problem was with the armament section: although the team sent to the

William Tell meet that year had scored highest, the section was still seriously undermanned for a nuclear mission. One problem was that the 15-month tour at Goose Bay seriously undermined the ability of the unit to keep trained personnel on duty.

Nineteen-sixty four was a big year for nuclear weapons in Canada. The RCAF units using both the Bomarc missile and the CF-104 Starfighters had been armed and placed on alert, and the Army began duty with the Honest John rocket in Germany. For the United States, this was not to be the year they would arm the 59th air defence squadron at Goose Bay. With a loss of almost 90 personnel, it was an inauspicious start to the year. However, the unit still managed to fly 1627 operational sorties in the first quarter, and the NORAD operational readiness exercise (ORE) was held on 11 and 12 March. This was one of the final big steps prior to the acquisition of the warheads, and the 59th flew over 100 sorties, mostly in the middle of the night, to accomplish the review. The USAF also sent the 26th Tactical Evaluation Team to conduct an Alert Force Capability Test off the 59th. This gained the unit a "satisfactory" rating.

A lot more security was going to be needed for the 59th once they received nuclear warheads. HQ GADS and SAC were studying the problem and noted that another 61 personnel would be needed. Since the bunkers were only used for temporary, transient nuclear weapon storage, staffing did not have to be high. Full-time storage for the 59th would increase the demand on the Special Ammunition Storage Site (SAS).[490]

HUGHES FALCON GAR-11, AIM-26A MISSILE

The Falcon Air Interceptor Missile 26A was the only Falcon air-to-air missile type to be armed with a nuclear warhead. This unique weapon carried the very small W-54 atomic warhead for the destruction of incoming Soviet bombers. Originally called the GAR-11, the name was changed with the modernization of all military terms to the AIM-26A. Hughes was given a contact in March 1958, and the first unguided flight took place on 13 May 1958. The first guided flight was on 22 May. At this point the Joint Chiefs of Staff approved a nuclear warhead for the new Falcon system.

The missile itself was 2.28 m long, with a 0.28 m diameter body, and a 0.91 m tail fin/wing span. It was capable of reaching 8-16 km to a target at Mach 2 using a solid fuel Thiokol rocket motor. Fuzing of the warhead was accomplished by four long proximity fuzes placed laterally along the nose of the missile. The warhead and missile were thereby detonated by the proximity fuzing system when the missile came to within 56 m of the target.

While the rocket body worked, and the guidance seemed to function, the fuzing was very unreliable. In the flight testing between August 1959 and September 1960, 21 of the 36 tests failed due to fuze problems. In October the new fuse was ready and testing resumed. The warhead package was finally delivered and mated to the Falcon missile in December 1961, and testing was to resume. However, a lack of target drones, test missiles, and available test time at Elgin AFB in Florida again halted the program. The final weapons system testing took place between May and July 1962, two years behind schedule, and determined that the fuzing worked only half the time. Of 20 missiles which returned useful telemetry, 19 came within 10 m of the target aircraft. This was more than close enough to destroy any aircraft with even the most humble atomic bomb. The weapon was judged to have a kill probability against sturdy Soviet heavy bombers of at least 90%.

In the meantime, USAF ADC had provided 200 of the AIM-26A Falcon to operational units in December 1961, even though it had not finished testing and there was no functional warhead. The MDU-6/A was the training device for the Falcon/W-54 unit, and was used when the 59th FIS underwent certain inspections and exercises. Over the 10-year service life, some 1900 of the AIM-26A Falcons were produced. By the late 1960s the missile was considered of little use, and retirement of the system began in July 1967 and ended when the final unit was withdrawn in April 1972.

W-54 NUCLEAR WARHEAD[491]

Nuclear weapons for air defence rockets were born with the mating of the W-25 warhead and the Genie rocket body. The problem was that the early system depended on an unguided rocket and an aircraft-based fire control system. The USAF wanted a more independent missile which would track the target itself. The other problem was that the original F-102A could not be armed with the Genie atomic rocket system.

With fewer F-102A aircraft than originally planned entering and staying in the inventory, the USAF demanded more bang for their buck, and this meant that the Delta Dagger would have to have the follow-on nuclear missile. In December 1957 USAF General Curtis LeMay called for the development of a small warhead for a Falcon missile. The idea was approved, and Hughes fired the first test missile in March 1958. After this came the approval of the nuclear warhead by the Joint Chiefs of Staff in May 1958, and on 23 June the U.S. Atomic Energy Commission was allowed to proceed with development of the W-54. Given the demand for other, easier-to-produce weapons, the warhead for the Falcon was not expected before February 1961. Both Los Alamos and Lawrence Livermore came up with designs, Wee Gnat and Quail respectively, for the Falcon warhead. The Wee Gnat would be renamed as the XW-54, and it was design-released in December 1959.

The W-54 warhead was developed for three uses: as the warhead for the U.S. Army's Davey Crockett small atomic weapon fired from a recoilless gun, as the warhead for the U.S. Army's Special Atomic Demolition Device", and for carriage in the U.S. Air Force's new Falcon AIM-26A air-to-air missile.

There were warhead problems. The Atomic Energy Commission told the USAF that the warhead would not be ready for the 1959 release date, now expecting to hand over a complete warhead in October 1960. There had been accidents involving high explosives at Los Alamos and production techniques were altered. Production stopped, and the delivery date was again pushed back to February 1961. Another problem with the warhead was that the high explosives would not compress the fissile core enough to attain the design yield. The entire high-explosives package had to be re-designed, and delivery was again pushed back until May 1961. The warhead package was finally delivered and mated to the Falcon missile in December 1961.

The W-54 had an even smaller nuclear yield than the W-25 Genie warhead, and could produce as little as 0.1 kt of atomic explosion or up to 1 kt. The actual warhead was only 0.38 m long and 0.28 m in diameter, and had a cylindrical shape. Its total weight was about 26.6 kg. It was equipped with a mechanical combination Permissive Action Link (PAL) which would have to be unlocked prior to the interceptor aircraft leaving the alert hangar.

Developed at Los Alamos labs, the W-54 was design-released in December 1959, and production of the W-54 Mod 0 and Mod 2 began in April 1961 and lasted until February 1965. In five years, between 1000 and 2000 of these warheads were manufactured for various uses, the majority going to the USAF. However, due to operational requirements which the AIM-26A Falcon did not meet, the need for the warhead decreased, and retirement of the W-54 began in July 1967, and the final warhead was removed from service in April 1972.

FURTHER PREPARATIONS

Outside of Goose Bay, preparations for the arrival of nuclear weapons for the 59th were also under way. In Ottawa, the Department of Trade and Commerce had insisted that there be export permits for whatever equipment the USAF moved out of the leased bases in Newfoundland. Nuclear weapons were no exception, and the deputy minister of National Defence had to act as the agent for the USAF in dealing with the transit of nuclear warheads. A similar permit had been issued for the Bomarc warheads on about 25 October 1963.[492] DND applied for the permit on 13 January 1964 and External Affairs was consulted on the matter on 17 January for their approval. There was no reason not to give it, so the permits were signed. Strangely, there is a note indicating that the trade control division of the Department of Trade and Commerce cancelled the application on or about 23 April.[493] There is no explanation for this. The permit application is interesting and worth seeing.

> Export Permit APPLICATION No. 486695 has been received from Deputy Minister of National defence, Dept. Of National Defence, Ottawa. Dated January 13, 1964 for permission to export to U.S.A. the following: Nuclear air-to-air defensive weapons brought into Canada under the Canada-US Agreement of September 28 and 30, 1963 and any amendments thereto, and exported in accordance with the provisions of that Agreement. (See copies of letters attached) This equipment is valued at $___ and is consigned to United States of America.[494]

The service-to-service arrangement to cover the provision of nuclear weapons to the 59th at Goose Bay was finally signed during the first week of May 1964.[495] This paved the way for the arrival of warheads.

When all was ready, the nuclear warheads would be scheduled to arrive much sooner than expected. The arrangement had been signed by the RCAF and the USAF for the provision of nuclear warheads to Goose Bay, and SAC had provided extra Munitions Maintenance Squadron (MMS) crews to Goose Bay. The USAF was therefore able to move the delivery date up from 1 October 1964 to 15 July 1964.[496] However, the 59th would not be certified to use the W-54 nuclear warhead once it arrived.

In the spring of 1964 the munitions section experienced a 55% changeover in staff, with little overlap between the departing and arriving servicemen. Most were not familiar with ADC nuclear weapons, and quality of work fell. An interesting note to the unit diaries read: "Missile Maintenance Section personnel assigned to the ADC Special Storage Site were moved to the site. This provided and increased responsiveness and insures that the Storage Site is operational under any circumstances."[497] It was still difficult for the personnel to keep the 20 combat-ready aircraft armed and secure.

The New Year saw the 59th operating 31 of the F-102A fighter-interceptors, two of the TF-102A training versions, and 8 of the T-33 general proficiency aircraft with 65 officers and 565 airmen. In the first quarter of 1965 the unit flew 1836 sorties with their primary aircraft in 2499 hours.[498] Aside from two annual inspections which fell during that time, and which were passed, there was little excitement except for the arrival of CBC television crews. The CBC filmed two 30-minute documentaries, including one about a day in the life of a fighter pilot, and another for the film *Eyes of the North*.

The unit now had to pass the dreaded Initial Capability Inspection (ICI). The ICI team from USAF ADC office of the command inspector general stayed for four days in June 1965 and measured every aspect of operations and maintenance performed by the 59th. The ICI team found that the 59th was limited by the fact that "the existing alert facilities did not meet the physical security standards ... for the protection of alert aircraft armed with warheads. Furthermore, they did not meet the explosive safety distance requirements." However, on 23 June, the team gave a positive general evaluation, saying, "The unit is ready to receive weapons/warheads."[499] The nuclear warheads arrived in July, but that the aircraft could not be armed with them to stand alert in the alert hangars due to the limiting factor. A subsequent inspection in November 1965 showed exactly the same limiting factors.[500] ADC therefore adjusted the unit mission away from a nuclear one.[501] As per the leases and agreements and arrangements, the RCAF sent an observer to the inspections, and he was able to report in detail that the limiting factor meant that the 59th was prohibited from using the "present alert facilities with nuclear armed aircraft during peacetime" as neither the physical security nor explosive safety distances met USAF standards. The director of nuclear weapons for National Defence W/C Charko reported that the 59th had "only been assigned a five and fifteen minute alert commitment for identification purposes hence has no requirement to place nuclear armed aircraft in the alert facilities." The director reported that only under DefCon 1 or higher alert condition could the aircraft at Goose Bay be armed in a mass load area.[502]

The Canadian military was kept fully informed at all times of the progress of the deployment. Wing Commander Charko, DNW, wrote after observing the ICI of 1965 that the second limiting factor pertains to equipment and expandable supplies for warhead maintenance and must be rectified before the unit receives warheads.[503] Although the unit was technically allowed to use the weapon in an Air Defence Emergency or at DEFCON 1 in the mass load area, there is no indication that the weapons were ever brought out of storage to stand regular 5 and 15 minute alerts. W/C Charko stated that a certification of rectification will be obtained before authorization for import of warheads is granted.[504] This last statement clearly indicates that htere were no W-54 warheads at Goose Bay as of June 1965.

With the ICI out of the way, NORAD scheduled a regular operational readiness inspection (ORI) for 22–24 July, and a no-notice ORI on 12 August 1965. The 59th had successful results in both inspections. The unit diary notes that the ADC readiness exercise was passed by the maintenance section without limiting factors during the summer.[505] What the record did not show was the base facilities for the alert aircraft were insufficient, and that limiting factors would continue to be listed against the Goose.

While 1964 and 1965 showed slow progress towards nuclear arming of the unit, 1966 showed a great downturn. Detachment 1, 59th FIS was informed that it was being deactivated as of 1 April 1966. All alert commitments would cease at 2400 hours on 31 January. The F-102 fighters were returned to Goose Bay and all activity ended on 25 March with the last member flying back to Goose Bay.[506] In closing, Major Marcus Oliphant wrote that his detachment acted "with the same high motivation and spirit it had possessed during former years."[507] The 59th, aside from losing their only off-site detachment, was also losing aircraft. At the end of 1965 they had 32 F-102 and TF-102 aircraft, but March saw the unit drop to only 26 F-102 and 2 TF-102 fighters.[508]

The unit did not have long to live. In December 1965 the U.S. Department of Defense had announced that the F-102A interceptors would be phased out of the active forces and delivered to the Air National Guard to replace obsolete F-89 fighters. In light of this decision, the 59th at Goose Bay and their F-102 interceptors would probably be inactivated, according to the State Department in early November, as of 1 January 1967.[509] Back on 31 December 1965, the U.S. embassy in Ottawa told External Affairs that the unit would be deactivated by 1 July 1967, and informal talks with the U.S. air member at the PJBD confirmed this. However, it had become necessary to accelerate the process of moving the aircraft to other units and sending the air crew to more pressing assignments in southeast Asia. The U.S. secretary of state told Canadian ambassador Ritchie that "it is planned to deactivate 59th Fighter Interceptor Squadron by Dec 31/66."[510]

Six days later, on 22 November, the chief of the Defence Staff told the minister that "the US Government has found it necessary to deactivate the 59th" at Goose Bay earlier than originally anticipated and programmed. General Allard stated that the 59th would not be replaced, but that the deactivation would not affect the nuclear mission of Goose Bay. Allard informed the MND that the USAF still wished "to continue to maintain nuclear weapons storage facilities at Goose Bay to support a possible future deployment to the base," and that the withdrawal would not affect the continued SAC mission of the base.[511]

On that same day, Marcel Cadieux, the under-secretary for state for External Affairs, informed Prime Minister Pearson of the withdrawal. Pearson was told that the aircraft would all be gone by the end of that year, but that "the US authorities have indicated that they wish to retain nuclear weapons storage rights at Goose Bay although the nuclear weapons stored there, which were exclusively designed for use by the interceptors, are also being withdrawn, beginning this week."[512]

With this decision, the W-54 nuclear warheads for the AIM-26A nuclear Falcon missiles were withdrawn from the Goose Bay Air Base SAS facilities between 20 and 30 November 1966.[513] US records indicate a removal date of December. The nuclear duty had lasted a very short time, and even if it had gone on longer, the eventual withdrawal of the AIM-26 Falcon from the USAF inventory would have made the 59th a conventional unit regardless.

The departure of the 59th from Goose Bay did not leave the Goose Air Defence Sector (GADS) vacant of defending aircraft. Six F-101 VooDoo interceptors were stationed on a rotational basis to Goose Bay from Loring AFB[514] in Maine and may have been part of the 27th Fighter-Interceptor Squadron. These six aircraft were eventually themselves withdrawn on 31 December 1967. The U.S. embassy in Ottawa recommended that the State Department advise both External Affairs and Newfoundland premier Joseph Smallwood of the withdrawal "sooner rather than later," as so much political capital had been spent on the question of interceptors at Goose Bay over the past 17 years.[515] The reply came three days later, on 3 November, when the State Department told the U.S. embassy that all matters were being handled through military channels by NORAD since it was only a six-aircraft F-101 detachment and had minimum impact on the local economy.[516]

The footnote to the history of the 59th Fighter Interceptor Squadron was that they were reactivated on 30 September 1968 at Kingsley Field, Oregon, and assigned to the 408th Fighter Group. They continued as an all-weather nuclear air defence interceptor squadron flying 19 F-101 VooDoo aircraft with two on five-minute alert, and two on one-hour alert.[517]

Chapter Seven

HARMON AIR FORCE BASE

Stephenville Air Base was constructed by the U.S. Army Air Force following its acquisition from the British in 1940. It was one of the many sites Winston Churchill gave to Roosevelt in exchange for war materials to aid in the fight against Germany, and the United States therefore got a very nice 99-year lease. The name of the site was changed in June 1941 to honour the memory of U.S. Captain Ernest Harmon. The site was officially referred to as an Air Force Base, and not as an Air Base as in the case of Goose Bay. This is because the United States had total control of the entire facility and almost total discretion over their own actions.

Harmon was one of the three bases which the United States maintained under the 1941 U.S.-U.K. leased bases agreement. The others were Pepperrell Air Force Base, which had no airfield, and Argentia Naval Station, which had no fleet. Pepperrell was closed in 1961, followed by Harmon in 1966, and finally Argentia in the 1970s. Reconstruction of the base, from its smaller wartime form to a larger strategic bombing and tanker role, began in 1953. This included all new heavy capacity runways, new fighter hangars, new port facilities, a new waterway, a new highway and a few hundred buildings.[518]

The purpose of Harmon in the new Cold War world was to provide support to both permanently stationed and temporary-duty heavy tanker aircraft. These KC-97 tankers from Strategic Air Command (SAC) would refuel the SAC heavy bombers on their way to destroy the Soviet Union and eastern Europe. Harmon was the last link in the "leap frog" chain of tanker facilities. In this operation, bombers would take off from zone of the interior (ZI) bases along with their tankers and immediately take on fuel. The tankers would land at the northern-most U.S. bases and refuel. The tankers from the northern-most U.S. bases would then meet the bombers and off-load more fuel, then land at Harmon and Goose Bay AB. The tankers at Harmon and Goose Bay would fly out over the north Atlantic to provide a final fuelling before the bombers penetrated Soviet airspace.[519]

The U.S. government felt in 1952 that as long as the Canadian and British governments had firm commitments from the United States that actual strikes from their territories would be a matter of joint decision, they were willing to allow the USAF to engage in various deployments and pre-positioning operations.[520]

But tankers are not nuclear delivery systems, even though they are integral to the nuclear weapons infrastructure. Harmon's nuclear weapons would not be strategic heavy weapons, but defensive systems deployed on fighter-interceptor aircraft. The 59th Fighter- Interceptor Squadron was one of only a few air defence units which were deployed to Harmon AFB. Others included the 61st FIS which flew the F94B between 10 July 1953 and November 1957; and, the 323rd FIS which flew the F102A between October 1957 and 6 June 1960.

Since it was obvious to the U.S. government that Ottawa was not about to move quickly to allow the USAF to arm systems in Canada, the military-to-military channel was utilized as a way of getting around the blockage in Cabinet. The RCAF Air Staff was sent a copy of the U.S. draft agreement on Harmon and Goose Bay AB on 22 September 1959[521] The chief of the air staff then had to decide how to approach Cabinet. SAC had offered the chief a full briefing on storage so that he could in turn brief Cabinet. SAC was especially interested in this as they were aware that there had been a submission to Cabinet on the topic which had been sitting unattended for 18 months. This was clearly not the time for any moves which would cause anxiety to political persons. So when the U.S. Navy in October asked permission to send the submarine USS *Swordfish* to Esquimalt, National Defence promptly informed them that the visit "at this juncture would be untimely. It is not approved to extend an invitation."[522]

The air staff was now deeply engaged in working out the Canadian response to the U.S. proposal. It is interesting to note that the military had the same interests in Canadian control as the politicians. The VCAS suggested that the sixth paragraph be altered to reflect that removal of the weapons from storage at Harmon for the arming of interceptors would be carried out only whenever a condition of Air Defence Readiness or higher state of alert was declared by CINC NORAD.[523] However, military consideration was not enough, and an almost total lack of action by the Diefenbaker government would prevent the nuclear weapons from arriving for another eight years.

By 1962 the U.S. servicemen at Harmon numbered over 2500, and with the civilians, took in over a million dollars in salaries monthly. In northern Newfoundland, this was a great windfall, and the local economy was very much dependent on the spending of the military and local civilian employees. The storage of the Genies would have little impact on the local economy, as the increase in personnel would be so small in relation to the total already deployed as to be negligible.

It was not until the spring of 1963 that Harmon finally saw the nuclear light at the end of the long negotiating tunnel. The Diefenbaker Conservatives had been defeated by a minority Liberal government, and the new prime minister, Lester Pearson, had sworn that he would conclude all the prior commitments of the Canadian government. By mid-September, Cabinet allowed that the United States be informed that Canada would expedite agreement on Harmon and Goose Bay if the negotiations were restricted to that topic.[524] Two weeks later, on 26 September 1963, Cabinet finally agreed to allow the signing of the Goose Bay/Harmon agreement.

At this crucial Cabinet meeting, arrangements were made to allow the secretary of state for External Affairs to sign an agreement with United States, and for the prime minister to issue a possible statement on the storage at Harmon. As originally planned, Pearson was to tell the House of Commons that

> it is in the form of an Exchange of Notes and specifies the conditions under which nuclear, air-to-air defensive weapons will be stored for United States Air Force interceptor aircraft under the operational command of the Commander-in-Chief of the joint North American Air Defence Command stationed at the leased base area at Goose Bay and the leased base known as Harmon Field at Stephenville.

The United States government was horrified and politely demanded a change. The U.S. change came on 2 October and altered the reference to the named bases to a vague reference to leased bases.[525] The PMO made the changes, and Pearson's office gave a copy of the revised statement to Ross Campbell to show the State Department.

In the meantime, the storage agreement was finally signed by both countries on 28 and 30 September. Even the NATO general secretary conveyed his approval and said he was happy this long outstanding problem seemed to now have been solved.[526] The question of U.S. fighters at Harmon and Goose Bay had been a possible thorn for NATO, as many people wondered why Canada was sending squadrons to Europe when Canadian territory itself needed defending by the U.S. Air Force. This question did not go away, but it was now too late for the public to use it as an argument.

The USAF moved quickly once the agreement was signed, and they told Canada that they estimated it would take approximately three months to select and have the appropriate personnel on site preparatory to the receipt of the weapons. They therefore figured that, at best, the weapons should be available for use at Harmon in early January 1964.[527] USAF HQ indicated an intent to proceed as expeditiously as possible to achieve an operational F-102/GAR-11 nuclear capability at Goose Bay in January 1964 and "at Harmon as soon thereafter as facilities will permit."[528] During October Captain Donald L. Mang travelled from Goose Bay "to establish possible site locations for the proposed ammo storage complex at Harmon AFB. Three sites were considered acceptable for the proposed ammo storage complex, each with some reservations. One site was selected for the proposed ammo storage area. The programming documents are to be prepared by the 4081st but the justification will be supplied by GADS and the 59th FIS. As soon as definite action is authorized the projects can be justified and forwarded to 26th Air Division as a 'late starter' P341 package."[529]

In fact, they were moving too fast for Canadian comfort. It seemed possible, at least at the moment, that the USAF was prepared to move so fast that an arrangement governing the nuclear weapons would not be in place. External Affairs asked Canadian diplomats in Washington to tell the U.S. government that Canada would prefer to have the service-to-service arrangement on Harmon and Goose Bay AB concluded before nuclear weapons arrived at either place. External Affairs warned the embassy to watch for signs that the United States might be pushing ahead with their delivery schedule.[530]

The one problem nobody anticipated was that the Department of National Revenue, Customs and Excise Division, was intent on inspecting the imported warheads so that duty could be waived. This was another idea which horrified the U.S. government, and DND took action to minimize the requirements of Revenue Canada. The two departments negotiated, and in line with the legal requirements imposed by the Atomic Energy Commission security regulations in the United States, certain information was deleted from the import/export forms which would be seen by the customs inspectors at Harmon airfield.[531]

The original text of the letter was what DND and the USAF considered a security leak under U.S. law.

National Revenue Canada
Customs and Excise

December 2, 1963

Secret and Confidential
JER Simms, Esq.,
Collector of Customs and Excise,
Stephenville, Newfoundland

   This is to advise that within the near future the USAF is to commence stockpiling nuclear weapons and components at Ernest Harmon Air Force Base.

   Notwithstanding the fact that it has not been the practice at Stephenville to accept Reports Inward covering aircraft of the USAF, in all instances where this material is imported it will be compulsory for reports to be filed, followed in due course by Import Entries. Value for duty will be indicated as NCV. (no commercial value)

   Mr. DA McLeod, Traffic Advisor, RCAF, Ottawa, will arrive at Harmon Field prior to the first importation to brief the American authorities on Canadian responsibility. At that time, he will also call upon you.

National Defence insisted that references to Harmon and Stephenville, except in the case of the address of the recipient, be removed and replaced with "in Canada" or deleted altogether. The letters to the inspectors at both Stephenville and Goose Bay were duly altered. Of course, the news of the storage at these sites had already appeared in newspapers, so there was no real secret to protect at this point.

But even before this problem would become real, there was the constitutional question of who in Canada was allowed to deal with nuclear weapons. Who had the authority? E.B. Armstrong, the deputy minister of National Defence, asked the Atomic Energy Control Board to issue a general order authorizing the MND to permit dealings in nuclear weapons under the 28/30 September 1963 agreement. Armstrong pointed out that this would be substantially similar to the order issued by the board for the purposes of the earlier agreement of 16 August.[532]

SECRET

Permission is hereby given under the atomic energy Control Regulations for dealings in nuclear air-to-air defensive weapons, pursuant to the agreement constituted by the Canada-US Exchange of Notes of September 28 and 30, 1963, and any subsequent amendments thereto, as authorized from time to time by the Minister of National defence or persons thereunto authorized by him, and for the granting by the appropriate officers of the Departments of Trade and Commerce and National Revenue of export and import permits as required in relation to the export and import of such nuclear air-to-air defensive weapons.

This Order is made on the understanding that before dealings under the said agreement or amendments thereto are authorized by the Minister of National Defence or persons authorized by him consultation between appropriate officials of the Department of National Defence and the atomic Energy Control Board will be held to ensure that procedures satisfactory to the Atomic Energy Control Board are to be taken which will:

    (a) safeguard such nuclear air-to-air defensive weapons; and

    (b) safeguard health and safety in the storage, handling and transportation of such nuclear air-to-air defensive weapons.

Dated at Ottawa this 18th day of December, 1963.
ATOMIC ENERGY CONTROL BOARD
By   (signed GC Lawrence)
President

Now that the minister had the authority, he promptly passed it on to a competent operational officer. The National Defence Judge Advocate General prepared a ministerial designating order which would designate the director of Air Force movements as authorized for "dealing in" nuclear weapons.[533] This was basically a copy of the order which had been drawn up following the 16 August agreement.

MINISTERIAL DESIGNATING ORDER

I, Paul T. Hellyer, Minister of National defence, pursuant to authority vested in me by Order of the atomic Energy Control Board dated the 18th day of December 1963, do hereby

---

> authorize the officer from time to time holding the appointment of Director of Air Force Movements (DAFM) or, in his absence, the officer from time to time holding the appointment of Deputy Director of Air Force Movements (D/DAFM), to permit dealings in nuclear air-to-air defensive weapons destined for the United States Air Force in Canada pursuant to the agreement constituted by the Canada-United States Exchange of Notes of September 28 and 30, 1963, and any subsequent amendments thereto.

Everything was now in place except the safety rules. USAF HQ gave the Joint Staff a copy of the TF/F-102A/GAR-11 Weapons System Safety Rules for transmission to Ottawa. At the prodding of the safety specialists at both the AECB and the RCAF, the USAF was told not attempt to perform maintenance on more than one warhead at a time in either the maintenance building or storage facilities at both Harmon AFB and Goose Bay AB.[534] The USAF advised the Canadian military team in Washington that an initial capability inspection and safety inspection would be conducted on the 59th at Harmon AFB prior to delivery of the warheads.[535]

USAF 122-23 - SAFETY RULES FOR THE TF/F-102A/GAR-11 WEAPONS SYSTEM. SECRET.
(Selected)

14c. Whenever an aircraft is loaded with ready missiles, the Armament Selector Switch will be in the "SNAKE" position; the Igniter Control Switch will be in the "OFF" position with the guard safetied and sealed; the Special Weapon Switch will be in the "DISARM" position with the guard safetied and sealed; and the Armed-Safe Switch will be in the "SAFE" position with the guard safetied and sealed.

15. Peacetime aircrew proficiency flights and/or practice intercepts with the TF/F-102A/GAR-11/Mk054 Weapons System are prohibited.

15b. Except where separate bilateral or other international agreements prohibit, the TF/F-102A/GAR-11/Mk054 Weapons System may be flown on active air defense and deployment missions as indicated below

(1)In areas for which CINCONAD/CINCNORAD have air defense responsibilities:

(a) For active air defense deployment missions under DEFCON 3 or higher states of readiness.
(b) For target identification missions elsewhere under DEFCON 3 or higher states of readiness.
(c) at any time that an object has been declared or designated HOSTILE by proper authority in accordance with the applicable rules of engagement.

Locals all knew that nuclear weapons were soon to arrive, and this was hardly distressing news. As the U.S. diplomatic staff in Canada knew, Newfoundland exhibited one of the most pro-U.S. attitudes in Canada.[536] Mayor Gillis of Stephenville favoured the new weapons on the grounds; they would lend more permanence and stability to the bases' civilian payrolls. The two air bases, plus the U.S. Naval Station at Argentia, were estimated to provide the province's third-ranking economic activity.[537] Little did the mayor know, but his facility had only a couple of years to live. The deployment was coming, but so was unemployment.

Progress was made in bringing the Harmon detachment up to speed, and by the spring of 1964 they successfully completed an unannounced operational readiness inspection.[538] However, there were limiting factors, and this would prevent full use of the systems. Harmon seemed ready to receive nuclear weapons.

At the detachment site in Harmon, the munitions staff were just receiving the trailers and storage racks for the nuclear Falcons. Goose Bay staff visited to brief the detachment staff from the 59th on the theory of operations of AIM-26A's and associated air defence techniques. During the summer the armament section was able to do mass loads under conditions 2 and later 6. However, with only nine qualified load teams to service the 27 aircraft, four of which were on alert at Harmon, there were problems. The 26th Air Division (SAGE) Munitions Standardization Team visited and witnessed a mass load and turnaround exercise during 8 to 10 September. All aspects of the 59th Weapons Release Section were found to be functioning in a satisfactory manner.[539] The meaning of this seems to be that there were warheads available for the AIM-26A Falcons, but that they could not be used on a regular basis until the limiting factors were lifted.

All the limiting factors were finally removed, and the units passed a regular operational readiness inspection from 22 to 24 July, and a no-notice ORI on 12 August 1965. The unit diary notes that the ADC ORI was passed by the maintenance section without limiting factors during the summer.[540] This meant that warheads could now be used without restriction at Harmon. The nuclear warheads were delivered during or immediately after July 1965.

But even as the inspections were being passed and the warheads being uncrated, briefings telling of the doom of Harmon were being given. Paul Martin was told that SAC, ADC and TAC could dispense with the facilities they now had at Harmon, providing that they were allowed to transfer some of the activities to Goose Bay and Argentia.[541] He was told that the U.S. government was counting on Goose Bay during the 1970 time period and on Argentia for the foreseeable future. U.S. authorities were rather concerned about Premier Smallwood's probable reaction when he heard the news.[542] Thus, the highest levels of the Canadian government knew in June 1965 that the closure date was June 1966.[543]

By mid-1965 Harmon was providing SAC with 13 KC-97 alert tankers from the 376 Air Refueling Squadron, down from 14 the previous year. Other tankers would "reflex" into Harmon from the 384th Air Reserve Refueling Squadron at Westover AFB in Massachusetts.[544] By August 1965, SAC was requesting that the USAF delete the reflex force at Harmon.[545] All operations were about to wind down.

The State Department was greatly concerned about the news of changes at Harmon which began leaking out in October 1965, quite close to a federal election. Embassy officials feared that a leak which damaged the current Liberal government could have serious implications for the future co-operation of that government with the desires of the U.S. military and political establishment.[546] SAC told the Newfoundland base commanders that the Department of State "must not be pre-empted in its actions with the Government of Canada."[547] It was of little help, and the military actions and loud talk made it obvious that change was coming. It got so bad that Dean Rusk sent a bitter note to Robert McNamara saying, "You guys aren't doing your job very good and you're making my job hard by putting the word out on Harmon."[548]

The entire leak started because somebody did not realize that Harmon was part of a large program in the continental United States called Fast Fly. Fast Fly was thought to be a program exclusive to the Zone of the Interior (ZI), (continental United States) and therefore, would have no international relations implications. This was not the case, and officials became most upset that this information had leaked out to the Canadian and Newfoundland governments. Ambassador Butterworth was "hopping mad because of what he learned about Harmon, more so what the Canadians may have learned."[549]

The bad news did not stop some people from saying silly things. Newfoundland premier Joey Smallwood told an audience in Stephenville that a full year of U.S. occupancy of Harmon remained. He also strongly intimated that civilian employment at the air base would not deteriorate until after December 1966. The general tone of the speech was that the local populace should not be unduly alarmed about the U.S. base closure announcement.[550]

Strangely, while all this was going on, Harmon was still preparing for nuclear duty: nobody had communicated the reality of their situation to them. At that time the missile storage site was being painted by personnel assigned to Detachment 1.[551] The base was now engaged in arranging deck chairs on the *Titanic*. Harmon was still a busy place, and in the middle of 1965 hosted numerous units.

```
4081 Strategic Wing HQ
4081 Consolidated Aircraft Maintenance Squadron
4081 COS Group
4081 Combat Defense Squadron
4081 Field Service Squadron
4081 Civil Engineering Squadron
4081 Support Squadron
4081 Transport Squadron
 867 Medical Group
 376 Air Refueling Squadron
1624 MATS Support Squadron
  59 FIS Detachment #1
 640 Aircraft Control & Warning Squadron
  54 Air Rescue Squadron
1933 Communication Squadron
   7 Air Post, Detachment #7
USATTC, US Army Transport Terminal Unit (Arctic) Detachment
#1
USAF Auditor
OSI Detachment #1, Office of Special Investigation
4440 Aircraft Delivery Group, Detachment #4
```

In total, this was a complement of 281 officers and 2340 airmen. In addition, and so important to the local economy, the USAF employed 103 U.S. civilians and 1007 local Newfoundland civilians as base support workers.

The United States already knew that the truth was that on 1 July 1966 all civilian permanent appointments would be terminated.[552] The war in

Southeast Asia was far more important, and ballistic missiles had challenged the role of the manned bomber. It was now economically desirable and operationally feasible to close Harmon by 1 January 1967. Harmon was told to prepare programming plans to discontinue 59 FIS, det 1, no later than 1 April 1966 and to return all personnel and equipment to Goose Bay. Internally, U.S. officials conceded that this decision would be communicated to Canadian authorities by the end of 1965.[553]

The U.S. embassy in Ottawa delivered the message to External Affairs on a cold afternoon in late November. The Canadians were informed "of the decision of the US Government to close out Harmon Air Force Base as of 01 January 1967." U.S. officials also informed Paul Hellyer and Premier Smallwood.[554] It was little consolation that various bases in the United States were also being closed. To the Canadians, it was a mixed blessing: closure would finally be brought to the nuclear deployments question, but it would also happen so soon after the Liberals had expended so much political capital in allowing the deployments.

It was now a public fact. Walt Butterworth, who had visited Harmon, gave Paul Martin the formal note on the closure. All it said was that "the United States Government hereby notifies the Government of Canada of the intention of the United States Government to abandon Harmon Air Force Base, Newfoundland, on December 31, 1966. The United States will cease all regular air operations by July 1, 1966, at Harmon Air Force Base and will abandon the base on December 31, 1966."[555] The next day, on 8 December, SAC told the 8th Air Force that Harmon was dead. There was to be complete withdrawal of mission support aircraft by 1 April 1966, and any emergency requirements would be covered by Goose Bay and Loring AFB in Maine. Harmon would remain open 18 hours a day, as Air Canada was flying in four times a day.[556] It would close at 00:45 each morning.

The W-54 nuclear warheads for the AIM-26A nuclear Falcon missiles were withdrawn from the Goose Bay Air Base SAS facilities between 20 and 30 November 1966.[557] It is not known when they were removed from Harmon, as these records are not as complete and clear. Since all mission aircraft were sent back to Goose Bay from Harmon by 1 April 1966, it is fairly certain that the nuclear weapons were also removed to either Goose Bay or the continental United States earlier that spring. I suspect that the airlift of warheads was done during the final two weeks of March 1966.

As the warheads were again being crated, Cabinet met in Ottawa to discuss the disposition of Harmon Field at Stephenville. Paul Hellyer told them that the U.S. government had given one year's notice of its intention to give up its base at Harmon Field, this to be effective on 31 December

1966. It was intended to discontinue operations on the first of July. Hellyer said that Smallwood had been in touch with the federal government concerning future use of the base and, pursuant to a Cabinet decision of 8 December 1965, a committee of senior federal and Newfoundland officials had decided that the property should be deeded to Newfoundland with the reservation that lands needed for federal purposes would be made available to the Department of Transport. Cabinet was told that because the base had been given to the United States prior to entry of Newfoundland into Confederation, the precise legal position of Canada was not clear. This had happened before in the case of the closure of Pepperrell, and the action in that case rested on an ad hoc agreement between the province and the federal government.[558]

The Minister of Transport said that Harmon field, just like Pepperrell and Argentia, "had never, strictly speaking, been Canadian territory." Cabinet agreed that since these were the only three bases in this special category, there was no need to establish the legal position and it was preferable that all three be settled by an agreement.[559] Canada would simply assert that the land was Canadian and promptly give it to Newfoudndland.

Ernest Harmon Air Force Base was officially closed on 16 December 1966.

Chapter Eight

ARGENTIA NAVAL STATION

The United States Navy site at Argentia, Newfoundland, contained one of only three nuclear weapons storage facilities in Canada for the use of U.S. forces. Weapons at this site were to be used against Soviet submarines operating in the north Atlantic. It was, therefore, the only nuclear weapons site in Canada for the use of the United States Navy. Argentia was one of the areas given by the British to the United States during World War II in exchange for war materials, and the 1941 lease was to be in place for 99 years. The United States would finally turn the site over to Canada in 1994, a mere 53 years later.

Because some of the sites in Newfoundland which were occupied by the U.S. military were leased bases, over which the United States had total and more-or-less sovereign control, there were many incidents of conflicting jurisdiction. Usually, this happened because the U.S. forces felt they could simply do whatever they liked as though they were back in their own country, or even worse, in the view of the Canadian government, in the country of a defeated enemy.

One of the most infamous incidents involved the threatened shooting of Customs officials near Argentia. On 9 July 1948, local Customs officials stopped a car coming from Argentia Naval station to inspect it for smuggled goods, specifically cigarettes. The officials found certain contraband items and were in the process of taking the vehicle into custody. One of the U.S. personnel from the car telephoned the base, and a car with two U.S. Navy police and Captain Prevoneau arrived. Captain Prevoneau, who was in a highly excited state, pointed his service revolver, which had the safety catch off, at the Customs officials and demanded the release of the car and personnel. In a Cabinet meeting, the minister of National Defence observed that U.S. forces would have to be better controlled than this, and that if the RCMP had been present, "a most unfortunate incident might have resulted."[560] This meant that the RCMP could have shot the misguided U.S. officer dead on the spot for having pointed his loaded and non-safetied revolver at government officials.

This and other incidents come up repeatedly in the records of continuing problems Canada had with the poorly disciplined U.S. soldiers in the immediate post-war world. Another troubling incident involved the USAF ordering an RCAF Lancaster reconnaissance aircraft to cease photography of Canadian territory and land under U.S. control at Thule on 5 March 1952. In another case, and in total disregard for both aviation safety and national sovereignty, the USAF established a navigation beacon in Canada without telling the Department of Transport.[561] The crux of the problem was a basic legal question as to who really owned Argentia and the other leased sites. This would come up again and again, and be of great concern to Cabinet during the Argentia negotiations.

The U.S. Navy asked for nuclear rights at the site for 10 years prior to their wish being fulfilled. In the end, they got their desire only because the USAF interceptor squadron detachment was to leave Harmon AFB at Stephenville in 1967 when that site closed, and the U.S. military wanted to maintain storage rights at two sites in Newfoundland after Harmon closed. This would be the rationale for the transfer of the storage rights from Harmon to Argentia in 1967.

In the 1950s and early 1960, Argentia was the western anchor of the U.S. Navy airborne Distant Early Warning (DEW) line. Squadrons of modified Super Constellation long-range aircraft patrolled the north Atlantic watching for the feared Soviet attack. Aside from the aviation part of the base, there was also a naval facility. This facility was a processing station for the sound surveillance system (SOSUS), and operated acoustic hydrophones planted on the bottom of the north Atlantic to listen for Soviet submarines. The facility also hosted a missile tracking instrumentation station (MTIS), a remote ranging station supporting missile tests from U.S. east coast ranges, and a SAC Green Pine station for northern communications with USAF bombers. Recently the work of the station was moved to Halifax and now operates with a remote connection to the SOSUS terminal at Argentia.

The theory of using nuclear weapons in an anti-submarine warfare role goes back to the work of the Massachusetts Institute of Technology

(MIT) in 1950. They had theorized that even a very expensive atomic bomb would be worth using in an anti-submarine warfare role as the increased probability of a kill could save a much greater value of convoyed material and naval task forces no longer subject to submarine attacks. Later this theory would be altered, as convoy protection became less important, and protection of cities and military sites gained pre-eminence.

The Joint Chiefs of Staff, prompted by the U.S. Navy, approved the search for atomic weapons for anti-submarine warfare use in April 1951. The study produced the mating of the W-7 warhead with a new depth charge casing, together called the Alias Betty. Production of this 20 kt yield weapon began in June 1955, and the last of the 225 weapons were retired by 1960. In 1955 the U.S. Navy had its first atomic bomb for use against Soviet submarines, and therefore its first opportunity for foreign basing of such a weapon. Its early withdrawal ensured that the Betty would never see service in Canada.

The Betty was replaced by the smaller (one-half the weight and one-quarter the volume) Mk101 Lulu atomic bomb. Using the 10-15 kt W-34 warhead first deployed in 1958, the Lulu was approved by the Pentagon in February 1956. The Mod 0 Lulu came out in 1958, the Mod 1 in 1959, the Mod 2 in 1960, and the Mods 4 and 5 in 1962. With the deployment of the Mk57 beginning in 1963, Lulus began retirement in July 1964, with the final three versions withdrawn during 1971. Some 2000 of the W-7 warheads for the Lulu were built between August 1958 and late 1962. This makes the weapon a prime candidate for deployment to the Argentia site in the 1967–70 period, although it was likely replaced at most sites by the more advanced Mk57.

The final anti-submarine warfare nuclear weapon of the U.S. Navy is the Mk57 depth bomb. Requested by the U.S. Navy, but made for the USN, the U.S. Marines, and the U.S. Air Force, this 5 to 10 kt atomic bomb was deployed in six versions from 1963 through to today. Versions 1, 2 and 5 continued in service from 1963 until at least 1990, while models 3,4 and 6 were deployed in 1966 and retired in 1972. With three services using the weapon, and a number used by NATO allies, demand was great and some 3100 units were built at Pantex between January 1963 and May 1967. The anti-submarine warfare version had two flooding ports to allow water into the hydrostatic fuzing sections. In addition, the parachute used to slow descent would be jettisoned upon impact with the water's surface. This nuclear anti-submarine warfare weapon saw the widest service with the U.S. Navy, and was stored at NAS Argentia.

The military purpose of storing nuclear anti-submarine weapons for

U.S. Navy forces at Argentia was to increase the capabilities of these forces to deal with a perceived growing threat from Soviet conventional and nuclear-powered submarines carrying sea-launched ballistic missiles (SLBM) and sea-launched cruise missiles (SLCM). The U.S. naval forces on the American east coast, like most U.S. forces arranged against the Soviet Union, were designed for optimal use with nuclear weapons. Thus, the United States government indicated to the Canadian government early on that the forces at Argentia could not operate at their full capability without nuclear depth bombs. The threat was assessed as having changed from a bomber to a missile threat, and increasingly towards a sea-based missile threat. For this reason, the U.S. Navy was increasingly tasked not with protecting shipping in the North Atlantic as had been the case in World War II, but with destruction of the Soviet fleet in order to protect the U.S. homeland from nuclear destruction.[562]

HISTORY

During 1956 the U.S. Navy undertook an extensive construction program at Argentia, spending $10.5 million for various projects including the relocation of eight magazines for conventional ammunition for the anti-submarine warfare forces. But conventional weapons were only part of the story. In the "pentomic" era, when the Pentagon met the 1950s with atomic weapons of every kind, the U.S. Navy moved to an increasingly nuclear stance, and their anti-submarine warfare forces at Argentia were to be thus equipped.

The Pentagon brought the State Department in and requested that urgent moves be made to push the deployment. More bluntly, the military wanted to know if they even had to ask the Canadians at all. The State Department sympathized and suggested wrapping the request for Argentia and SAC storage all together. They advised the Pentagon of their firm belief that the Canadian government should be consulted and informed of U.S. plans before nuclear weapons were introduced at any base in Canada.[563] In addition, Parsons from the State Department also knew that "to assume that we have complete liberty of action with respect to Argentia in the face of the agreed minute of June 14, 1951, on the deployment of atomic weapons would, I am convinced, seriously irritate the Canadians. It could even jeopardize our existing base rights, as well as make infinitely more difficult the over-all implementation of our nuclear weapon storage plan.[564] The negotiations would have to be full and include Canada at every stage."

The State Department then developed the plan for this rather difficult request. The head of the European Division would invite Norman Robertson, the Canadian ambassador, to a meeting and tell him that the U.S. Navy would soon begin talks with the Royal Canadian Navy concerning the introduction of nuclear anti-submarine devices at the U.S.-leased base in Argentia. The ambassador was told to expect further consultation at the diplomatic level at an early date.[565] By the start of December 1957, discussion between the two navies had already begun.[566] In fact, by the time Robertson was informed of the decision, the naval talks had already begun.[567]

NATO was quickly becoming more and more of a nuclear alliance. At the December 1957 NATO Heads of Government meeting in Paris, the members adopted the concept of nuclear weapons as central to NATO military policy. This relates to Argentia, as the forces there fell under the control of the Supreme Allied Commander Atlantic (SACLANT) of NATO, which was far more of a NATO command than NORAD. This lent another dimension to the problem.

National Defence leaped on the subject and quickly produced a memorandum for the minister of National Defence to present to Cabinet. Due to the lack of details, the memo said little other than that the U.S. sought permission for the USN to store and use nuclear anti-submarine weapons in Canada.[568] It was considered at the 10 January 1958 Cabinet meeting, but nothing was done politically.

The Canadian military was already on the side of the U.S. request. In January 1958 the chairman of the chiefs of staff told the chief of the naval staff and the chief of the air staff that they should immediately prepare to discuss the proposal for nuclear anti-submarine devices to be used by the RCN and USN, and the implications of storage and use at locations on both coasts.[569] The RCAF had not yet been involved in any discussion on this storage requirement at Argentia. "However, in the interest of mutual defence it is considered that this requirement should be supported."[570] Despite military support, the issue fell dormant in Canada for over 18 months. Nothing was to be done on this most difficult request.

Fed up with waiting, the U.S. government re-issued their request in the spring of 1959, telling External Affairs that they wanted to be allowed the right of "storage of nuclear anti-submarine weapons at the United States Naval Base in Argentia, NFLD, for use by USN forces operating under the control of the SACLANT."[571] This 9 April prodding did not produce any real action until October, when the issue again went to Cabinet for indecision. More details were now available, and the minister took the entire subject to the Cabinet Defence Committee a couple of weeks later. He was then able to tell his colleagues that the U.S. authorities had indicated that only the one site would be required, that operational anti-submarine warfare flights would be undertaken from Argentia, and that no alternative or emergency facilities would be built.[572]

At the first face-to-face joint meeting of the ministers to deal with Argentia, it was quickly revealed that there was no full meeting of minds on this subject. The November 1959 meeting at Camp David saw the Canadian team state that Canada wanted to reserve the right to disapprove release from Argentia to a ship. The United States responded by pointing out that placing nuclear weapons on a ship is a form of storage and that the significant control is that they may not be used unless approved by the president as required by United States law. It was also pointed out that the authority for use can extend from the president through SACLANT if necessary, and that if this were restricted by a special authority for removal from storage there might be no time for them to be put into use.[573] The question of authorization was now front and centre, and the U.S. side was trying to make it go away. The U.S. secretary of Defense said that the use of weapons from Argentia on ships assigned to NATO forces would be exercised through SACLANT, and that adding a requirement of Canadian approval for their removal to a ship might be too cumbersome. As if to clinch the argument, the U.S. team stated that all of their agreements with other countries reserved to the country of storage only the right to approve or disapprove use — not the right to control removal from storage.[574] As the meeting closed, both Pearkes (MND), and Green (secretary of state for External Affairs) said they foresaw no difficulty for anti-submarine weapons in Argentia.

At their next meeting nine months later, the U.S. secretary of Defense, Gates, mentioned that the United States had not heard anything at all from Canada about Argentia. There followed a discussion about the difference between the Argentia proposals and the Air Defence proposals, and it developed that these stemmed from the interpretation of control by External Affairs and the chief ministers in Canada of nuclear weapons in Canadian territorial waters. Pearkes pointed out that there was no overflight agreement for ships, and it ended up that there should be some form of transit agreement worked out to permit the carriage of the weapons from the base through Canadian territorial waters to the high seas.[575]

Sidney Green, the secretary of state for External Affairs, made the point that he had no control over the use of the weapon once it had been put on the ship and therefore the problem was control of release to the ship or of the loading. Gates countered by suggesting that "what is needed is some form of transit approval across Canadian territorial waters."[576] The Canadians would provide the first draft.[577] There is no evidence that this was ever done. By this point work on nuclear issues had come to a standstill in the Diefenbaker government.

Another nine months went by with little or no response from Canada, and CINCLANT (U.S. Navy Commander-In-Chief, Atlantic) was now pushing for the Argentia storage. The Pentagon therefore asked Dean Rusk in April 1961 to take the initiative and push for the negotiations which Prime Minister Diefenbaker had already suggested. The problem now, as the Pentagon saw it, was that Diefenbaker wanted any agreement to provide for both joint control and joint custody. Of these, joint control presented the simpler problem. Such joint control over the use of nuclear weapons was already provided in the MB-1 Agreement, and comparable control procedures could doubtless be devised to meet the USN situation at Argentia. The joint custody concept posed more of a serious problem in light of U.S. legislation. It was suggested to Rusk that Canadian desires be explored in more detail.[578]

Dean Rusk agreed to pursue the subject, but held out little hope. He recognized that there would be little or no likelihood of making progress towards any agreement on nuclear weapons for anti-submarine warfare units at Argentia and Comox at the political and diplomatic level. He did, though, advise the Pentagon that his office saw no problem in holding informal sessions with various individual outside negotiating sessions.[579] Rusk felt that the sensible approach would be to limit the discussion to a few points and see if agreement could be reached. He proposed that the United States make three points: 1. Canada provided the land, and the United States provided construction and units; 2. USN keeps custody; and 3. release would be subject to consultation where practical.[580] If the United States could get Canada to agree to the basic points, the rest would be fairly straightforward, or at least so they thought.

The U.S. Navy was already preparing for full nuclear duty. The commanding officer at Argentia had been told that he was to provide support for advanced underwater weapons operations, and that the new unit would "perform classified tasks."[581] This means that the USN was already preparing for the deployment and operation of nuclear weapons at Argentia by June 1962, only four months before the Cuban missile crisis. As part of his duties as the head of U.S. affairs in Canada, Ambassador Walt Butterworth visited Argentia and stayed overnight.

Everything was now at a complete stand-still. The Diefenbaker government had essentially closed all nuclear options, and Argentia was at the bottom of a list with which they were unwilling to deal. All further negotiations would have to await the election of the Pearson Liberal government in the spring of 1963. However, the U.S. forces in Newfoundland were a secondary priority of the new minority government. First they were interested in arming the Canadian units in Canada and Europe. Second, they would proceed to discuss the requirements for U.S. nuclear air defence units in Newfoundland. Only after all this was accomplished would Pearson and Martin and Hellyer move on to discuss Argentia.

In fact, External Affairs was seriously worried about this issue and went so far as to tell Paul Martin not to bring it up with Dean Rusk. Martin was told that because there was "a custody problem to do with anti-submarine warfare weapons, and there is NO Canadian commitment in this area," he should not raise the subject at the September 1963 foreign ministers' summit. In fact, he was to put off Rusk if the issue came up.[582] Back in Ottawa Pearson was giving the Cabinet information but making no proposals for further action. He briefed them on the new U.S. proposal which covered both the air defence units at Goose Bay and Harmon, as well as the anti-submarine warfare forces at Argentia. In his view this introduced a lot of complicating NATO standard language into the equation.[583]

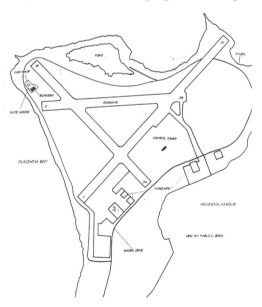

U.S. Naval Station Argentia, Nfld.

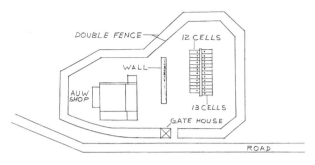

ARGENTIA NUCLEAR
WEAPONS STORAGE FACILITY
DRW. BY: PABLO C. ZEISS

Argentia nuclear weapons storage facility

No decision was reached by the full Cabinet, but it was considered by the Cabinet Defence Committee. The CDC decided that it should not be proceeded with until the review of Canadian naval policy had been concluded, as the proposal at that time covered weapons for both the Canadian and U.S. anti-submarine forces.[584] It was now the autumn of 1963, and another four years would elapse before the question was resolved. One year later the first full-time Canadian liaison officer was sent to Argentia as the sole representative of Canadian sovereign interests.

In Washington, the war between guns and butter was slowly being lost as more effort went into Viet Nam. Robert McNamara, the secretary of Defense, told President Johnson that the USN and his office had undertaken a re-appraisal of the Soviet naval threat and the marked increases in U.S. capabilities associated with the qualitative improvements the United States was making in all anti-submarine warfare areas. He stated that this made it possible to revise upward the estimates of USN capabilities with regard to Bloc forces. McNamara then recommended the procurement of another 45 P-3A patrol aircraft for $181 million. The USN had 36 of the new aircraft in 1963, and 57 in 1964. The plan was to eventually build some 234 of this amazing and effective aircraft.[585] This was the primary weapon system at Argentia, and it would be armed with both conventional depth charges and torpedoes, and with the Mk57 nuclear weapon.

The Canadian anti-submarine warfare forces in 1964 were rated as effective as those of the U.S. Navy, and far better than any other in NATO or the Pacific. The RCAF Argus operating on the east coast was determined to be the equivalent of the U.S. systems. The United States also had a great deal of respect for Canadian anti-submarine warfare capabilities on the aircraft carrier *Bonaventure*.[586] This helps to explain why the United States would consider aiding Canada with nuclear anti-submarine warfare systems, as the RCN was already a top-rated and professional service. After unification in the late 1960s, and once the admirals' revolt had ended, Maritime Command proved to be a fully capable anti-submarine warfare service but never up to the level of excellence displayed by the RCN and RCAF in earlier years.

By November 1964 the U.S. Marine Construction Battalion No. 1 had completed a number of major projects, including an inner perimeter security fence and the station advance underwater weapons installation.[587] It was also that month that a P-3A Orion tragically crashed in Placentia Bay, killing all 10 crew. Although the USN was engaged in construction projects, the Pentagon was already talking about scaling back at the remote site.

The security Cabinet met on 1 March 1965, and "there had been mention of the projected contraction of the United States Base at Argentia." Pearson wondered if it would be possible to preclude the closure by allowing the USAF to use it for the forward deployment of air defence interceptor aircraft, thus making a contribution to the solution of the "dispersal" problem which had been under discussion for a long time.[588] As it was explained to Paul Martin, the proposed reduction of activity at Argentia is one element of the U.S. plans to phase out certain elements of the North American air defence facilities. As part of these general plans it was the U.S. intention to phase out some of the airborne early warning radar aircraft which constitute the seaward extension of the DEW line, and this meant phasing out two squadrons of Super Constellation aircraft at Argentia.[589]

Martin would be briefed on the situation and would pass the information on to Pearson. As Martin understood, the dispersal proposal, which related to the declining manned bomber threat, was of little interest to the United States now. The message was that if nuclear force dispersal was an acceptable use for Argentia, as the prime minister had intimated at the recent meeting, it might be reasonable to think of introducing nuclear anti-submarine weapons for naval defence. This was more in keeping with the nature of the Argentia base and related to an increasing threat to North American security in contrast to the dispersal proposal which related to the declining manned bomber threat.[590]

Autumn came again, and 1965 was nearly over. Captain (N) R.G. Neal (USN) was appointed as the Argentia commanding officer for a two-year term. In September USN Admiral Thomas Moorer (SACLANT) visited

Paul Hellyer in Ottawa and again raised the question of the storage at Argentia. Hellyer said nothing could be done until after the elections in Canada, but that he would raise the matter with the prime minister and the minister of National Defence. Hellyer remarked to Basil Robinson that he did not think Canada could any longer delay satisfying United States Navy wishes. Moreover, he said that "if we could get the Americans off our backs" it would give the Canadian authorities longer to consider whether they wished to acquire nuclear equipment for Canadian anti-submarine warfare purposes.[591] Hellyer would therefore tell Robert McNamara that he was now prepared to take this question up in Cabinet.[592]

MOVE TO GANDER

The mid-1960s were a time of change and consolidation in the U.S. military as the war against Viet Nam grew ever larger. This is demonstrated by the fact that even as negotiations were under way to allow nuclear weapons to be stored at Argentia, the United States was in the process of changing its deployment plans. U.S. secretary of Defense Robert McNamara wrote a letter of election congratulations to Paul Hellyer and told him, "Our plans on Argentia are in no way firm at this time. We are in the midst of a series of reviews with the Navy and these will not be completed until sometime in March. However, it would be of assistance to us to know that if the alternative of relocating the patrol aircraft and weapons storage to Gander is feasible, we could develop plans to store nuclear ASW (anti-submarine warfare) weapons at that location."[593] Hellyer, given the messages at the time, must have been more than a little shocked at this sudden change in direction.

Hellyer soon went to see Jack Pickersgill, the Liberal point man on Newfoundland. Pickersgill told him that Gander was not the ideal place for a U.S. military base, "particularly in view of the special security arrangements required in connection with nuclear weapons." Hellyer communicated this to the prime minister, and said he would tell McNamara that "we would not be willing to entertain a proposal to move the ASW squadrons to Gander. I would at the same time confirm that I was recommending to the government our concurrence in the American desire to store nuclear weapons in the compound already constructed at Argentia."[594]

Hellyer replied to McNamara's original letter almost two months later, telling his friend Bob that the MND had made enquiries about the feasibility of transferring the USN air organization from Argentia to Gander. Hellyer advised him that this "would not be acceptable to the Canadian Government, for a number of reasons which I will not elaborate, but which are well known to your Ambassador here." The minister closed by inviting McNamara's people, if they were still interested in storage at Argentia, to make a request through the normal channels. Hellyer assured his friend that the request would be given sympathetic consideration and would have his full support.[595] With this, the U.S. quest to move to Gander ended.

NEGOTIATIONS

Nineteen sixty-six would see the negotiations on Argentia finally reopened. Early in the year Paul Martin was presented with a draft memo to Pearson which had been worked out between External Affairs and DND during December and January. Talks had been held in abeyance following the prime minister's meeting with Kennedy at Hyannisport in May 1963. Pearson was told that the United States had shown considerable forbearance in withholding pressure on this matter during the past two years, and that their request for suitable storage facilities in Canada for this purpose rested on very strong grounds.[596] In reality, the USN had organized the entire east coast anti-submarine operation on the assumption that nuclear weapons would be available to all U.S. forces. A notation in the margin by Martin asked, "Why could we not use this as a bargaining chip in our Law of the Sea problem."[597] Linkage was rearing its ugly head, and it looked as though both sides were preparing to fight a dirty fight.

The United States was first to enter the mud ring by telling Paul Martin that "the leased bases agreement might give them a legal right to store at Argentia any weapons they might wish. A tenable but not conclusive argument can be developed in support of this contention." Martin warned Pearson of this development, but pointed out that the United States had never tried to press this as an advantage.[598] There was little chance for retaliation, and Martin was warned that Canada had no history of using linkage on joint defence matters. In addition, Marcel Cadieux told him that the negotiations on Argentia would be of the type which would not be conducive to using the item as a bargaining chip on Law of the Sea.[599]

The deputy minister Cadieux feared that if Canada tried to push too hard, "the Americans could also seek to establish a legal case that under the Leased Base Agreement they do not require our consent to the installation of defence facilities."[600] At Cabinet it was noted that Argentia, like Harmon Field and Pepperrell, "had never, strictly speaking, been Canadian territory."[601] This was a political minefield, and one the Pearson government wished to avoid at all costs.

Activities continued at Argentia, and the regular deployments of maritime patrol aircraft came and went. In the first half of the year, VP 44, Detachment 17, operated five P-3A aircraft at Argentia until they were replaced by four P-3Bs from VP 26, Detachment 17, for the second half. On the weapons side, the advanced underwater weapons detachment was now staffed by one officer and 14 men, and was commanded by the station commanding officer.[602]

The regular February meeting of the Permanent Joint Board on Defence was the site of the next move. The U.S. Navy member reiterated the continuing keen interest of the United States, indicating that current plans foresaw use at current or higher levels at least through 1971.[603] The Canadians were told that none less than SACLANT had endorsed the requirement for anti-submarine warfare at Argentia. This information, although in the hands of the prime minister, produced no actions by Canada. It was again up to the United States to broach the subject.

The broaching came in June when the U.S. embassy in Ottawa received instructions to prepare to deliver a formal note "requesting the approval of the Canadian Government for the storage of anti-submarine nuclear weapons at Argentia for the use of US forces stationed there."[604] The embassy sought the advice of J.S. Nutt in the defence liaison division at External Affairs. Nutt told their counsellor that the United States would be better advised to put forward the anti-submarine warfare proposal separately and prior to putting forward the dispersal proposal, as the dispersal option was going nowhere in Ottawa. Ottawa also did not want to offend too many at once. The dispersal question was closed in Canada, and if the United States put it up for consideration with Argentia, the USAF would go away disappointed while the USN would be seen as getting what they wished. As Nutt put it, "The foregoing leads me to support the one-at-a-time approach with ASW first and dispersal perhaps never."[605] The United States took his advice. Butterworth had requested that his people keep Argentia and dispersal as separate issues. This did not stop the U.S. embassy from delivering a formal note on dispersal a month later, but it was now completely divorced and could be quietly left to die.[606]

On 9 September 1966 Mr. Scott from the U.S. embassy visited External Affairs to deliver a note requesting dispersal of USAF interceptor aircraft to Canada. The United States was to hold off on this until after the Argentia matter was settled, but they referred to "the tyranny of passing time" as having forced them to proceed. Jim Nutt wrote that "I think I left him with the impression, however, that by putting in this Note at the present time, the US authorities might have complicated the prospect of getting an early decision on Argentia." Paul Martin then told the prime minister of the new complication.[607] They solved the problem by doing nothing.

The U.S. proposal was verbal, but Butterworth left behind an aide-memoire.[608] The portion on operational authorization for the use of the nuclear weapons bears examination, as it was heart of the problem as far as Canada was concerned.

> In normal circumstances, the nuclear ASW weapons under consideration would not be removed from storage except for logistical transfers. Neither nuclear-loaded training flights nor routine alert loading of aircraft is contemplated. It is considered that the minimum threat situation warranting alert-loading of airborne patrol with these weapons would be (1) circumstances of heightened international tension or (2) intelligence indications sufficiently serious to justify precautionary measures. In case (1), the consultations which the two Governments would in any case be holding under the agreement of September 17, 1965 will cover, as well, the alert-loading of aircraft with ASW weapons or airborne patrol with such weapons, or both. In case (2), the Government of the United States would consult prior to taking these measures if time permitted and in any event as quickly as possible.

Butterworth also said that there would be no public announcement concerning the agreement and that in the event of any public enquiry the presence of the weapons in Canada would neither be confirmed nor denied.

There was now another complicating factor. Canada had negotiated an air transport agreement with the Soviet Union, and the United States was none too happy about this bit of Canadian independence. Marcel Cadieux told Paul Martin that positive consideration of the Agentia proposal "might help in some degree to mitigate the adverse reaction in Washington which seems inevitable if we proceed with the air agreement. Although a favourable decision on the US request on ASW would in itself be a difficult one, it might help in the present situation and make somewhat easier the decision to proceed with the air agreement."[609]

Martin was aware that Lyndon Johnson had actually yelled at Pearson over the Cuban element of the air agreement which allowed flights to Cuba to stop in Canada, yet he was still concerned with the provisions for authorization. As he noted on the bottom of the page, "The weapons would be on Canadian soil without any Canadian control." They all recognized that in the case of Argentia a full-fledged NATO Command was involved and it would be difficult to provide for Canadian government control under a formula similar to that for the MB-1 and the Canadian nuclear forces. NORAD operations over Canada were controlled under rules of engagement approved by the appropriate Canadian authorities, but the government was uncertain if there were analogous rules of engagement applying to SACLANT operations on the open sea.[610]

Paul Martin therefore felt that he had no real choice but to tell Pearson that a rejection of the request would cause some difficult problems. "A rejection would be taken very seriously by the United States, and might give rise, among other things, to a US decision to close the Argentia base to the serious detriment of the local economy. It would also add an important new item to the list of current Canadian positions about which Washington is unhappy, whereas a favourable decision could help to affect adverse US reaction on such matters as the Soviet air agreement."[611] It was then that Martin made a proposal which would actually become the rationale for the storage at Argentia. He wrote to Pearson:

> If the US does not wish to retain storage rights at Goose Bay after withdrawal of the interceptor units, we could terminate the present agreement. Such an arrangement might then be presented, with I think considerable validity, as the transfer of a commitment from an area in which the threat is declining to one in which it is increasing, rather than as the acceptance of an additional commitment.[612]

Pearson agreed with Martin and directed that the memo to Cabinet on the subject first go through his office.

External Affairs continued low-key work on the proposal, reviewing the new U.S. draft. They concluded that Canada would have no physical control over the nuclear weapons. The draft provided that the Argentia weapons would be released for operational use in the emergency circumstances defined in paragraph 8(e) of the agreement of 17 September 1965. In other words, where time permitted, consultation would take place prior to release, "but in an actual or indisputably imminent attack it has been agreed in advance that the President and the Prime Minister will grant the required authority to CINCNORAD without consultation." The deputy minister told Martin that "if we were to agree to the principles in the present US draft we would not be conceding to the United States anything which we have not already agreed upon with them."[613] In his briefing before a mid-summer foreign ministers' meeting with Rusk, Martin was told to assure him that the proposal was "receiving careful consideration at the highest level," but that difficulties could arise from premature disclosure that the matter was under consideration by Cabinet.[614]

Time is the enemy of action, and the summertime is the enemy of action in Ottawa and Washington. When Scott from the U.S. embassy inquired on the status of the work, Jim Nutt in the defence liaison division at External Affairs told him that the summer was a bad time as everyone was away, and nothing was expected before September.[615] Scott had come as much to push as to take the pulse of the situation. He reminded Nutt that the USN and Admiral Moorer were hoping that it would be dealt with very soon. Nutt did tell Scott that he personally felt the draft now had a good chance. But some action was happening. The idea that some of the nuclear weapons might be deployed to ships had now been swept away. Only aircraft would carry the anti-submarine warfare weapons held at Argentia, and this was confirmed by the U.S. team. The Canadian position that the word "AIRBORNE" be inserted before all references to nuclear weapons in the exchange of notes was accepted in August.[616] DND had no professional opinion, and simply wanted External Affairs to get on with the work.[617] The new draft of 26 August 1966 was then approved by MND on 14 September 1966.[618] Now it was time to go back to Cabinet.

Martin's staff at External Affairs worked through September to prepare the submission to Cabinet, as it was now expected to actually be given a real hearing. Basically the memo covered the facts that the United States could act unilaterally due to the 1941 agreements covering the bases, that the United States now sought to exchange Harmon rights for Argentia, and that the nuclear weapons were property of and would remain in the custody of the United States. Importantly, as discussed in Chapter 1, was that consultation with the Canadian government before release from storage was limited by agreement and circumstance. The draft required "Timely authorization" from the prime minister to SACLANT for use without consultation by both prime minister and president, as was the case with NORAD.[619] The secretary of state for External Affairs sent this document to the prime minister for a first look, as Pearson had requested.[620]

With the approval of Pearson, the memorandum was presented to Cabinet by the two Pauls on 27 October 1966.[621] Cabinet heard that the United States had vacated Harmon Field and subsequently wanted to utilize Argentia for nuclear weapons. Pearson pointed out that under the 1941 bases agreements, the United States was virtually sovereign in those areasand could therefore do whatever they wished. Withdrawal from Argentia due to a refusal to agree to the deployments would cause economic hardship in an already depressed region. Paul Hellyer said that closure of Harmon would mean that the number of nuclear sites would not increase, just that the task would change. The minister of Manpower and Immigration, questioned whether Canadian compliance with the U.S. request was consistent with the Liberal government's declared intention of reducing its nuclear commitments. Cabinet noted that to the public it would appear as an extension of the Canadian involvement in nuclear matters. "The Prime Minister said that the US leased bases were an embarrassment generally." Then nothing was done: Pearson asked that the whole subject be held over until the next meeting as he was going to consult certain people in the United States.[622]

Less than a week passed, and with no indication from the United States that this issue was going to soon die, Pearson had it raised at the 1 November Cabinet meeting. In a much quicker fashion, the group decided that the United States would be "permitted to store airborne nuclear weapons at the US leased base in Newfoundland, subject to the negotiation of a mutually satisfactory agreement" and that the negotiated agreement would "be consistent with and not to exceed the provisions of existing Canada-United States Agreements."[623]

Regular duties continued at Argentia as the new year started. Naval Patrol Squadron VP 49 Detachment 17 deployed two, then four, P-3A aircraft to Argentia from January through June 1967. VP 49 was then replaced by VP 45, Detachment 17, with two and then four P-3A through December. As the end of the year approached, the alert patrol was augmented by an additional three aircraft from VP 8, Detachment 17. The advanced underwater weapons detachment continued to do little with its one officer and fourteen enlisted men.

The Canadian government was now actually working on the issue, yet this still had to be communicated to the highest levels of the U.S. government. Pearson had to tell Johnson that this was a most difficult issue, and that it "was difficult and painstaking work due to the need for the authorization paragraph dealing with non-NORAD, non-air defence forces."[624] The fact that the entire issue would be dealt with by the Cabinet Defence Committee also served to appease Washington.

With the agreement finally in sight, the militaries turned to the much easier problem of the service-to-service technical arrangement. This document would provide for the transport, import, export, custody, safety, maintenance, storage, inspections, salvage and use of information. The meeting between the Canadian military and the USN in Ottawa on 28 June 1967 produced substantial agreement on the content and rough draft wording.[625] Official Washington was, however, a bit more concerned with what they saw as a new danger to the deal. The U.S. embassy warned Washington that Walter Gordon would be attending a NATO meeting, and that Gordon, the president of the Privy Council, advocated leaving NATO and NORAD, and urging an end to the U.S. war against Viet Nam.[626] On a second occasion, the embassy worried that Gordon and the influential ministers such as Pearson and Martin wished to de-emphasize the military roles of Canada. None too diplomatically, they wrote that "they [Gordon et al.] all have support in Cabinet of naive ministers like Pennel and LaMarsh."[627] The agreement was in no danger and would be signed within two weeks.

AGREEMENT

While the summer of 1966 had been slow in Ottawa, 1967 saw a mad rush to complete the work. At the Cabinet Committee on External Affairs and Defence, Paul Martin briefed the inner Cabinet. He emphasized that the draft agreement was consistent with and did not exceed the provisions of the existing Canada-United States agreement on nuclear weapons and was patterned after the Canada-United States exchange of notes in 1963 and by a further exchange in 1965. Martin pointed out that provision had been made for various conditions under which the United States might wish to release the weapons for alert loading, airborne patrol, or possible employment and that, despite the fact that the weapons would be under the control of the U.S. National Command or, in time of war SACLANT, the conditions for release and for Canadian consultation and authorization were no less stringent than those pertaining to the 1965 agreement relating to NORAD.[628] Most importantly, "the question of 'timely authorization' by the prime minister would in all probability be resolved, as had been done in 1965 by an exchange of letters." Lastly, the CDC was informed that "no authority will be sought from Council since the agreement is to remain secret."[629] News of the 18 July Cabinet Defence Committee meeting was immediately communicated directly to Dean Rusk in Washington. Bissonette had told the U.S. embassy, and Rusk was informed, that it was expected that the full Cabinet would give approval nearly automatically.[630]

With the final approval of Pearson, the definitive memorandum (No. 439/67) was presented to the full Cabinet on 20 July 1967. Martin now sought final approval to sign the agreement for storage of nuclear weapons earmarked for SACLANT at an unnamed base in Newfoundland.[631] The full Cabinet was informed that agreement had been reached ad referendum with U.S. officials which was consistent with and did not exceed the provisions of past bilateral agreements on nuclear weapons. The draft agreement had conditions which were exactly the same as those contained in the 1963 agreement. However, there was new wording to take into account the differences in the factual situation. There would be no specific mention of NORAD in the agreement since the forces in question were not under NORAD command but under U.S. national command. However, the draft agreement has retained the same controls concerning authorization and possible use as those related to NORAD forces.[632] Since Cabinet had fought long and hard over the consultation and authorization agreement, this prior knowledge eased the way for the Argentia agreement.

Due to the rather hostile nature of the USN to any public knowledge of their real military activities in the nuclear field, Cabinet had to agree that the agreement and the location would remain a secret. All they would be allowed to say was that the new agreement was designed to meet a new threat and that it was a transfer of a commitment from one base (Harmon) to another. To conform with standard U.S. military security requirements, the statement did not identify the base involved.[633] The Canadian government was authorized by the U.S. government to state that

> US rights to maintain nuclear storage facilities for US aircraft at a leased base in Newfoundland have been relinquished by the US Government. Meanwhile, the threat to this continent persists and there is a NATO requirement to have nuclear weapons available to US aircraft. The Canadian Government has agreed to a transfer of nuclear storage rights to another leased base to facilitate this requirement.
>
> This transfer does not involve the provision of nuclear weapons for Canadian forces.

U.S. NUCLEAR WEAPONS IN CANADA

> The employment of nuclear weapons is subject to the same
> controls already in effect for NORAD defence weapons.[634]

The only possible problem the United States faced was that the Canadian government was not totally under control and proposed to answer questions about the agreement. One answer in particular made the Pentagon and State Department shudder. When asked about controls over the use of weapons, Canadian government spokesmen or ministers were going to say that this question was answered by the statements made by the prime minister at the time of the August 1963 agreement. The State Department was blunt and expressed the hope that the Government of Canada would not feel called upon to make this statement "because of the likelihood that such a statement would create difficulties for the United States in negotiations now going on with another country."[635] This probably meant the Federal Republic of Germany.

The Cabinet meeting that day was difficult, and ministers clearly discussed the possibility of withdrawing from the anti-submarine warfarecommitment. It was agreed that "it would not be possible for the government to withdraw from commitments which had been made in relation to the storage of nuclear weapons in Canada."[636] By the end of the day, they had given approval to Paul Martin to sign the agreement and had approved the use of the contingency press statement in case of "leaks" in relation to the storage of weapons at the base.[637] The next day, Martin signed for Canada. The text is presented in full in Annex C to this book.

Exchanged as Canadian note No. DL-1711 and U.S. note No. 32, the agreement embodied the understanding that the anti-submarine warfare nuclear weapons would be under the ownership and custody of the United States; that the United States would provide reasonable security; that a service-to-service arrangement covering transport, loading, delivery and salvage was to be signed by the CAF and USN; and that Canada would authorize the import of the weapons. Most important, the agreement stipulated that

> the weapons will be released by the United States for alert loading, airborne patrol or employment, only
>
> (1) upon Defence Condition One or a higher state of alert as authorized by both Governments for CINCNORAD as provided in the Agreement of September 17, 1965 between the two Governments;

(2) in the emergency circumstances set forth in paragraph 8(E) of the Agreement of September 17, 1965 between the two Governments;

(3) When otherwise authorized by both Governments. Authorization for the employment of the weapons will be effected by the Canadian Government under the conditions specified in (1) and (2) above. To provide for the emergency circumstances set forth in (2) above in which prior consultation is not practicable, it is agreed that the Prime Minister, acting on behalf of the Government of Canada, will provide to the President of the United States, timely authorization for the employment of these weapons. The weapons will be employed in accordance with the United States Navy rules of interception and engagement and the United States Navy nuclear weapons employment procedures.

PRIOR AUTHORIZATION

The most difficult issue for Ottawa was, of course, authorization. As the two Pauls explained on 29 May, the "fact that the draft agreement is dealing with U.S. forces under U.S. national command and not NORAD forces has not however affected the application of the basic principles set out in the agreement of 17 September 1965."[638] (This agreement was discussed in detail in Chapter 1.) As explained to the Cabinet, in brief, "it provides that in these circumstances, when there is time for consultation, authorization for employment will be given at the time" and "it also stipulates that, if prior consultation is not practicable, the Prime Minister will provide to the President of the US 'timely authorization'. Paragraph 6 does not itself constitute timely authorization. This is not defined and remains a matter to be resolved between the Prime Minister and the President; as was the case for the 1965 Agreement."[639]

Even more important than the agreement itself is the "prior authorization" note signed by the prime minister and given to the U.S. ambassador for transmission to the White House in Washington. While the actual letter remains classified by both Canada and the United States, the letter of transmission of this document from Paul Martin, the secretary of state for External Affairs, to the prime minister is now open. Here we see the first conclusive evidence that the Canadian government, as represented by the prime minister, had signed away possibly the most significant aspect of national sovereignty: the right to decide to go to war.

Paul Martin gave the prime minister a text of the "timely authorization for the employment of the weapons" which Pearson could sign and forward to the U.S. ambassador. The 27 July 1967 exchange between Martin and Pearson makes it clear that authorization was given in advance, and that Canada could be cut out of the decision-making loop by virtue of having given prior authority.

---

27 July 1967, Top Secret
Memorandum for the Prime Minister

re: Agreement Between Canada and the United States for the Storage of Nuclear Weapons at a United States Leased Base in Newfoundland for United States Forces.

Cabinet authorized me yesterday to sign the above-mentioned Agreement which I have done today.

As you know the Agreement requires that the Prime Minister acting on behalf of the Government of Canada, will provide to the President of the United States timely authorization for the employment of the weapons .

Attached for your signature, if you agree, is the text of the timely authorization in question. You will recall that the text was sent to you in a Memorandum of May 26 which I had signed together with Mr. Hellyer. You then approved the text. It will be provided to the Ambassador of the United States when signed by you at the same time as the Agreement.

Paul Martin

Prime Minister Lester Pearson's letter of timely authorization to the U.S. president is now held in the National Security Files of the Lyndon Baines Johnson Presidential Library in Austin, Texas. It remains classified as top secret and is not yet available for public research. This single-page letter is the subject of a prolonged and ongoing mandatory review request which began prior to the first volume of this series being published.

There was a third note that day, and it has never been released to the public either. The U.S. Navy was so sensitive, paranoid and concerned that U.S. and allied citizens would discover the location of nuclear weapons and protest that they forbade any mention of the specific location or site name. The base was never to be referred to directly, and thus the final agreement talks only of a "leased base" in Canada. The third note, containing the name "Argentia," was classified ZED[640] (controlled information), and its distribution was tightly controlled. This was ultimately nonsense, as the whole thing had been written out in full on many documents spanning a 10-year period. External Affairs was forced to tell the Canadian embassy in Washington that it was not able to send a copy of the third note naming the base, but that it could be seen in the ZED registry at National Defence.[641] Although the Argentia agreement and the supporting technical arrangement contain no "Restricted Data or Formerly Restricted Data" as defined by the U.S. Department of Energy and the atomic Energy Act, the U.S. Navy insisted on treating the entire matter as a ZED control issue, and all documents were to be handled accordingly.

ARGENTIA ACTIVITIES

With the agreement now signed, and the substantive negotiations between the militaries already done, the chief of the Defence Staff sent to the USN chief of Naval Operations a Canadian draft of the service-to-service technical arrangement for his concurrence and possibly signature.[642] The only U.S. Navy objection was to the provision for customs formalities when entering or exporting items to and from Canada. The USN felt that since they essentially "owned" Argentia, and as they had not been directly subject to customs inspections for some years, they were not willing to accept such. It turned out that Canada Customs had forgotten about the Argentia situation, but would re-establish itself. External Affairs pointed out that even though the U.S. military was in a "tax-exempt" status in Canada, that did not make them exempt from the normal formalities of Customs clearance.[643] Revenue Canada finally concluded in late July that the U.S. Navy Base commander could sign as the importer of nuclear weapons, that nuclear weapons are subject to the normal customs regulations, and that Tariff Item 708 would be applicable.[644]

With the arrival of nuclear weapons expected shortly, the U.S. Marine barracks in 1967 was brought up to necessary strength with four officers and 106 troops. On 1 August, Captain (N) G.I. Tarleton became base commanding officer, and served until July 1969. Captain Tarleton was in command when Argentia passed the necessary inspection and when nuclear weapons were delivered to the storage site on base.

Nineteen sixty-eight was the year of nuclear weapons at Argentia. The long-suffering advanced underwater weapons (AUW) detachment with its one officer and 15 enlisted men was ready to receive weapons. The main alert duty was assumed by VP 8, Detachment 17, which had 3 P-3A aircraft on site from about April through to the end of the year, with three aircraft and three crews rotated every two weeks. During this period, VP 8 would maintain an operational readiness state of 92.7%. Prior to the return of VP 8, VP 49 Detachment 17, brought in seven P-3A aircraft in January, with two in the pipeline for the base. However, it seems that VP 49 may only have stayed at Argentia for the first quarter or half of 1968. The year ended with VP 16 augmenting VP 8 with one additional P-3A aircraft during the final quarter.

VP-8, the "Tigers," was the most common unit to do rotational alert duty at Argentia during the short nuclear period. One unit wag wrote that in comparison to the Argentia weather, one of their other duty sites at Keflavik, Iceland, was like Miami Beach. The unit spent the Argentia nuclear years supporting operations at Argentia, Bermuda and Iceland. In October 1962 VP-8 had become the first squadron equipped with the new P-3A Orion and immediately dispatched a handful to Argentia. Unit records have not been retained by the U.S. Navy, so little is known about the daily operations of the unit during its time at Argentia.

Naval Station Argentia, now awaiting full operational capability with nuclear weapons, underwent their initial U.S. Navy technical proficiency inspection (NTPI) during 22-25 January 1968. "This activity represents the final step required prior to the positioning of weapons." The U.S. Navy inspectors rated Argentia and the weapons detachment as satisfactory and therefore qualified and certified to receive nuclear weapons.[645] Weapons were then delivered in February 1968, and it is known that between 23 and 25 September 1968, the base had a regular Navy technical proficiency inspection and was rated as satisfactory with no limiting factors.[646] The U.S. Marine guards, the standard naval storm-trooper unit at a U.S. naval site, provided the security for the nuclear weapons. They underwent a physical security inspection on 5 and 6 February 1968 as part of the "special projects" at Argentia. The last known NTPI took place between 22 and 25 September 1969, and the site was rated as satisfactory.[647]

The Canadian government always knew exactly what was going on with the warheads stored at Argentia. Section 7(b) of the service-to-service arrangement specified that the USN would "keep the Canadian Forces through the US Naval Attaché at Ottawa advised of the numbers and types of weapons present at the Base." Although the channel was through the U.S.

Naval attaché in Ottawa to the Canadian Forces, there does not seem to have been a way to move this information to necessary offices within National Defence. For this reason, the director general of intelligence and security for National Defence wrote to External Affairs and asked to be placed on the distribution list for further items related to nuclear weapons storage at Argentia. He argued that he was ultimately responsible for security in Canada, and that his people might have to provide added support to the U.S. Marine security at the site in case of troubles.[648] External Affairs would later inform the brigadier that he could find certain information, such as the location, in the ZED registry at National Defence.[649]

ARGENTIA 1969[650]			
Activities/Units Supported	Aircraft	Pers	Admin Superior
COMFAIRARGENTIA			COMNAVAIRLANT
Marine Barracks		93	CO NAVSTA
Navy Commissary Store		13	CO NAVSTA
Navy Exchange		18	CO NAVSTA
Fleet Weather Facility (NWSED)		26	CO NAVSTA
Air Traffic Control No. 15		38	CO NAVSTA
OIC Construction		1	DIRLANTDOCKS
AUW Det.		16	CO NAVSTA
Oceanographic Facility		182	
COMOCEANSYSLANT			
Naval Communition		111	HD NAVCOMSYSHQ
Coast Guard Radio Station		14	Cmdr 1st CG Dist.
Int'l Ice Patrol		22	COMEASTAREA
VP Sqdn Det.	3P3A/B	71	COMFAIRARGENTIA
NAVSTA	1 C54S		
	2 HU16D		
	1 UH34J	675	COMNAVAIRLANT

Time was now short for Argentia as Captain (N) C.A. McCarthy (USN) became commanding officer in July 1969 for a two-year term. He would oversee the final removal of the nuclear weapons from the storage site in June 1970. The advanced underwater weapons detachment had 16 men assigned and maintained this number until the unit was withdrawn in total by mid-1970. The alert aircraft continued to rotate in and out on a sporadic basis during 1969. The year started with VP 16 Detachment 17, deploying three P-3A in January. They were replaced by the regular group of three P-3A aircraft of VP 8 Detachment 17, from February to June 1969. One aircraft arrived from Jacksonville, Florida, to replace VP8. The VP 5 Detachment Argentia would soon send another three P-3A aircraft and maintain the alert through September when they were replaced by VP 16 Detachment 17 for the final quarter of 1969.

It was already obvious in late 1968 that Argentia was not going to last forever and that it might close in the near future. Labour concerns were expressed, and the U.S. consulate in St. John's wrote that they had tried to dispel any anxiety. The consulate may not have been all that helpful, as what they told labour leaders was that while the United States did not intend to abandon the base, it could not foresee the future, and the 1941 lease allowed them to give one year's notice before abandonment.[651]

By the end of 1969 closure was imminent. The Pentagon began discussions of proposals to "to cut back sharply operations and manning of NAVSTA Argentia." The contemplated reductions would begin in January 1970 and be completed within six months. It seems that the Pentagon had planned to reduce personnel to a bare minimum, and only U.S. naval personnel would be employed: all Canadian civilian employment would be terminated. The U.S. embassy in Ottawa was horrified at the prospect and shot back that firing of Canadian employees would be seen as closure of the base. They also noted for both the State Department and the Pentagon that every effort would have to be made to ameliorate the effect of the closures, as "this is the least we can do in recognition of excellent cooperation we have had in province for almost 30 years and may continue to need in the future."[652]

The news of the U.S. reductions had already leaked to the Canadian Forces. Vice Admiral O'Brien told the U.S. government that the CAF would not be able to assume full responsibility for Argentia due to the limited budget, but that the Department of Transport might have been able to take over tower operations and airport maintenance. DND also feared the problems created by the rise in unemployment among so many local workers.[653] The Liberal government feared this prospect even more.

Through 1970 the U.S. Navy kept a sub-unit of three P-3A patrol aircraft on station at Argentia from VP 16 Detachment 17. However, the advanced underwater weapons detachment had been removed during the personnel reductions. Therefore no nuclear weapons remained. In the end, Argentia saw the storage of airborne nuclear anti-submarine weapons for the short time between February 1968, and June 1970: about twenty-eight months.

By 1970 the Marine Barracks was down to 101 personnel in total, and by the following year there ceased to be any on the Station nominal roll. Marines were told of the deactivation of the Marine Barracks, Argentia, in the June 1970 newsletter. The date of deactivation was 25 June, immediately after the weapons removal. With the nuclear weapons redeployed, and the patrol aircraft gone, there was no longer a need for the storm troops.

Nineteen-seventy-one saw the staff at Argentia total 39 officers and 394 enlisted personnel. This was a huge drop from 1968 when there were 118 officers and 1216 enlisted personnel. In a 1972 audit of the remaining facilities at Argentia, the U.S. Navy determined that Building 606, the "Special Weapons Shop," was worth $401,586 ($US); while Building 615, the "Special Weapons Magazine," was worth $146,214 ($US).[654] Readiness Hangars numbers 1 and 2 were worth almost half a million dollars each. The special weapons facilities would be demolished and the ground scraped flat. All physical evidence in Newfoundland that the nuclear weapons had ever been there was now gone; only sparse records in Washington, and sketchy records in Ottawa remained.

THE AIRCRAFT

Lockheed P-3A ORION

The Lockheed Orion was a military derivative of the successful civilian commercial airliner, the Electra. Lockheed won the contract for the new U.S. Navy anti-submarine warfare patrol aircraft in April 1958 and the first prototype flew on 19 August that year. The first P-3A flew on 15 April 1961, and the first deliveries to the U.S. Navy were made on 13 August 1962, just prior to the Cuban missile crisis. The first aircraft served with VP-8 and VP-44. The Orion can fly 1600 km to a patrol zone, then patrol for eight hours, then return to base without refueling.

P-3A ORION

Wing span: 30.4m
Length: 35.6m
Tail: 10.3m
Engines: 4 x Allison T56-A-14 turboprop
Max. weight: 57.7 t
Max. speed: 765 km/h
cruising speed: 640 km/h

```
patrol speed: 370 km/h
Ceiling: 8500m
Crew: 12
Bomb load: 3.29t in bomb bay
Bomb Bay 3.9m long x 2.0m wide x 0.88m high
Bomb load: 3 x Mk57 or 2 x Mk 101
```

WEAPONS

Mk 101 LULU[655]

The Mk 101 Lulu nuclear depth bomb was carried internally on anti-submarine warfare patrol aircraft of the U.S. Navy. Built by General Mills, better known for more consumer-oriented products, the 544 kg snub-nosed bomb was 2.35 m long and 0.48 m in diameter. Armed with the W34 warhead, the Lulu would have a yield of about 10 to 15 kt.

Lulu was designed by the U.S. Naval Ordnance Laboratory and U.S. Navy Bureau of Ordnance with assistance from the U.S. Atomic Energy Commission. The bomb was nothing more than a cylindrical atomic bomb device with a hollow aft-body, and four fins with a ring of sheet steel surrounding their ends. Fuzing was both by hydrostatic depth fuzes, and by a backup timer should the primary system fail. There was also a form of contact fuze which would detonate the weapon on contact with the sea floor below. One of the few safety features prevented the bomb from detonating in less than 30 m of water. Lulu also carried a small retardant parachute for drops from higher speeds, which fell off as Lulu entered the water.

The design was approved on 28 July 1957 and tested during Operation Plumbbob that year. After the tests, approximately 2000 W34 warheads were built for Lulu bombs between August 1958 and late 1962. The U.S. Navy began to replace the Lulus with B57 bombs starting in July 1964, with the final Lulu being withdrawn from service in 1971, as the B57 nuclear depth bomb had completely taken over the nuclear anti-submarine warfare job. A Lulu practice shape and trolley can be viewed and examined in the National Atomic Museum at Kirtland AFB, New Mexico.

B57[656]

The B57 bomb arming the P-3A Orion naval patrol aircraft was the internally carried, free-fall or parachute retarded, depth-fuzed for underwater burst, sealed-pit nuclear fission weapon. It had a Permissive

Action Link (PAL), which had to be operated on the ground by U.S. Navy advanced underwater weapons personnel prior to flight.

The W57 warhead was a Nominal yield weapon, like the Hiroshima bomb, of less than 20 kt, and this is often referred to as a 5 to 10 kt bomb, but is more likely actually in the 15 to 20 kt range. This low-yield weapon was the smallest free-fall atomic bomb in the U.S. arsenal. It was one of the very few atomic gravity bombs originally developed for the U.S. Navy and U.S. Marine Corps. They had requested a small (size and yield) tactical atomic bomb for both land attack and anti-submarine work. The B57 weighed 231 kg, and was 3.02 m long with a maximum body diameter of 0.37 m. Given the low yield, the B57 was probably a fission bomb containing a plutonium core and contained no secondary stages necessary for thermonuclear fusion. The fuzing option was probably selected on the ground prior to flight for air or ground burst.

The naval versions were equipped with depth pressure sensors, or hydrostatic fuzes, to have an anti-submarine capability, and these versions were used at Argentia on board the P-3A patrol aircraft. The bomb body had two flooding ports for allowing water to reach the hydrostatic fuzes. When the parachute-retarded bomb struck the water, the parachute would be jettisoned and the fuzes would be activated. Practice shapes for the weapon included the BDU-11A/E for loading, and the BDU-12A/B as a drop shape. Samples of some training shapes can be viewed in the National Atomic Museum at Kirtland AFB, and in the Smithsonian Museum of U.S. History in Washington, D.C.

Production of some 3100 units began at the Pantex Plant near Amarillo, Texas, in January 1963 and ended there in May 1967. The final weapon was retired in June 1993. Seven different Mods were produced in the 1960s, with the USAF and USN getting Mods 0, 1, 2 and 5 in 1963, and Mods 3, 4 and 6 in 1966. Mods 5 and 6 were designed for carriage by the massive B-52 strategic bomber. The USN could have used any of the first four versions, as their external characteristics were virtually identical.

Chapter Nine

SOURCES, FILES, ARCHIVES, LIBRARIES, AND AGENCIES

U.S. NATIONAL ARCHIVES

The National Archives at College Park, Maryland, just outside of Washington, D.C., have tremendous holdings of both military and civilian documentation. State Department files for the 1950–68 period dealing with nuclear weapons for and in Canada, although sometimes grossly censored, are now available to the public. The State Department Decimal Files and Central Files on CANUS Defense Relations are the researcher's best friend. The sad fact for Canadians is that there is more information from and about Canada available in the Washington files than is available from the Canadian government through the National Archives of Canada. Researchers are encouraged to make their own copies at one of four available copy machines for 10 cents per page.

The National Archives also has an extensive collection of USAF and USN photographs on the fifth floor, including many of nuclear weapons, aircraft and bases which are available for researchers to copy on their own. Many excellent photos of weapons systems and military sites are available. All of the photographs can be copied on regular machines, laser machines, Polaroid machines, or copied using photographic equipment. Photographs pertinent to this study are found in the colour and black and white collections of the USAF.

NATIONAL SECURITY ARCHIVE

The National Security Archive, a research and publication organization in Washington, D.C., has one of the single largest private collections of U.S. government documents on the history of nuclear weapons and nuclear weapons policy, in the world. The collection, by its very nature, includes material dealing with U.S. nuclear weapons activities around the world. This archive has provided documentation for both volumes in this series.

U.S. AIR FORCE HISTORICAL OFFICE

The U.S. Air Force maintains a large historical section at Maxwell Air Force Base, Montgomery, Alabama. The records of all the USAF units which supported nuclear weapons in Canada are on file at this facility. However, the files of many units which had custody of the nuclear weapons are under the jurisdiction of the U.S. Department of Energy and cannot be released without a formal declassification process outside of the USAF. The records of USAF flying units which operated in Canada from time to time are often accessible.

U.S. NAVY and MARINE CORPS ARCHIVES

The Washington, D.C., Navy Yard is home to the Naval Historical Centre and the associated U.S. Marine Corps History Archives. Both facilities are excellent research centres with helpful and knowledgeable staff. However, little in relation to naval nuclear activities in Canada has been retained. In addition, the USN is far more secretive than the USAF about their nuclear activities. The records for Argentia have been destroyed, and only a slim microfiche package of a few annual reports of the site commander are now available. The Naval Air archives has some records from units which served at Argentia, but these too are spotty and not all that helpful. The researcher is best off using the Pentagon and State Department records at the U.S. National Archives. Better naval air information was available on the Internet than in the USN history offices within this narrow topic.

SOURCES, FILES, ARCHIVES, LIBRARIES, AND AGENCIES

THE NATIONAL ARCHIVES OF CANADA

The National Archives on Wellington Avenue, Ottawa, is a superb repository of material on nuclear weapons in Canada. However, the collection is not a homogeneous mass, and the researcher will spend days looking in disparate places for various scraps of information in various unrelated files.

The Government Archives Division (GAD) of the National Archives is the unit best equipped to help. Within the GAD there are archivists who specialize in military files, Cabinet documents, and External Affairs. Each will be able to guide the researcher through various and massive finding aides.

Through the efforts of the author, many of the National Archives files dealing with nuclear weapons have been opened for public viewing or are under review by one or more government departments in Canada and the United States.

The one downside is that the National Archives of Canada is now charging illegal fees to access to information requesters, possibly in an attempt to discourage requests for documents. This unconscionable action had been repeated several times with numerous clients, so I filed a case in the Federal Court of Canada against the minister of Canadian Heritage, Sheila Copps, who is responsible for the National Archives, charging that the minister had violated the Access to Information Act, the Treasury Board regulations governing the act, and the National Archives Act. The case is officially known as T-1-99 (Ottawa).

THE DIRECTOR OF NUCLEAR WEAPONS

Probably the single greatest wealth of nuclear weapons information in Canada is contained in the records of the Director of Nuclear Weapons files held in three boxes at the National Archives of Canada. Although certain items are withheld for the moment, the author has been successful in having the vast bulk of this material opened for public inspection. Unfortunately, some of the material dealing with U.S. activities in Canada continues to be held as secret by the National Archives. The most important of the files is as follows:

File Locator Number: RG24 Accession No. 1986-87/165, Box 16, Box 17, Box 18

- file 3312-2 Plans, Operations, & Readiness. Nuclear Weapons. Field Activities. USN Base.
- file 3313-23 Plans, Operations, & Readiness. Nuclear Weapons. Safety, F-102A, Harmon/Goose Bay
- file 3314-2 Plans, Operations & Readiness. Nuclear Weapons. Storage. Maritime Weapons.

DEPARTMENT OF FOREIGN AFFAIRS

At External Affairs, now known as Foreign Affairs and International Trade, in the Lester Pearson Building on Sussex Drive in Ottawa, there is a considerable body of political history available to qualified researchers. Through their academic history program, the staff at External Affairs will grant certain academics the right to inspect original files generated by that department. In addition, much material has been released by their Access to Information Office either through direct requests or through consultations with other government departments and the National Archives.

PRIVY COUNCIL OFFICE

The Prime Minister's Office and the Privy Council Office (PMO and PCO) in Ottawa are the primary source for documents generated by or for the Cabinet and the Cabinet Defence Committee (CDC). The Access to Information Office at the PCO was able to provide all the Cabinet and CDC documents and minutes used in this study.

NATIONAL DEFENCE HEADQUARTERS

Almost none of the material used in this study came directly from National Defence Headquarters. This is because National Defence holds almost no older historical material itself, preferring to transfer it to the National Archives. However, the Access to Information Office at NDHQ was instrumental in declassifying a vast amount of documentation as a third party to the National Archives. They were both helpful and forthcoming at all times.

DIRECTORATE OF HISTORY AND HERITAGE

The DND Directorate of History and Heritage (DHH) in Ottawa holds a vast array of documentation useful to this research. Although the records are often not complete for various bureaucratic reasons, they are second to none. Without the input of staff at DHH at Holly Lane in Ottawa, and their provision of files, this study would have been impossible. Entries included such items as photographic books, Goose Bay documents, nuclear accidents, PJBD journal entries, Joint Staff memos, and arrangements with the USAF and USN. Sadly, due to government spending cuts, the office is now open only two days per week. Copies of the documents used in the researching and production of both this book and the previous *Canadian Nuclear Weapons* have been deposited at DHH and are available without restriction to any researcher. They are filed under the heading Clearwater Nuclear Weapons Fond.

PHOTOGRAPHIC ARCHIVES IN CANADA

The Canadian Forces Photographic unit in Ottawa is the repository for all important negatives, films and videos in the military. The collection is arranged with a cross-referenced index, and photographs of nuclear weapons can be found under the name or number of the user unit, the base or station, or the name of the weapon. The facility also has some films and videos of historical interest. The staff was of great help in finding old negatives of nuclear weapons activities in Canada and especially in Newfoundland. There is no single reference which will yield all required photographs.

The National Archives photographic section is not particularly useful to the nuclear researcher. The photographs of the construction of the various sites in Newfoundland are generally too long before the introduction of nuclear weapons to yield useful information. In addition, an overly restrictive policy about photo use and reproduction makes the photo section extremely uninviting.

ANNEX A

THE MB-1 AGREEMENTS

19 February 1957, Agreement on Carrying Air-to-Air Nuclear Rockets on US Fighters in Canadian Air Space. USA Note, Signed by John Foster Dulles.

I have the honour to refer to conversations between representatives of our two governments regarding the proposed incorporation of nuclear weapons in the air defence of Canada, the Continental USA and Alaska. Such a move would greatly enhance the joint-defence capabilities which our two countries have been developing over a period of years. As has already been indicated to the Canadian Chiefs of Staff Committee, the initial nuclear capability visualized for air defence is in the form of an air-to-air rocket (MB-1). This weapon was issued around January 1, to the USA Air Force in small numbers for use in air defence activities. In order that this new weapon may be given maximum scope in defence activities which affect both Canada and the USA, this Government wishes to propose that the MB-1 be carried by USA military aircraft over Canada under the following terms and conditions:

1) The initial period during which the Canadian Government will authorize the carriage of MB-1 weapons over Canada will extend to 1 July 1957. More permanent arrangements will have to be worked out to cover the period after July 1957.

2) USA Air Force planes so armed will enter Canadian air space only in the event an Air Defence Warning Yellow or Red is declared. In such an event, the USA planes will confine their activities in the main to Canadian territory bordering on the Great Lakes and extending northward to about 50 degrees north latitude. USA planes armed with MB-1 weapons, under Air Defence Warning Yellow or Red, will be authorized by the Canadian Government to land at, or take off from, Canadian bases in the territory over which they have authority to operate.

3) In the circumstances visualized above, rules of interception and engagement over Canadian territory shall continue to be those established from time to time by the Canadian Government for interceptor aircraft of the Royal Canadian Air Force operating over Canada. Attached for your information is a copy of the USA

Interception and Engagement instructions and procedures, which have been reviewed for their applicability to the employment of atomic weapons and which became applicable in 1 January 1957.

4)   The USA Government has taken the utmost precaution in designing the weapon, and will exercise equal caution in establishing operational procedures, to insure a minimum possibility of public hazard when employment of the MB-1 is necessary. Representatives of the Royal Canadian Air Force have been thoroughly informed by the USA Air Force concerning safety procedures.

5)   In accordance with current agreed procedures, crashes of aircraft from either country in the territory of the other are reported on a service-to-service basis. During the term of this agreement, the USA will take measures to insure that the Canadian Government is immediately notified of any crash in Canadian territory of a USA aircraft carrying MB-1 rockets.

6)   Detailed arrangements will be made between the USA Air Force and the Royal Canadian Air Force to provide designated RCAF personnel with training necessary for the salvage of MB-1 weapons following an accident. In the event salvage is necessary, the USA Air Forces willing to send at any time, upon request, trained personnel to assist in the operation.

7)   Any information released jointly or separately by the two Governments concerning this subject will be processed in accordance with the current understanding of 19 March 1951, which governs the release of publicity relating to joint Canadian-USA defence plans and operations.

If these conditions are acceptable to your Government, I suggest that this note and your reply shall constitute an agreement effective from the date of your reply.

Accept, however, the renewed assurances of my highest consideration. (signed) John Foster Dulles.

19 February 1957, Canadian Note No. 91.

Sir,

I have the honour to refer to your Note of 19 February 1957, proposing that under certain terms and conditions the MB-1 Air-to-Air rocket may be carried by USA military aircraft over Canadian territory.

ANNEX A: THE MB-1 AGREEMENTS

The terms and conditions set out in your Note under reference are acceptable to my Government which concurs as well with your suggestion that your Note and this reply shall constitute an agreement affective the date of this Note, and to extend to 1 July 1957.

Accept, Sir, the renewed assurances of my highest Consideration. (signed) A.D.P. Heeny

30 June 1959, Amendment to MB-1 Agreement, USA Note. Top Secret.

Excellency:

I have the honour to refer to the exchange of notes of February 19 and June 28, 1957, and May 12 and June 30, 1958, between our two Governments, authorizing the carriage of MB-1 weapons over Canada by the United States interceptors under certain conditions. These agreements have greatly enhanced the joint air defence capability of our two countries. This capability, the United States Government believes, can be still further enhanced, particularly in view of the recently established North American Air Defence Command, by modifying the existing agreement in the respects set forth hereinafter.

There are three features of the existing agreements which the United States Government believes should now be reconsidered and modified to reflect prospective technological advances and the long-range air defence needs of NORAD.

First, the existing interim agreement concerns only the MB-1, a specific model of air defence weapons. The United States Government believes that the language should take account of the fact that technological advances may produce weapons of different nomenclature during the many years NORAD may continue.

Second, the interim arrangements apply to an area which geographically is much smaller than the area of NORAD responsibility. In view of the present and prospective range of nuclear-capable interceptors, operating from the United States, including Alaska, it seems advisable to the United States Government that existing geographical limitations should be removed in order that these interceptors may carry out their functions everywhere within the area of NORAD's responsibilities.

Finally, the interim arrangement could impair the potential effectiveness of the interceptors involved by limiting their nuclear-capable flights to conditions of Air Defence Warning Yellow or Red. The effect of this restriction is to preclude overflights during the critical period between the first warning of approaching air attack and actual hostile penetration of the air defence combat zone. The United States Government considers that warning of approaching air attack justifies the taking of prompt defensive measures in response and that, therefore, it is necessary to launch these flights when a condition of at least Air Defence Readiness has been declared by CINC NORAD.

Accordingly, the United States Government proposes that henceforth United States interceptor aircraft under the operational control of NORAD be authorized to carry nuclear air-to-air defensive weapons over Canada in accordance with the following principles:

1. The authorization shall continue in force for one-year period at which time it will be reviewed.
2. Such aircraft armed with nuclear air-to-air defence weapons may enter Canadian air space whenever a condition of Air Defence Readiness, or a higher state of alert, is declared by CINC NORAD. Such aircraft may land at, and take off from military airfields in Canada.
3. The rules for interception and engagement of hostile aircraft over Canadian territory shall be those established from time to time by the Canadian Government for Canadian military aircraft over Canadian territory, or as authorized by CINC NORAD upon approval by the appropriate authorities for the two Governments.
4. The United States will continue to take the utmost precautions in designing nuclear air-to-air defence weapons, and will exercise equal precaution in establishing operational procedures, to insure a minimum possibility of public hazard when employment of such weapons is necessary. Representatives of the Royal Canadian Air Force will continue to be thoroughly informed by the United States Air Force concerning both storage and operational safety measures.
5. The United States Government will take measures to insure that the Canadian Government is immediately notified of any crash in Canadian territory of a United States military aircraft carrying nuclear air-to-air defence weapons.
6. In accordance with such agreements as have been or may be concluded between the two Governments with respect to the transfer of atomic information, and pursuant to detailed arrangements between the United States Air Force and the Royal Canadian Air Force, designated RCAF personnel will be provided with training necessary for appraisal, monitoring, and decontamination in the event of accident involving nuclear air-to-air defence weapons. In the event

salvage is necessary, the United States Air Force will send trained personnel at any time, upon request of the Royal Canadian Air Force, to assist in the operation.

7. Any information released jointly or separately by the two Governments concerning this subject will be processed in accordance with the current understanding of 19 March 1951, which governs the release of publicity relating to joint Canadian/United States Defence Plans and Operations.

If the forgoing principles are acceptable to your Government, I propose that this note and your reply shall constitute an agreement between our two Governments, replacing the current MB-1 overflight agreement effective on the date of your reply.

Accept, Excellency, the renewed assurances of my highest consideration.

(signed) Robert Murphy.

(on behalf of Christian A. Herter, Secretary of State)

30 June 1959, Canadian Note No. 390, Top Secret.

Sir,

I have the honour to refer to your Note of 30 June 1959, proposing on behalf of your Government that United States interceptor aircraft under the operational control of NORAD be authorized to carry nuclear-air-to-air defence weapons over Canada in accordance with the principles set out in your Note.

I am pleased to inform you that my Government concurs in the principles set forth in your Note. My Government agrees with your further proposal that your Note and this reply shall constitute an Agreement between the Canadian and United States Governments effective on this date which will replace the Agreements between the two Governments concluded in the Exchange of Notes of February 19 and June 28 1957, and May 12 and June 30, 1958.

Accept, Sir, the renewed assurances of my highest Consideration.

(signed) A.D.P. Heeney

ANNEX B

THE GOOSE BAY AND HARMON AGREEMENT

28 September 1963, Canadian Note No. 162. From the Secretary of State for External Affairs, Paul Martin, to the U.S. Ambassador to Canada, W.W. Butterworth. Secret.

Excellency,

I have the honour to refer to discussions between representatives of the Canadian and United States Governments concerning the strengthening of the continental air defences by an increase in the numbers of air defence weapons with nuclear capability. These discussions have taken into account recommendations by the Commander-in-Chief, North American Air Defence Command, as to the immediate military requirement for the storage at certain points in Canada of nuclear air-to-air defensive weapons for United States forces under the operational command of the Commander-in-Chief, North American Air Defence Command.

As a result of these discussions, the Canadian Government is prepared to permit the storage of nuclear air-to-air defensive weapons at Goose Bay and Harmon Air Force Base for United States forces in accordance with the following conditions:

1) Unless the context otherwise requires, "Canada" means the Government of Canada, "United States" means the Government of the United States of America, "NORAD" means the North American Air Defence Command established by Canada and the United States in an Exchange of Notes dated May 12, 1958, and "CINC NORAD" means the Commander-in-Chief of NORAD. The weapons under consideration are such nuclear air-to-air defensive weapons as may from time to time be made available to United States forces under the operational command of CINC NORAD.

2) Ownership and custody of these weapons shall remain with the United States. United States personnel will be provided for this purpose. The status of such personnel in Canada will be governed by the provisions of the NATO Status of Forces Agreement and any other supplementary arrangements which may be agreed upon. These weapons may be stored within the leased areas at Goose Bay and at the leased base at Harmon Air Force Base, Newfoundland. The cost of the

establishment, maintenance and operation of the storage facilities shall be the responsibility of the United States Government.

3) The United States shall provide and be responsible for the security of the storage sites in accordance with the terms of the existing agreements concerning leased areas, i.e., the Agreement of March 27, 1941, concerning Leased Bases in Newfoundland in respect of Harmon Air Force Base and the Exchange of Notes of December 5, 1952, in respect of the leased areas situated within RCAF station Goose Bay.

4) The safety procedures for storage, maintenance, transport, loading, delivery and salvage of nuclear weapons will be at least equivalent to U.S. standards and will be the subject of arrangements between the appropriate authorities of the United States and Canada, taking into consideration classified (atomic) information which can be transferred under existing agreements between the two Governments.

5) Authorization of transportation of these weapons in Canadian territory will be subject to the requirements of Canadian law. The United States will be responsible for transportation between the United States and storage sites in Canada including security during transit.

6) The release of nuclear warheads to meet operational requirements will be the subject, where practical, of prior inter-governmental consultation. They will be used, when authorized by both Governments, only in accordance with procedures established by CINC NORAD. The MB-1 Agreements, of June 30, 1959 and June 1, 1962, shall apply to the removal of these weapons for operational reasons from the areas utilized by U.S. forces at Harmon and Goose Bay under existing agreements between the two Governments.

7) The provisions of this agreement will be applied in such a manner as to permit the return of the weapons to the United States at any time at the request of the United States Government.

8) The terms of this Agreement will be reviewed by the two governments at the request of either government and after such review may be terminated by either government upon six months' notice.

9) Supplementary arrangements between the appropriate military authorities of the two governments may be made from time to time for the purpose of carrying out the intent of this Agreement.

I have the honour to propose that if these conditions are acceptable to your Government, this note and your reply indicating such acceptance will constitute an agreement between our two Governments, to take effect on the date of your reply.

Accept, Excellency, the assurances of my highest consideration.
(signed)
Paul Martin
Secretary of State
for External Affairs

30 September 1963, United States Note No. 112. From the U.S.
Ambassador to Canada, W.W. Butterworth, to the Secretary of State
For External Affairs, Paul Martin. Secret.
(The final text of this Note has not yet been declassified)
Accept, Excellency, the renewed assurances of my highest consideration.
signed
W.W. Butterworth
US Ambassador to Canada
The Honorable
Paul Martin, P.C., Q.C.,
M.P., M.A., LL.M., LL.D., D.C.L.,
Secretary of State for External Affairs,
Ottawa.
SECRET

TERMINATION

The U.S. State Department says that the 28/30 September 1963 agreement
was terminated on 9 March 1987.

THE GOOSE BAY AND HARMON AIR FORCE BASE
AGREEMENT SERVICE-TO- SERVICE ARRANGEMENT

15 May 1964, Service-to-Service Arrangement Between the United States
Air Force and the Royal Canadian Air Force to Provide for Implementation
of the Government-to-Government Agreement of 28 and 30 September
1963 Concerning Nuclear Weapons for United States Air Defense Forces at
Goose Bay and Harmon Air Force Base.

The Chief of Staff, United States Air Force and the Chief of the Air
Staff, Royal Canadian Air Force agree to the provisions contained herein.

SECTION I

U.S. NUCLEAR WEAPONS IN CANADA

GENERAL

1. PURPOSE: The purpose of this RCAF/USAF Supplementary Arrangement, hereinafter referred to as "this agreement", is to establish and describe the procedures governing the receipt, storage, maintenance, transport, loading, delivery, salvage, custody, security, and control of the nuclear warheads for air-to-air missiles of the United States air defense units based in Canada at Goose Bay and Harmon Air Force Base, in order to provide an operational capability while ensuring compliance with the applicable US laws and regulations (such as the United States Atomic Energy Act of 1954, as amended) and applicable Canadian laws and regulations.

2. BACKGROUND: The USAF air defense units with which this agreement is concerned are assigned to the USAF Air Defense Command, and are under the operational command of CINC NORAD. The status of these units in other respects is governed by the terms of the relevant inter-governmental agreements, in particular the Goose Bay Lease Agreement expressed in the Exchange of Notes of 5 December 1052 and the Agreements concerning Leased Bases in Newfoundland.

3. AUTHORITY: This agreement implements and draws its authority from the Canada/United States agreement effected by the Exchange of Note 162 (Canada) and 112 (United States) dated 28 September 1963 and 30 September 1963 respectively

4. POLICY: This agreement prescribes the procedures necessary for both the USAF and RCAF to exercise their respective responsibilities under the aforementioned Government-to-Government agreement. This agreement further establishes procedures to insure nuclear safety. The RCAF and USAF each assume responsibility for ensuring compliance with the terms of this agreement by their own personnel and any non-RCAF/USAF personnel sponsored by them, respectively.

PROCEDURES
TRANSPORTATION, IMPORT AND EXPORT

5. Nuclear warheads will be transported to the two bases by USAF airlift, conducted in accordance with approved procedures, and, while in Canada, in conformity with applicable Canadian laws and regulations. Authorization of transportation of these weapons in Canadian territory will be subject to the requirements of Canadian law. The provisions of this agreement will be applied in such a manner as to permit the return of the weapons to the United States at any time.

6. The RCAF will:

    (a) Authorize shipments of warheads into or out of Canada or between the two bases.

    (b) Arrange for the issue of import and export permits as required by Canadian regulations.

    (c) Arrange for the clearance through customs of each shipment of warheads.

    (d) Obtain any necessary waivers with respect to customs entries that would reveal Restricted or Formerly Restricted Data.

7. The USAF will:

    (1) Provide for the airlift, when authorized, of warheads into, out of, or between the two bases.

    (2) Keep the RCAF, through CINC NORAD, advised of the numbers of weapons stored at each base.

    (3) Prepare and present customs import and export entries for nuclear weapons, warheads and components at Goose Bay and Harmon Air Force Base in accordance with agreed procedures.

CUSTODY OR CUSTODIAL CONTROL

8. As used in this agreement, custody or custodial control is defined as the guardianship and safekeeping of nuclear weapons and their components, including source and special materials. This includes:

    (a) Accountability for warheads and classified Restricted Data or Formerly Restricted Data which remains with the US as US property;

    (b) Control of access to the warheads or material classified Restricted Data or Formerly Restricted Data in that it would take an act of force against a US National, and therefore, against the US Government, to obtain or use without proper authority the warheads or material classified Restricted Data or Formerly Restricted Data and obtain information concerning them.

[9....]

SECURITY

10. Security of all facilities within Harmon Air Force Base and the leased areas at Goose Bay is the responsibility of the USAF. This security responsibility will be exercised in a manner consistent with security standards prescribed in current USAF security directives for similar USAF installations.

STORAGE AND MAINTENANCE

11. Storage facilities at Goose Bay and Harmon Air Force Base will be of a

standard satisfactory to the RCAF and consistent with USAF criteria for similar facilities within the United States.

12. The United States Air Force will:

(a) Be responsible for all costs of the establishment, maintenance and operation of the storage and alert facilities and associated equipments at Goose Bay and Harmon Air force Base.

(b) Provide the RCAF with site plans, drawings and specifications of the storage, maintenance and alert facilities.

(c) Ensure that warhead storage, maintenance and handling are in accordance with the US Approved Nuclear Weapons Systems Safety Rules.

INSPECTIONS

13. The RCAF will have the right of inspection, at agreed times, of the storage and alert areas and facilities with a view to ensuring the adequacy of security and safety arrangements and procedures. However, the RCAF agrees that after nuclear warheads or other United States Restricted Data or Formerly Restricted Data materials are in place this right of inspection, including the right of the Commanding Officer RCAF Station Goose Bay, as stipulated in the Goose Bay Lease Agreement, to free access to any part of the Goose Bay Leased Area, will not be exercised in circumstances where a compromise of Restricted Data or Formerly Restricted Data would result.

14. An Initial Capability Inspection (ICI), as prescribed in applicable USAF regulations, must be accomplished with a satisfactory rating at each base prior to delivery of nuclear warheads.

15. The RCAF may provide representatives who will participate as observers in the ICI and subsequent USAF inspections to the extent permitted by United States law.

16. The USAF will arrange for RCAF participation in the ICI and subsequent USAF inspections and provide the RCAF the results of such inspections to the extent permitted by United States law.

SAFTY

17. Applicable Canadian laws and regulations, US Approved Nuclear Weapon System Safety Rules, and NORAD orders and regulations, are binding at all times on both US and Canadian personnel. These are intended to:

a. Prevent weapons involved in accidents or incidents, or jettisoned weapons, from producing a nuclear yield;

b. Prevent deliberate arming, firing, or launching except when authorized and directed by competent authority;

c. Prevent inadvertent arming, firing, launching, or jettisoning;

d. Ensure adequate security.

18. The RCAF will provide the USAF with copies of applicable Canadian laws and regulations.

19. The USAF will provide to the RCAF a copy of the pertinent US Approved Nuclear Weapon System Safety Rules together with a copy of the relevant Technical Orders, Safety Directives and Technical Manuals.

SALVAGE AND EXPLOSIVE ORDNANCE DISPOSAL (EOD)

20. The organization and procedures for salvage and EOD within the leased areas will be the subject of further agreement between the USAF and RCAF.

21. For incidents or accidents involving a possible nuclear hazard which occur outside the leased base areas, the provisions of the "Service-to-Service Agreement Between the United States Air Force and the Royal Canadian Air Force on the Responsibilities for Response to Nuclear Weapons Incidents Involving Canadian Territory", dated 20 July 1961, will apply.

22. The RCAF will:

a. when requested, provide EOD assistance to the USAF Base Commanders in response to nuclear accidents or accidents occurring within leased base areas;

b. Assume control of nuclear weapons incidents or accidents occurring outside the leased base area.

23. The USAF will:

a. Maintain at each base an adequate organization for dealing with nuclear incidents or accidents which may occur within leased base areas. At Goose Bay, this organization will also be responsible for dealing with nuclear incidents or accidents which may occur outside the leased areas during delivery or removal of the warheads; however, overall control of such incidents or accidents will be exercised by the RCAF as prescribed as paragraph 22(b) above;

b. Immediately advise the RCAF and other appropriate Canadian authorities of the nature and extent of the hazard whenever a nuclear hazard exists;

c. Provide to the RCAF full details of any nuclear accident, excluding Restricted Data, together with a report of subsequent EOD actions;

d. Provide to the RCAF a copy of base disaster control plans.

U.S. NUCLEAR WEAPONS IN CANADA

CONTROL

24. Channels for United States national release of nuclear weapons will be established by CINC NORAD in accordance with directives from higher authority.

25. The release of warheads to meet operational requirements will be the subject, where practical, of prior inter-governmental consultation. They will be used, when authorized by both governments, only in accordance with procedures established by CINC NORAD. The MB-1 Agreement of June 30, 1959, as amended, shall apply to the removal of these weapons for operational reasons from the areas utilized by US forces at Harmon and Goose Bay under existing agreements between the two governments.

ATOMIC INFORMATION

26. Any US Atomic Information (Restricted Data or Formerly Restricted Data) provided to Canada under the terms of this agreement will be subject to the terms of the agreement between the Government of the United States of America and the Government of Canada for Co-operation on the Use of Atomic Energy for Mutual Defence Purposes, 22 May 1959, and associated administrative procedures.

PUBLIC INFORMATION

27. Public Information policy will be in accordance with the joint Canada-United States Publicity Directive Governing the Release of Information Relating to Joint Defence Plans and Operations dated 1 March 1951.

ANNEX C

THE ARGENTIA AGREEMENT AND ARRANGEMENT

27 July 1967, External Affairs Note No. DL-1711, to the U.S. Ambassador in Canada, W.W. Butterworth, from the Secretary of State for External Affairs, Paul Martin. Secret.

I have the honour to refer to recent discussions between representatives of the Canadian and United States Governments concerning the strengthening of North American defences through the storage of airborne nuclear anti-submarine weapons in Canada for the use of United States forces. In the discussions, particular account was taken of the recommendation by the Supreme Allied Commander, Atlantic, that such weapons should be available in Canada to United States forces which are earmarked for his operational control in the event of war.

As a result of those discussions, the Canadian Government is prepared to permit the storage of airborne nuclear anti-submarine weapons in Canada for US forces in accordance with the following conditions at a site to be agreed.

(1) Unless the content otherwise requires, "Canada" means the Government of Canada, and "United States" means the Government of the United States of America. The weapons under consideration are such airborne nuclear anti-submarine weapons as may from time to time be made available to United States forces in Canada.

(2) Ownership and custody of these weapons shall remain with the United States. United States personnel will be provided for this purpose. The status of such personnel in Canada will be governed by the provisions of the NATO Status of Forces Agreement and any supplementary arrangements which may be agreed upon. The cost of the establishment, maintenance and operation of the storage facility shall be the responsibility of the United States.

(3) The United States shall provide and be responsible for the security of the storage sites in accordance with the terms of the existing agreements.

(4) The safety procedures for storage, maintenance, transport, loading, delivery and salvage of nuclear components will be at least equivalent to U.S. standards and will be the subject of arrangements between the appropriate authorities of the United States and Canada, taking into consideration classified (atomic)

information which can be transferred under existing agreements between the two Governments.

(5) Authorization of transportation of these weapons in Canadian territory will be subject to the requirements of Canadian law. The United States will be responsible for transportation between the United States and the agreed site, including security during transit.

(6) The weapons will be released by the United States for alert loading, airborne patrol or employment, only

    (i) upon Defence Condition One or a higher state of alert as authorized by both Governments for CINC NORAD as provided in the Agreement of 17 September 1965 between the two Governments;

    (ii) in the emergency circumstances set forth in paragraph 8(e) of the agreement of 17 September 1965 between the two Governments;

    (iii) when otherwise authorized by both Governments. Authorization for the employment of the weapons will be affected by the Canadian Government under the conditions specified in (i) and (ii) above. To provide for the emergency circumstances set forth in (ii) above in which prior consultation is not practicable, it is agreed that the Prime Minister, acting on behalf of the Government of Canada, will provide to the President of the United States timely authorization for the employment of these weapons. The weapons will be employed in accordance with the United States Navy rules of interception and engagement and the United States Navy nuclear weapons employment procedures.

(7) The provisions of this agreement will be applied in such a manner as to permit the return of the weapons to the United States at any time at the request of the United States Government.

(8) The terms of this Agreement will be reviewed by the two Governments at the request of either government and after such review may be terminated by either government upon six months' notice.

(9) Supplementary arrangements between the appropriate military authorities of the two governments may be made from time to time for the purpose of carrying out the intent of this Agreement.

I have the honour to propose that if these conditions are acceptable to your Government, this Note and your reply shall constitute an agreement between our two Governments, to take effect on the date of your reply.

Accept, Excellency, the renewed assurances of my highest consideration.

ANNEX C: THE ARGENTIA AGREEMENT
AND ARRANGEMENT

27 July 1967, U.S. Department of State Note No. 32, to the Secretary of State for External Affairs, Paul Martin, from the U.S. Ambassador in Canada, W.W. Butterworth. Secret.

Sir:

I have the honor to refer to your Note No. DL-1711 of July 27, 1967, proposing on behalf of the Government of Canada the conditions under which the storage of nuclear anti-submarine weapons in Canada for the use of United States forces would be permitted.

I am pleased to inform you that the conditions set forth in your Note are acceptable to my Government. My Government further agrees that your Note and this reply shall constitute an agreement between the two Governments effective today.

Accept, Sir, the renewed assurances of my highest consideration.

(signed)

W.W. Butterworth

The Honorable

Paul Martin,

Secretary of State for External Affairs,

Ottawa.

U.S. NUCLEAR WEAPONS IN CANADA

THE ARGENTIA SERVICE-TO-SERVICE ARRANGEMENT

c. August 1967, "Canadian Forces - United States Navy Supplementary Arrangement for US Naval Forces at a Leased Base in Canada," Secret. (DND dated 18 December 1967)

FOREWORD

The governments of the United States and Canada have agreed to the storage of airborne nuclear anti-submarine warfare (ASW) weapons in Canada for the use of the United States Navy.

The location for storage in Canada of airborne nuclear ASW weapons for use of the United States Navy is specified in a US Formerly Restricted Data/Canadian ZED document (FRD/ZED). For Canadian authorities, the document is ZED Doc. No. 67/22 and is controlled by the DND ZED control office in Canadian Forces Headquarters (CFHQ). For US authorities the document is categorized as FRD and is identified as the Dept of External Affairs letter to the US Ambassador, concerning the storage of nuclear anti-submarine weapons in Canada for use by United States Forces, dated 27 July, 1967. For purposes of these supplementary arrangements site location will be hereinafter be referred to as "the Base."

In accordance with assigned responsibilities the United States Navy and the Canadian Forces have jointly prepared these supplementary arrangements to provide for implementation of the intergovernmental agreement. Contained in this document are procedures governing the transportation, import and export, custody, security, storage, maintenance, inspection, safety and salvage of the United States nuclear airborne ASW weapons at the Base while these weapons are in Canada. Procedures for control of these weapons are governed by the US/Canada Exchange of Notes of 27 July, 1967 and by the US/Canada Exchange of Notes on Authorization and Consultation, dated 17 September 1965.

(signed)
F.R. Sharp, Air Marshal
Vice Chief of the Defence Staff
(Signed)
T.H. Moorer, Admiral
U.S. Navy Chief of
Naval Operations

ANNEX C: THE ARGENTIA AGREEMENT
AND ARRANGEMENT

"Service-to-Service Arrangement Between the United States Navy and the Canadian Forces to Supplement and Provide for the Implementation of the Government-to-Government Agreement of 27 July, 1967 Concerning United States Airborne Nuclear ASW Weapons at the Base."

The Chief of Naval Operations, United States Navy and the Chief of the Defence Staff, Canadian Forces agree to the provisions contained herein.

SECTION I
GENERAL

1. PURPOSE: The purpose of this Canadian Forces/United States Navy Supplementary Arrangement, hereinafter referred to as "this agreement", is to establish and describe the procedures governing the transportation, import and export, custody, security, storage, maintenance, inspection, safety and salvage of the nuclear airborne ASW weapons at the Base, in order to provide an operational capability for United States Naval Forces in Canada while ensuring compliance with the applicable United States laws and regulations (such as the United States Atomic Energy Act of 1954, as amended) and applicable Canadian laws and regulations.

2. BACKGROUND: The United States Naval Forces with which this agreement is concerned are assigned to the United States Atlantic Fleet and are under the operational command of CINCLANTFLT. The status of these forces in other respects is governed by the terms of the relevant inter-governmental agreements.

3. AUTHORITY: This agreement implements and draws its authority from the Canada/United States agreement effected by the Exchange of Canadian Note DL-1711 and United States Note No. 32 dated 27 July, 1967.

4. POLICY: This agreement prescribes the procedures necessary for both the United States Navy and the Canadian Forces to exercise their respective responsibilities under the aforementioned Government-to-Government agreement. This agreement further establishes procedures to insure nuclear safety. The Canadian Forces and the United States Navy each assume responsibility for ensuring compliance with the terms of this agreement by their own personnel and any non-Canadian Forces non-United States Navy personnel sponsored by them, respectively.

PROCEDURES

TRANSPORTATION, IMPORT AND EXPORT

5. Nuclear weapons will be transported into, and exported from, Canada in accordance with approved procedures. Authorization of transportation of these weapons in Canadian territory will be subject to the requirements of Canadian law. The provisions of this agreement will be applied in such a manner as to permit the return of the weapons to the United States at any time.

6. The Canadian Forces will:

a. Arrange for the issue of import and export permits as required by Canadian regulations;

b. Authorize shipments of nuclear weapons into or out of Canada;

c. Arrange for the clearance through customs of each shipment of nuclear weapons;

d. Obtain any necessary waivers with respect to customs entries that would reveal Restricted Data or Formerly Restricted Data and associated classified information;

e. Prepare export entries for nuclear weapons on behalf of the Base.

7. The United States Navy will:

a. Provide for transportation when authorized of nuclear weapons into or out of the Base;

b. Keep the Canadian Forces through the US Naval Attaché at Ottawa advised of the numbers and types of weapons stored at the Base.

c. Prepare and present customs import entries for nuclear weapons at the Base and provide the Canadian Forces with information for the preparation of export entries for nuclear weapons in accordance with agreed procedures.

CUSTODY OR CUSTODIAL CONTROL

8. As used in this agreement, custody or custodial control is defined as the guardianship and safekeeping of nuclear weapons including source and special materials. This includes:

a. Accountability for warheads and classified Restricted Data or Formerly Restricted Data which remains with the United States as United States property;

b. Control of access to the nuclear weapons or material classified Restricted Data or Formerly Restricted Data in that it would take an act of force against a United States National, and therefore, against the United States Government, to obtain or use without proper authority the warheads or material classified Restricted Data or

Formerly Restricted Data and obtain information concerning them.

9. The United States Navy will exercise custodial responsibility for the nuclear weapons at the Base.

SECURITY

10. Security of all facilities within the Base is the responsibility of the United States Navy. This security responsibility will be exercised in a manner consistent with security standards prescribed in current United States Navy security directives for similar United States Navy installations.

STORAGE AND MAINTENANCE

11. Storage facilities at the Base will be of a standard satisfactory to the Canadian Forces and consistent with United States Navy criteria for similar facilities within the United States.

12. The United States Navy will:

a. Be responsible for all costs of the establishment, maintenance and operation of the storage and alert facilities and associated equipments at the Base;

b. Provide the Canadian Forces with site plans, drawings and specifications of the storage, maintenance and alert facilities;

c. Ensure that nuclear weapons storage, maintenance and handling are conducted in accordance with the United States approved Nuclear Weapons Systems Safety Rules for the specific weapons systems involved.

INSPECTIONS

13. The Canadian Forces will have the right of inspection, at agreed times, of the storage and alert areas and facilities with a view to ensuring the adequacy of security and safety arrangements and procedures. However, the Canadian Forces agree that after nuclear weapons or other United States Restricted Data or Formerly Restricted Data materials are in place this right of inspection will not be exercised in circumstances where an unauthorized release of Restricted Data or Formerly Restricted Data would result.

14. A Navy Technical Proficiency Inspection, as prescribed in applicable United States Navy regulations, must be accomplished with a satisfactory rating at the Base prior to delivery of nuclear weapons.

15. The Canadian Forces will provide representatives who will participate as observers in the initial and annual ASW nuclear weapons

inspections to the extent permitted by United States law.

16. The United States Navy will arrange for Canadian Forces participation in the Initial and annual ASW nuclear weapons inspections and provide the Canadian Forces the results of such inspections to the extent permitted by United States law.

SAFETY

17. Applicable Canadian laws and regulations and United States Approved Nuclear Weapon System Safety Rules for the specific weapons/weapons systems involved are binding at all times on United States personnel. These are intended to:
a. Prevent weapons involved in accidents or incidents, or jettisoned weapons, from producing a nuclear yield;
b. Prevent deliberate arming, firing, or launching except when authorized and directed by competent authority;
c. Prevent inadvertent arming, firing, launching, or jettisoning;
d. Ensure adequate security.

18. The Canadian Forces will provide the United States Navy with copies of applicable Canadian laws and regulations. The United States Navy will provide the Canadian Forces with copies of appropriate US Navy Weapons Systems Safety Rules.

SALVAGE AND EXPLOSIVE ORDNANCE DISPOSAL (EOD)

19. All salvage and EOD functions, including radiological monitoring and decontamination, as may be required for nuclear accidents and significant incidents occurring within the Base will be the responsibility of the United States Navy Base Commander. The Canadian Forces and other appropriate Canadian authorities will be advised immediately of the extent and nature of the hazard and of the action being taken when a nuclear hazard exists within the Base.

20. For incidents or accidents involving a possible nuclear hazard, which occur outside the Base, the provisions of the "Service-to-Service Agreement Between the United States Air Force and the Royal Canadian Air Force on the Responsibilities for Response to Nuclear Weapons Incidents Involving Canadian Territory", dated 20 July 1961, will apply.

21. The Canadian Forces will:
a. when requested, provide EOD assistance to the United States Navy Base Commander in response to nuclear accidents or accidents occurring within the Base;

b. Assume control of nuclear accidents or significant incidents outside the Base.

22. The United States Navy will:

a. Maintain an adequate organization for dealing with nuclear accidents or incidents which may occur within the Base;

b. Immediately advise the Canadian Forces and other appropriate Canadian authorities of the nature and extent of the hazard whenever a nuclear hazard exists;

c. Provide to the Canadian Forces full details of any nuclear accident, excluding Restricted Data, together with a report of subsequent EOD actions;

d. Provide to the Canadian Forces a copy of base disaster control plans.

ATOMIC INFORMATION

23. Any United States Atomic Information (Restricted Data or Formerly Restricted Data) provided to Canada under the terms of this agreement will be subject to the terms of the agreement between the Government of the United States of America and the Government of Canada for Co-operation on the Use of Atomic Energy for Mutual Defence Purposes, 22 May 1959, and associated administrative procedures.

PUBLIC INFORMATION

24. Public Information policy will be in accordance with the joint Canada-United States Publicity Directive Governing the Release of Information Relating to Joint Defence Plans and Operations dated 1 March 1951.

ANNEX D

CONSULTATION AND AUTHORIZATION FOR THE OPERATIONAL USE OF NUCLEAR WEAPONS

AUTHORIZATION FOR THE OPERATIONAL USE OF NUCLEAR WEAPONS

10 July 1964, Redraft of Proposed Canadian Note, and, U.S. State Department Letter No. 138 of 27 January 1965 from Washington, Secret, Draft.
Final version: Canadian Note 352, 17 September 1965.

Sir:

1. I have the honour to refer to the Exchange of Notes of August 16, 1963 between our two Governments; in particular to paragraph 5 of the Secretary of State for External Affairs' Note No. 125 of that date; to the Letters of understanding of the same date, concerning consultation prior to the release of nuclear warheads to, and authorization for their operational use by NORAD forces in Canada; to the Exchange of Notes of September 28 and 30, 1963; in particular to paragraph 6, of the Secretary of State for External Affairs' Note No. 162 of September 28; and to the review by officials of the two Governments of existing arrangements between our two Governments providing for certain measures which might be taken when hostilities involving North America appeared likely or possible and for various forms of consultation concerning situations which might lead to the outbreak of such hostilities.

2. The general pattern reflected in these various arrangements is that the measures envisaged require governmental authorization, which normally would be given only at the time and following inter-governmental consultation. The possibility of surprise attack is reflected by the qualification, explicit or implied, that the time factor might not always permit prior inter-governmental consultation and might in certain circumstances require some of these measures to be undertaken on the basis of prior authorization.

3. The Canadian Government wishes to propose the conclusion of a comprehensive Agreement with the United States Government, in the terms set out below, both concerning bilateral consultation

between the two Governments with regard to situations which might lead to the outbreak of hostilities involving North America, and hence might call for the release of nuclear warheads to NORAD forces, and concerning procedures relating to the authorization to CINC NORAD for operational use of nuclear weapons. The object of this agreement would be:

(a) to consolidate relevant provisions of existing agreements and to define more precisely (1) the relationship between such consultation and measures relating to North American defense which might be undertaken in a situation of rising tension or to prepare for possible war, and (2) the procedural arrangements and channels of communication applicable to such consultation;

(b) to specify the procedures for authorizing CINC NORAD to use operationally forces equipped with nuclear weapons.

CONSULTATION

4. (a) As the NORAD Agreement recognizes that the air defense of North America is single and indivisible, there is a special obligation of both Governments to maintain the closest consultation in any situation which could develop into a direct military threat to North America and consequently would lead to such precautionary steps as the raising of NORAD's state of readiness. It is agreed that in a situation of increasing international tension which could give rise to hostilities involving North America, a meeting of representatives of our two Governments will be convened, on the initiative of either Government, (1) to examine jointly that situation in both its political and military aspects, and (ii) to consider, and to coordinate as appropriate, the courses of action which the two Governments might decide to undertake in relation to that situation.

(b) In a situation involving so urgent a risk of hostilities involving North America that is not considered practicable to convene such a meeting, either Government may initiate consultations concerning that situation through the medium of telecommunications, this to be known as "emergency consultation."

(c) Rapid and reliable telecommunications facilities will be provided which will, with due regard for security, permit the simultaneous participation in such emergency consultation of the President, the Secretary of State, the Secretary of Defense, and the Chairman of the Joint Chiefs of Staff for the United States, and the Prime Minister, the Secretary of State for External Affairs, the Minister of National Defence, and the Chief of the Defence Staff for Canada, and the Commander-in-Chief, NORAD (CINC NORAD).

(d) Consultation between our two Governments in a situation of increasing international tension will be fully effective only if each has an adequate understanding of the views of the other concerning the background of that situation. Accordingly senior civilian and military representatives of our two Governments shall be prepared to meet at intervals of approximately six months to discuss situations which, in the view of either Government, might so develop as to lead in due course to a risk of hostilities involving North America. These discussions will be informal and exploratory and will not be regarded as involving or implying any commitment on the part of either Government as to the action it would take or the position it would adopt in particular circumstances not yet arisen.

PREPARATORY MEASURES

5. (a) In the course of consultation undertaken as provided in 4(a) or 4(b) above consideration shall be given to the advisability of implementing measures which might be proposed by either Government or by CINC NORAD in preparation for possible hostilities involving North America. Such measures could include:

(i) the institution by either country of military or civil alert measures on a national basis,

(ii) the increase by CINC NORAD of the state of readiness of the North American Air Defense Command,

(iii) measures by national authorities preliminary to operational use of nuclear weapons by NORAD forces,

(iv) the release by the United States Government of nuclear weapons to Canadian forces committed to NORAD, and the concurrent authorization by both Governments to CINC NORAD for the operational use of nuclear weapons.

(b) Except as provided in 5(c), 5(d), and 9 hereunder, measures of a joint nature such as those listed in 5(a), (ii) and (iv) above shall not be undertaken until they have been discussed and agreed in the course of inter-governmental consultation as provided in 4 above.

(c) If an attack on North America appears imminent or probable in a matter of hours rather than days inter-governmental consultation between CINC NORAD and the two Governments might, of necessity, coincide with or even follow certain actions of a preparatory nature such as those listed in 5(a) above. In that event, the other parties concerned will immediately be informed of the action taken, and consultation will take place as soon as possible.

(d) Where time or other factors preclude his first consulting national authorities, CINC NORAD's authority, as set out in his terms of reference, to increase the state of readiness of his forces is reaffirmed, and his authority in an emergency to authorize the use of nuclear warheads is affirmed in the manner hereinafter prescribed.

(e) In a situation in which general war appears likely or imminent, certain other preparatory measures, not relating directly to the air defence of North America but nevertheless of concern to both Governments, would probably be considered. It would be appropriate that such measures be discussed in the course of the inter-governmental consultation for which provision is made in this agreement.

PROCEDURES

6. (a) When time permits and communications and other facilities are available, the normal channel for the initiation by either Government of consultation as provided in 4(a) and (d) above shall be between the United States Department of State and the Canadian Department of External Affairs via the Canadian Embassy, Washington. procedures already established to permit rapid communication between our two Governments at any time by this channel may be used for this purpose.

(b) In addition to the channel indicated in 6(a) above, channels which may be used to propose emergency consultation as provide in 4(b) above include President-Prime Minister, Secretary of State-Secretary of State for External Affairs, Secretary of Defense-Minister of National Defence, Chairman of the Joint Chiefs of staff-Chief of the Defence Staff or between designated officials of the Department of State and of the Department of External Affairs. Such emergency consultation may be initiated at the suggestion or request of CINC NORAD and, in such circumstances, CINC NORAD should normally be invited to participate in any discussions bearing on North American defense and involving other senior military advisers of the two Governments.

(c) Each Government shall establish and maintain such internal arrangements as will permit it to participate, at any time and on short notice, in such emergency consultation. Each Government shall inform the other of the nature of those internal arrangements, to the extent that such information would facilitate the prompt and effective conduct of such emergency consultation.

(d) Arrangements will be made to provide for periodic exercises to test and practice the procedures for initiating and conducting such emergency consultation, such exercises to be held on occasion in conjunction, with appropriate military and civil defense exercises.

AUTHORIZATION FOR THE OPERATIONAL USE OF NUCLEAR WEAPONS BY NORAD FORCES

7. (a) Both Governments have placed nuclear armed Air Defense Forces under the operational control of CINC NORAD. Elements of these forces might be required to undertake Air Defense operations either in the event of a strategic attack upon North America or in connection with hostilities not involving such an attack but nevertheless involving the vital interests of either Government.

   (b) USA authorization for the release of nuclear weapons to Canadian Forces under the operational control of CINC NORAD, and Canadian and USA authorization for the use of nuclear weapons by forces under the operational control of CINC NORAD, including the cross-border deployment of nuclear armed forces and their employment in the airspace of both countries, will be effected upon declaration of Defense Condition one (strategic attack against North America is occurring) or in emergency circumstances as indicated in 8 below.

   (c) Authorization for use of nuclear weapons in connection with hostilities in the North American area but not necessarily involving a strategic attack against North America will be effected as indicated in 9 below.

STRATEGIC ATTACK AGAINST NORTH AMERICA

8. (a) In the case of a gradual build-up in international tension, the inter-governmental consultative machinery, both political and military, would be active. By this time, as international situations develop, NORAD readiness and defense conditions could be

changed to any of the defense conditions, or air defense emergency, as may be appropriate considering the seriousness of the situation.

(b) To provide for the emergency circumstances set forth in (e) below in which prior consultation is not practicable it is agreed that the President of the USA will provide for the timely release of nuclear warheads to Canadian NORAD Forces, and that the Prime Minister, acting on behalf of the Government of Canada, and the President, acting on behalf of the Government of the USA, will provide for the timely authorization to CINC NORAD to employ operationally nuclear armed forces.

(c) Nuclear weapons thus made available upon a declaration of Defense Condition one or Air Defense Emergency by CINC NORAD, either under emergency circumstances or through the consultative process covered by 4 above, will be used in accordance with the approved NORAD rules of interception and engagement (NORAD Regulation 55-6) and NORAD Nuclear Weapons Employment Procedures.

(d) Measures of a precautionary nature, the movement of forces in accordance with national preparedness procedures, and special deployment procedures applicable in areas such as Alaska where the period of warning could be very short may be undertaken as necessary in either country on the authority of the government of that country.

(e) The following circumstances referred to in this paragraph are as follows:

(i) A surprise attack in force against targets in Canada, or the USA, or both. In the absence of any advance warning that such an attack was imminent, or of any indication that large scale hostilities had started or were imminent in other theatres where USA or Canadian forces were involved, direct and unequivocal evidence that an attack in force had begun would be required. (Examples of developments which would be considered an "attack in force" would include the actual entry of substantial numbers of bombers into Canadian or USA sovereign airspace, or the detection of several missiles on trajectories originating from the USSR and terminating in North America, or a combination of several missiles and bombers penetrating the BNEWS and DEW Lines, respectively, on flight paths patently directed towards North America.)

(ii) Several nuclear bursts of unknown origin occurring in the space of a few minutes within the confines of the USA or Canada.

(iii) Reliable evidence that a large number of bombers had taken off or several ICBM's had been launched from bases in the USSR in circumstances preceded by a period of increased international tension.

(iv) A properly authenticated communication from any major NATO or USA commander clearly indicating that attacks involving the use of nuclear weapons had been launched in at least one theatre directly involving NATO or USA forces.

(v) Any circumstances in which in CINC NORAD's judgement a strategic attack against North America or an attack against Alaska, is imminent or occurring and in which delay might seriously prejudice the defense of the area involved.

GENERAL CONDITIONS

9. (a) In view of the possibility that situations might arise not involving a strategic attack against North America but nevertheless involving the vital interests of either government, each government shall, notwithstanding the other provisions of the agreement, retain for purposes of its own defense the freedom to take measures, at home or abroad, not inconsistent with the sovereignty of the other. Such measures would include the employment, under national control and not subject to any restrictions arising from this agreement, of forces otherwise under the operational control of CINC NORAD. In the event such forces are so employed, the other government concerned will be informed immediately of the action taken.

(b) In the circumstances envisaged in 9(a) above, each government shall be entitled to make use of the NORAD command and control facilities to the extent necessary for the effective employment of its forces.

10. This agreement when it comes into forces shall supersede the existing Agreements listed in Annex A.

11. This Agreement may be reviewed by the two governments at the request of either government, and after such review may be terminated upon six months notice. It may be modified or amended at any time, by agreement, upon the proposal of either government.

12 If the foregoing is acceptable to your government, I propose that this

Note and your reply thereto shall constitute an Agreement between our two governments on this matter which comes into effect on the date of your reply.

ANNEX A

I. On the date on which it comes into force the agreement to which this is annexed shall supersede the following earlier agreements concluded between the Governments of the United States of America and of Canada:

A. The agreed minute dated June 14, 1951 concerning frequent special consultations on mutual defense arrangements and related matters.

B. The Agreement relating to consultations respecting the alerting of the North American Air Defense System set out in the following four notes:
    (1) Note of May 14, 1956 from the Canadian Ambassador, Mr. ADP Heeney, to the Secretary of State, the Hon. John Foster Dulles.
    (2) Note of December 4, 1956 from the Deputy Under Secretary of State, Mr. Robert Murphy, to the Canadian Ambassador, Mr. ADP Heeney.
    (3) Note of March 1, 1957 from the Canadian Ambassador, Mr. ADP Heeney, to the Secretary of State, the Hon. John Foster Dulles.
    (4) Note of November 10, 1958 from the Deputy Under Secretary of State, Mr. Robert Murphy, to the Canadian Ambassador.

C. The so-called MB-1 Agreements relating to authorization for United States interceptor aircraft under the control of NORAD to carry nuclear air-to-air defense weapons over Canada, set out in the following exchanges of notes:
    (1) (a) Note of February 19, 1957 from the Secretary of State, the Hon. John Foster Dulles to the Canadian Ambassador, Mr. ADP Heeney.
         (b) Note No. 91 of February 19, 1957 from the Canadian Ambassador, Mr. ADP Heeney, to the Secretary of State, the Hon. John Foster Dulles.
    (2) (a) Note of June 28, 1957 from the Acting Secretary of State, Mr. Christian Herter, to the Canadian Ambassador, Mr. Norman A. Robertson
         (b) Note No. 362 of June 28, 1957 from the Canadian

Ambassador, Mr. Norman A. Robertson, to the Acting Secretary of State, Mr. Christian Herter.

(3) (a) Note of May 12, 1958 from the Acting Secretary of State, Mr. Christian Herter, to the Canadian Ambassador, Mr. Norman A. Robertson.

   (b) Note No. 262 of May 12, 1958 from the Canadian Ambassador, Mr. Herbert A. Robertson, to the Secretary of State, the Hon. John Foster Dulles.

   (c) Note of May 12, 1958 from the Canadian Ambassador, Mr. Herbert A. Robertson, to Mr. MG Parsons of the Department of State,

   (d) Letter of May 14, 1958 from Mr. MG Parsons of the Department of State, to the Canadian Ambassador, Mr. Herbert A. Robertson.

(4) (a) Note of June 20, 1959 from the from Mr. Robert Murphy, to the Canadian Ambassador, Mr. ADP Heeney.

   (b) Note No. 390 of June 30, 1959 from the Canadian Ambassador, Mr. ADP Heeney, to the Secretary of State, the Hon. Christian A. Herter, and subsequent notes on this subject up to and including the exchange of notes of June 30 and July 5, 1964 between the Canadian Ambassador, Mr. CSA Ritchie and the Secretary of State.

D. The agreements relating to increases in CINC NORAD's status of readiness, as set out in the following exchanges:

(1) (a) Letter of September 30, 1959 from the Canadian Ambassador, Mr. ADP Heeney, to the Secretary of State, the Hon. Christian A. Herter.

   (b) Letter in reply of October 2, 1959 from the Secretary of State, the Hon. Christian A. Herter, to the Canadian Ambassador, Mr. ADP Heeney.

(2) (a) Letter of June 11, 1960 from Mr. Saul F. Rae, Minister of the Canadian Embassy, to Mr. Woodbury Willoughby of the Department of State.

   (b) Letter in reply of January 14, 1951 from Mr. Woodbury Willoughby of the Department of State to Mr. Saul F. Rae, Minister of the Canadian Embassy.

II. On the date on which it comes into force, the agreement to which this is annexed shall modify the exchanges of letters of August 16,

1963 between the Secretary of State for External Affairs, the Hon. Paul Martin, and the American Ambassador, Mr. W. Walton Butterworth, relating to their exchange of notes Nos. 125 and 58 of the same date, regarding the provision of nuclear warheads for Canadian forces, as follows:

> "The reference on the first page of Mr. Martin's letter to Paragraph 5 of the exchange of notes concerning consultation which was to be understood to be in accordance with the procedures set out in the secret exchange of letters dated September 30 and October 02, 1959 and supplementary exchanges, all of which are now superseded. This reference shall now therefore be understood to refer to consultation in accordance with the procedures set out in the agreement to which this is annexed."

III. On the date on which it comes into force, the agreement to which this is annexed shall modify the agreement on the storage of nuclear air-to-air defensive weapons at Goose Bay and Harmon Air Force Base for United States forces, as set out in the exchanges of letters of September 28, 1963 (Note No. 162 from the Secretary of State for External Affairs, the Hon. Paul Martin, to the American Ambassador, Mr. W. Walton Butterworth) and September 30, 1963, (Note No. 112 from the American Ambassador, Mr. W. Walton Butterworth, to the Secretary of State for External Affairs, the Hon. Paul Martin), as follows: Paragraph 6 of Mr. Martin's Note No. 162 stated that:

> "The release of warheads to meet operational requirements will be the subject, where practicable, of prior intergovernmental consultation. They will be used, when authorized by both governments only in accordance with procedures established by CINC NORAD. The MB-1 Agreements, of June 30, 1959 and June 1, 1962, shall apply to the removal of these weapons for operational reasons from areas utilized by US forces at Harmon and Goose Bay under existing agreements between the two Governments."

This paragraph shall now be understood to read:

> "The release of warheads to meet operational requirements will

be the subject, where practicable, of prior intergovernmental consultation. They will be used, when authorized by both governments, in accordance with the provisions of the agreement to which this is annexed. They will be used, when authorized by both Governments through the consultative procedures or in the emergency circumstances set out in the agreement to which this is annexed and only in accordance with procedures established by CINC NORAD."

ANNEX E

U.S. MILITARY SITES IN CANADA DURING THE COLD WAR

The list of U.S. cold war military sites in Canada is largely derived from a declassified list produced for the Department of National Defence, DPILS office, under contract by F.J. McEvoy on 17 February 1995. Items have been added and subtracted from the list to bring it up to date and to remove unnecessary World War II sites.

Argentia, Newfoundland
naval base, reduced to partial maintenance facility 20 June 1970.

Armstrong, Ontario
Pinetree Line, to Canada 12 June 1961

Atkinson Point, Northwest Territories
DEW Line, closed 1963

Baldy Hughes Mountain, British Columbia
Pinetree Line, to Canada 12 June 1961

Barrington, Nova Scotia
Pinetree Line, to Canada 12 June 1961

Beaverlodge, Alberta
Pinetree Line, to Canada 12 June 1961

Beausejour, Manitoba
Pinetree Line, to Canada 12 June 1961

Bernard Harbour, Northwest Territories
DEW Line, closed 1963

Bray Island, Northwest Territories
DEW Line, closed 1963

Broughton Island, Northwest Territories
DEW Line, rebuilt as NWS

Burwell (n30), Newfoundland
Pinetree Line, deactivated July 1961

Byron Bay, Northwest Territories
DEW Line, closed 1993?

Cambridge Bay, Northwest Territories
DEW Line, rebuilt as NWS
Seismic Research Station (detection of nuclear blasts) 23 December 1968
- current

Cape Dyer, Northwest Territories
Cape Dyer-Thule tropospheric scatter (radar) system, 25 July 1957 - current
DEW Line, rebuilt as NWS

Cape Hooper, Northwest Territories
DEW Line, rebuilt as NWS

Cape Makkovik (N28A), Newfoundland
Pinetree Line, deactivated July 1961

Cape Perry, Northwest Territories
DEW Line, rebuilt as NWS

Cape Peel, Northwest Territories
DEW Line, closed 1963

Cartwright (N27), Newfoundland
Pinetree Line, deactivated June 1969
Chesterfield Inlet, NWT
rearward DEW Line site

Churchill, Manitoba
SAC refuelling base, 20 June 1958 - 1 July 1963
Churchill Research Range, rocket test facility, 29 August 1955 -
1 January 1966
rearward DEW Line site

Clifton Point, Northwest Territories
DEW Line, closed 1963

Clinton Point, Northwest Territories
DEW Line, closed 1993?

Cold Lake, Alberta
SAC refuelling base, 20 June 1958 - 1 September 1963

Coral Harbour, Northwest Territories
rearward DEW Line site

Cranberry Portage, Manitoba
rearward DEW Line site

Cutthroat Island (N27B), Newfoundland
Pinetree Line, deactivated July 1961

Dewar Lakes, Northwest Territories
DEW Line, rebuilt as NWS

Eskimo Point, Northwest Territories
rearward DEW Line site

Flin Flon, Manitoba
Seismic Research Station (detection of nuclear blasts) 1958 - current

Folly Island, Northwest Territories
DEW Line, rebuilt as NWS

Gander, Newfoundland
planned airfield deployment site for pre-positioned supplies and fuel

Gillam, Manitoba
rearward DEW Line site

East Melville Peninsula (Sarcpa Lake), Northwest Territories
DEW Line, closed 1963

East Simpson Peninsula (Keith Bay), Northwest Territories
DEW Line, closed 1963

Elliston Ridge (N22B), Newfoundland

Pinetree Line, deactivated July 1961

Ekalugad, Northwest Territories
DEW Line, closed 1963

Fort Chimo, Quebec
air base, transferred to Canada 1 November 1949
radio station

Fox Harbour (N26A), Newfoundland
Pinetree Line, deactivated July 1961

Frobisher Bay, Northwest Territories
air base, transferred to Canada 1 September 1950
SAC refuelling base, 20 June 1958 - 1 July 1963
USAF contingent deployed 1951 - ?
Pinetree Line, deactivated July 1961

Gander (N25) Newfoundland
Pinetree Line, to Canada 12 June 1961

Goose Bay Newfoundland
Goose Air Base, majority withdrawn 30 June 1976; final withdrawal 18
July 1991

Hall Beach, Northwest Territories
DEW Line, rebuilt as NWS main site

Hat Island, Northwest Territories
DEW Line, closed 1963

Horton River, Northwest Territories
DEW Line, closed 1963

Hopedale (N28), Newfoundland
Pinetree Line, deactivated June 1969

Jenny Lind Island, Northwest Territories
DEW Line, closed 1993?

Kamloops, British Columbia
Pinetree Line, to Canada 12 June 1961

Kay Point (Stokes Point), Yukon
DEW Line, closed 1963

King William Island, Northwest Territories
DEW Line, rebuilt as NWS

Kivitoo, Northwest Territories
DEW Line, closed 1963

Komakuk Beach, Northwest Territories
DEW Line, rebuilt as NWS

Lady Franklin Point, Northwest Territories
DEW Line, rebuilt as NWS

Lascie (N26B), Newfoundland
Pinetree Line, deactivated July 1961

Lowther, Ontario
Pinetree Line, to Canada 12 June 1961

Matheson Point, Northwest Territories
DEW Line, closed 1963

Melville (N24), Newfoundland
Pinetree Line, to Canada 1 July 1971

Mingan, Quebec
air base, transferred to Canada 1 October 1949

Moisie, Quebec
Pinetree Line, to Canada 12 June 1961

Namao, Alberta
air base, transferred to Canada 1 January 1946
SAC refuelling base, 20 June 1958 - 1 July 1964

ANNEX E: U.S. MILITARY SITES IN CANADA
DURING THE COLD WAR

Nanoose Bay, British Columbia
underwater weapons testing range, 1965-current

Nicholson Point, Northwest Territories
DEW Line, rebuilt as NWS

Padloping Island, Northwest Territories
DEW Line, closed 1963

Pagwa, Ontario
Pinetree Line, to Canada 12 June 1961

Pearce Point Harbour, Northwest Territories
DEW Line, closed 1963

Port Au Port, (N23) Newfoundland
Pinetree Line, deactivated 30 June 1971

Puntzi Mountain, British Columbia
Pinetree Line, to Canada 12 June 1961

Ramore, Ontario
Pinetree Line, to Canada 12 June 1961

Redcliff, Newfoundland
USN naval communications site, deactivated 1970

Repulse Bay, Northwest Territories
rearward DEW Line site

Resolution Island, Northwest Territories
Pole Vault South System, tropospheric scatter system, 1955 - current

Ross Point, Northwest Territories
DEW Line, closed 1963

Rowley Island, Northwest Territories
DEW Line, closed 1970

Saglek Bay (N29), Newfoundland

U.S. NUCLEAR WEAPONS IN CANADA

Pinetree Line, deactivated June 1970

St. Anthony's (N26) Newfoundland
Pinetree Line, to Canada 14 January 1971

St. John's, (Redcliff, N22) Newfoundland
Pinetree Line, deactivated July 1961

Saskatoon Mountain, British Columbia
Pinetree Line, to Canada 12 June 1961

Shepherd Bay, Northwest Territories
DEW Line, rebuilt as NWS

Shingle Point, Northwest Territories
DEW Line, rebuilt as NWS

Simpson Lake, Northwest Territories
DEW Line, closed 1963

Sioux Lookout, Ontario
Pinetree Line, to Canada 12 June 1961

Spotted Island (N27B), Newfoundland
Pinetree Line, deactivated July 1961

Stephenville, Newfoundland
Ernest Harmon AFB, closed 31 December 1966
USAF communications annex transmitter site near base, to Canada
09 May 1969

Sturt Point, Northwest Territories
DEW Line, closed 1963

Syndey, Nova Scotia
Pinetree Line, to Canada 12 June 1961

The Pas, Manitoba
air base, transferred to Canada 02 August 1945
radio range

Thicket Portage, Manitoba
rearward DEW Line site

Torbay, Newfoundland (St. John's,
Newfoundland)
USAF General Depot, withdrawn
1 July 1960

Tuktoyuktuk,   Northwest
Territories
radio station and airfield, 22 June
1973 - current
DEW Line, rebuilt as NWS

Tununuk, Northwest Territories
DEW Line, closed 1963

Quidi Vidi, Newfoundland
Fort Pepperrell, became Pepperrell
AFB June 1949. Closed 1960-61.

West Baffin Island, Northwest
Territories
DEW Line, closed 1963

West Melville Peninsula (Mackar
Inlet), Northwest Territories
DEW Line, closed 1993?

West Simpson Peninsula (Pelly
Bay), Northwest Territories
DEW Line, rebuilt as NWS

Young Point, Northwest Territories
DEW Line, closed 1993?

Endnotes

1   1 March 1957, U.S. Department
    of State despatch from M.C.
    Rewinkel at the U.S. embassy in
    Ottawa to Washington, re:
    United States Bases and
    Operating Facilities, Canada.
    Secret, Limited Distribution, No
    Outside Distribution.

2   21 March 1964, Letter to Robert
    McNamara, U.S. secretary of
    Defense, from Paul Hellyer,
    minister of National Defence, re:
    1964 White Paper. Secret.

3   6 December 1963, U.S.
    Department of State Incoming
    Telegram to the Secretary of State
    from the U.S. Embassy in
    Ottawa, re: 5 December Defence
    Debate in Ottawa. Confidential.
    The document talks about the
    need to readjust the arrangements
    for the continued use of the
    rocket facilities at Fort
    Churchill.

4   30 October 1968, Memorandum
    to P. Farley, G/PM, from J.

Leddy, EUR, State Department,
subject: Project Schooner. Secret.

5   4 May 1948, External Affairs
    memorandum for L. St. Laurent,
    secretary of state for External
    Affairs, from L.B. Pearson, under-
    secretary, re: U.S. Coloured
    Engineer Troops. DEA/11681-40.
    Secret. (Documents on Canada's
    External Relations [DCER],
    1948, p. 1631.)

6   4 May 1948, External Affairs
    Telegram No. EX-1206, to the
    Canadian Ambassador in
    Washington, from the Secretary
    of State for External Affairs, re:
    U.S. Coloured Engineer Troops.
    Secret. Important. (DCER,
    1948, p. 1632.)

7   25 August 1950, External Affairs
    memorandum for L.B. Pearson,
    under-secretary of state for
    External Affairs, from C. Eberts,
    DL(1) Division, re: U.S.
    Coloured Engineer Troops.
    DEA/11681-40. Secret. (DCER,

1950, pp. 1506-07.)

8   4 February 1969, Letter to the under-secretary of state for External Affairs, from the RCMP assistant commissioner, director, Security and Intelligence, re: CPC NATO Withdrawal Policy. Secret, By Hand. (And) 11 June 1968 Letter to the Under-Secretary of State for External Affairs, from the RCMP Assistant Commissioner, Director , Security and Intelligence, re: Voice of Women Communist infiltrated. Secret, By Hand. (Two items as examples.)

9   21 March 1969, Memo for the file, re: Protests and Demonstrations, CPC Delegation, Toronto. Special Investigation Bureau, Toronto, O Division. Code 90.

10   11 June 1968, RCMP Information Memo to File on Voice of Women - British Columbia, 7th Annual Meeting. Submitted by Inspector C.D. McArthur of Prince George, SIS Detachment, E Division.

11   24 May 1968, RCMP Information Memo to File on International Day of Protests on U.S. actions in Vietnam, 27 April 1968, Canada.Toronto Special Investigations Bureau. O Division. (Item No. 26.)

12   25 June 1969, Letter from Assistant Commissioner W.L. Higgitt, Director of Security and Intelligence, RCMP, re: Protests andDomonstrations: NORAD.

13   1 May 1968, Memo to File from theDirector, Security and Intelligence, RCMP, re: Protests and Demonstrations re: NORAD - Canada. Confidential.

14   Access to Information Request for RCMP files at the National Archives of Canada, re: Protests and Demonstrations re: NORAD, file 1027-98-A-00119.

15   8 January 1951, memorandum for the prime minister from the under-secretary of state for External Affairs, re: Consultations between Governments on the Possible Use of the Atomic Bomb. DEA/50069-C-40. Top Secret. (*DCER* 1951. pp. 1298-1329.)

16   17 June 1952, U.S. Department of State, memorandum for the file, subject: Use of British and Canadian Facilities for Atomic Weapon Strikes. Top Secret, Security Information. Four pages.

17   Ibid.

18   1 March 1957, Letter to U.S. secretary of state John F. Dulles, from A.D.P. Heeney, re: Consultation on Alert Measures. Top Secret.

19   Ibid. This was to constitute an agreement between Canada and the United States, using both this letter and the letter of 4 December 1956 from Robert Murphy, State Department. The 04/12/56 note has never been declassified.

20   1 March 1957, memorandum of conversation between Canadian embassy officials and U.S. State Department officials, re: Proposed Coordination of U.S.-Canadian Alert Arrangements. Top Secret.

21   25 March 1957, Letter to Charles Sprague, assistant secretary of Defense, from the secretary of state, re: Alert Measures. Top Secret.

22   9 May 1957, Letter to Robert Murphy, deputy undersecretary of state, from M.D. Sprague, assistant secretary of Defense, re:

Canada-USA Alert Consultations. Top Secret.

23 12 June 1957, memorandum for the president from the secretary of state, re: Canadian Proposal Regarding Consultation on Alert Measures. Top Secret.

24 Ibid.

25 10 July 1957, Department of State Telegram No. 18, from U.S. ambassador L. T. Merchant in Ottawa to Washington, re: Consultation on Alerts. Top Secret.

26 Ibid.

27 27 July 1957, memorandum of conversation between Prime Minister Diefenbaker and U.S. ambassador L.T. Merchant, re: Common Command Arrangements for Continental Air Defense. Secret. (*Foreign Relations of the United States*, 1955-57. Vol. XXVII. p. 906.)

28 29 January 1958, letter to Ambassador Norman Robertson, from C.B. Elbrick, assistant secretary of state, re: MB-1 Carriage Under State of Alert. Secret.

29 28 April 1958, Cabinet Defence Committee, Section 117,VI. Top Secret.

30 Ibid.

31 4 September 1958, Department of State Telegram No. 166, from Merchant in Ottawa to Washington, re: Alerts of NORAD forces by CINC NORAD. Top Secret.

32 Ibid..

33 13 October 1958, Memorandum from BNA, Mr. Dale, from the special assistant to the deputy undersecretary of state, re: Information for Canadians on

Nuclear Authority. Top Secret.

34 4 December 1958, letter to Ambassador A.D.P. Heeney, from Robert Murphy, deputy undersecretary of state, re: Consultations on Alerts. Top Secret.

35 29 April 1959, memorandum of conversation between Canadian embassy officials, and Department of State officials, re: Request for Canadian Concurrence to Increase Operational Readiness of NORAD Forces in Event Western Powers Are Denied Access to Berlin. Secret.

36 29 April 1959, aide-memoire from Department of State, re: CINC NORAD Direction to Increase Alert over Berlin Situation. Secret. Handed to Minister Saul Rae by Foy Kohler.

37 25 May 1959, aide-memoire from Canadian embassy, re: CINC NORAD direction to increase alert over Berlin situation. Secret.

38 18 June 1959, aide-memoire from Department of State, re: Operational Readiness of NORAD Forces During Berlin Situation. Secret. Handed to Canadian ambassador on 22 June 1959.

39 30 September 1959, letter to Secretary of State Christian Herter, from Ambassador A.D.P. Heeney, re: Consultations on NORAD Alerts During Times of International Tensions. Secret.

40 Ibid.

41 Ibid.

42 2 October 1959, letter to Ambassador Heeney from U.S. secretary of state Christian Herter, re: Increasing NORAD Operational Readiness. Secret.

43 24 October 1959, Cabinet Defence Committee, Section 127, V. Machinery for consultation with the United States. Top Secret.

44 6 November 1962, memorandum for the Canadian ambassador, from Rob Cameron, re: Agreements relating to Canada-United States consultations. Top Secret.

45 Ibid.

46 Ibid.

47 Ibid.

48 2 May 1963, 17:15, memorandum for the record, Subject: Meeting with the President on Canada. Top Secret.

49 8 January 1964, letter to Air Chief Marshal F.R. Miller, from Ross Campbell,assistant under-secretary of state for External Affairs, re: Draft Paper on Authorization for Use of Nuclear Weapons. 27-11-CDA/USA. Secret.

50 3 March 1965, draft memorandum to the Cabinet from the secretary of state for External Affairs, re: Authorization for the Use of Nuclear Weapons. Secret.

51 8 January 1964, memorandum to the prime minister from Paul Martin, secretary of state for External Affairs, re: Authorization for the Operational Use of Nuclear Weapons. Secret.

52 11 March 1964, memorandum for Bundy, National Security Council, from Smith, re: Release of Nuclear Weapons to Canada. Confidential.

53 Ibid.

54 14 March 1964, letter to Prime Minister Pearson from President Lyndon Johnson, re: Procedures for Control of NORAD Units. Top Secret.

55 Ibid.

56 13 March 1964, memorandum for the president from W.Y. Smith, National Security Council, re: Release of Nuclear Weapons to Canada. Top Secret.

57 Ibid.

58 16 March 1964, Paul Hellyer's interim instruction on authorization for the use of NORAD nuclear weapons.

59 4 May 1964, External Affairs memorandum to Ross Campbell from Kirkwood, DL(1) Division, re: Authorization for the Use of Nuclear Weapons. 27-1-1/USA-3. Secret.

60 4 May 1964, draft note from the Canadian ambassador to the U.S. secretary of state, re: Authorization for the Use of NORAD Nuclear Weapons. Secret.

61 Ibid.

62 Ibid.

63 8 May 1964, telex to Canadian embassy in Washington, from External Affairs, re: Authorization and consultation. Secret.

64 11 May 1964, External Affairs memorandum to Legal Division from Kirkwood, DL(1) Division, re: Authorization for the Operational Use of nuclear Weapons. 27-1-1/USA-3. Secret.

65 22 May 1964, message No. 1847 from Canadian embassy in Washington to External Affairs, re: Authorization and Consultation. 27-1-1-USA-3. Secret.

66 Ibid.

67 13 May 1964, telex from Ross Campbell in the Hague to Kirkwood in DL(1) Division, re: Meeting in Washington. Confidential.

68 14 May 1964, External Affairs
outgoing message from Kirkwood
in Ottawa to Ross Campbell at
Canadian embassy in Bonn. Re:
Draft agreement on Consultation
and Authorization. Confidential.

69 13 May 1964, telex from Ross
Campbell in the Hague to
Kirkwood in DL(1) Division, re:
Meeting in Washington.
Confidential.

70 28 May 1964, External Affairs
memorandum to Ross Campbell
from Kirkwood in DL(1) Division,
re: Authorization and
Consultation. 27-1-1/USA, and 3-
2-2-11-2. Secret.

71 Ibid.
72 Ibid.
73 Ibid.
74 Ibid.
75 Ibid.

76 2 June 1964, memo to Ross
Campbell from A.R. Menzies,
DL(1) Division, re: Authorization
and consultation – CINC
NORAD's authority to declare
DefCon 1. 27-1-1/USA-3. Secret.

77 Ibid.
78 Ibid.

79 3 June 1964, letter to CDS, Air
Chief Marshal Miller from Ross
Campbell, re: Authorization and
Consultation, 27-1-1-USA-3.
Secret.

80 Ibid.
81 Ibid.
82 Ibid.
83 Ibid.
84 Ibid.
85 Ibid.
86 Ibid.

87 11 June 1964, External Affairs
outgoing message to Ottawa from
Canadian embassy in Washington,

re: Authorization and
Consultation, 3-2-2-11-2. Secret.

88 11 June 1964, External Affairs
Outgoing Message DL1278, to
Canadian embassy in Washington
from Ottawa, re: Authorization and
Consultation, 3-2-2-11-2. Secret.

89 Ibid.

90 17 June 1964, memorandum for
the minister (Paul Martin), re:
Consultation Concerning and
Authorization for the Use of
Nuclear Weapons – Proposed
Agreement with the United States.
("Seen by the Minister"), 27-1-
1/USA-3. Secret.

91 17 June 1964, memorandum to
the Cabinet Committee on
External Affairs and Defence
from Paul Martin, re:
Consultation Concerning and
Authorization for the Use of
Nuclear Weapons, Proposed
Agreement with the United
States, 27-1-1/USA-3. Secret.

92 17 June 1964, Memorandum to
the Cabinet Committee on
External Affairs and Defence
from Paul Martin, re:
Consultation Concerning and
Authorization for the Use of
Nuclear Weapons, Proposed
Agreement with the United
States, 27-1-1/USA-3. Secret.

93 18 June 1964, memorandum to
the under-secretary from
Kirkwood in DL(1) Division, re:
Consultation Concerning and
Authorization for the Use of
Nuclear Weapons. 27-1-1/USA-
3. Secret.

94 18 June 1964, External Affairs
outgoing message No. 2213, to
Ottawa from R.P. Cameron at
Canadian embassy in Washington,

re: Authorization and Consultation, 3-2-2-11-2. Secret.

95 18 June 1964, External Affairs outgoing message No. 2214, to Ottawa from R.P. Cameron at Canadian embassy in Washington, re: Authorization and Consultation, 3-2-2-11-2. Secret.

96 22 June 1964, memorandum for the minister (secretary of state for External Affairs), from the DM, re: Consultation Concerning and Authorization for the Use of Nuclear Weapons, 27-1-1-USA-3. Secret.

97 Ibid.

98 Ibid.

99 Ibid.

100 24 June 1964, memorandum to the secretary of state, U.S. Department of State, from W.R. Tyler, European Office, re: Your Participation in the Canada-U.S. Ministerial Committee on Joint Defense, June 25: Information Memorandum. Secret.

101 July 1964, U.S. Department of State, Summary Record of Meeting, Canada-United States Ministerial Committee on Joint Defense, Washington, 25 June 1964. Top Secret. The parts of the document dealing with consultation and authorization are missing, and the deletions are under appeal through Freedom of Information Act in Washington.

102 30 June 1964, External Affairs outgoing message No. 2353, from Canadian embassy in Washington, to Ottawa, re Authorization and Consultation, 3-2-2-11-2, Secret.

103 30 June 1964, External Affairs outgoing message No. 2354, from

Canadian embassy in Washington, to Ottawa, re: Authorization and Consultation, 3-2-2-11-2, Secret.

104 1 July 1964, External Affairs outgoing message No. 2672, from Canadian embassy in Washington, to Ottawa, re: Authorization and Consultation, 3-2-2-11-2, Secret.

105 3 July 1964, letter to Air Chief Marshal R.F. Miller, from Ross Campbell, under-secretary of state for External Affairs, re: Authorization and Consultation on Use of Nuclear Weapons. 27-1-1/USA-3. Secret.

106 03 July 1964, External Affairs telex DL1390, from Ottawa to Canadian embassy in Washington, re: Authorization and Consultation, 3-2-2-11-2, Secret.

107 3 July 1964, External Affairs telex DL1392, from Ottawa to Canadian embassy in Washington, re: Authorization and Consultation, 3-2-2-11-2, Secret.

108 15 July 1964, Canadian minutes of 10 July 1964 discussions in Washington, Subject: Authorization and Consultation. Secret.

109 Ibid.

110 Ibid.

111 Ibid.

112 Ibid.

113 Ibid.

114 Ibid.

115 Ibid.

116 5 August 1964, letter to A.R. Menzies, Head DL(1) Division, External Affairs, Ottawa, from R.P. Cameron, Canadian embassy in Washington, re: Consultation and Authorization, 3-2-2-11-2. Secret.

117 28 August 1964, letter to A.R. Menzies, Head DL(1) Division,

External Affairs, Ottawa, from R.P. Cameron, Canadian embassy in Washington, re: Consultation and Authorization, 27-1-1/USA-3. Secret.

118 Ibid.

119 15 September 1964, briefing for prime minister, Columbia River Ceremonies, 16 September 1964, re: Authorization for Use of Nuclear Air Defence Weapons by NORAD Forces. 27-1-1/USA-3. Secret.

120 14 January 1965, memorandum for the president from the secretary of state, subject: Visit of Canadian Prime Minister Pearson. Secret.

121 25 January 1965, External Affairs outgoing message No. 242, from R.P. Cameron, Canadian embassy in Washington, to Ottawa, re: Authorization and Consultation. 3-2-2-11-2. Secret.

122 Ibid.

123 26 January 1965, letter to L. Cardin, acting minister of National Defence, from Paul Martin, secretary of state for External Affairs, re: Consultation and Authorization. 27-1-1-USA-3. Secret.

124 10 February 1965, letter to Air Chief Marshal R.F. Miller, chairman, Chiefs of Staff, from M. Cadieux, External Affairs, re: Consultation Concerning and Authorization for the Use of Nuclear Weapons by NORAD. 27-1-1/USA-3. Secret.

125 26 February 1965, letter to M. Cadieux, under-secretary of state for External Affairs, from Air Chief Marshal R.F. Miller, chairman, Chiefs of Staff, re:

Consultation Concerning and Authorization for the Use of Nuclear Weapons by NORAD. S3310-1 (DCPlans), Secret.

126 2 March 1965, External Affairs Telex No. DL426, to Canadian embassy in Washington, from Ottawa, re: Authorization and Consultation, 3-2-2-11-2. Secret.

127 5 March 1965, External Affairs outgoing message No. 275, to Ottawa, from R.P. Cameron at Canadian embassy in Washington, re: Authorization and Consultation. 3-2-2-11-2. Secret.

128 5 March 1965, memorandum for the minister (secretary of state for External Affairs), from the DM, re: Authorization for the Use of Nuclear Weapons in NORAD. 27-1-1/USA-3. Secret.

129 18 March 1965, memorandum to Cabinet, Cabinet Decision re: Authorization for the use of nuclear weapons by NORAD forces. 27-1-1/USA-3. Secret.

130 19 March 1965, memorandum for the minister (secretary of state for External Affairs) from H.B. Robinson, re: Authorization for the Use of Nuclear Weapons by NORAD forces. 27-1-1/USA-3. Secret.

131 3 March 1965, draft memorandum to the Cabinet from the secretary of state for External Affairs, re: Authorization for the Use of Nuclear Weapons. Secret.

132 Ibid.

133 5 March 1965, memorandum to Cabinet from the secretary of state for External Affairs and MND, Authorization for the Use of Nuclear Weapons by NORAD Forces. Secret.

134 3 March 1965, draft memorandum to the Cabinet from the secretary of state for External Affairs, re: Authorization for the Use of Nuclear Weapons. Secret.

135 Ibid.

136 23 March 1965, Cabinet Meeting Minutes, No. 22-65, Item: Authorization for Use of Nuclear Weapons by NORAD forces. Secret.

137 29 March 1965, record of Cabinet decision, meeting of 23 March 1965, Authorization for the Use of Nuclear Weapons by NORAD forces. 27-1-1/USA-3. Confidential.

138 19 March 1965, External Affairs telex No. DL-576 to Canadian embassy in Washington, from Ottawa, re: Authorization and Consultation "Points of clarification," 27-1-1/USA-3. Secret.

139 19 March 1965, External Affairs telex No. 885 to Ottawa, from Canadian embassy in Washington, re: Authorization and Consultation, 27-1-1/USA-3. Secret.

140 17 September 1965, memo for McGeorge Bundy, National Security Council, from R.C. Bowman, re: Consultation Agreement. Secret.

141 9 March 1965, memorandum for the minister (secretary of state for External Affairs) from the DM , re: authorization for the use of nuclear weapons by NORAD forces. 27-1-1/USA-3. Secret.

142 26 March 1965, External Affairs telex No. DL-605 to Canadian embassy in Washington, from Secretary of State for External Affairs Martin in Ottawa, re: Authorization and Consultation, 27-1-1/USA-3. Secret.

143 22 March 1965, External Affairs emergency telex No. 900 to Ottawa from R.P. Cameron at Canadian embassy in Washington, re: Authorization and consultation. 27-1-1-USA-3, and 3-2-2-11-2. Secret No Distribution.

144 23 March 1965, memorandum for the minister (secretary of state for External Affairs), from DM, re: Authorization for the Use of Nuclear Weapons by NORAD forces. 27-1-1/USA-3. Secret.

145 Ibid.

146 11 July 1966, memo for the secretary of state for External Affairs, re: U.S. Requirement for Storage of Nuclear Anti-submarine Warfare Weapons at Argentia. Secret.

147 30 March 1965, letter to Basil Robinson, under-secretary of state for External Affairs, from Air Chief Marshal R.F. Miller, chairman Chiefs of Staff, re: Authorization for the Use of Nuclear Weapons by Canadian Forces in Europe. S3310-3 (DCPlans) Secret.

148 Ibid.

149 3 June 1965, letter to J.T. McNaughton, assistant secretary of Defense for International Security Affairs, from Llewellyn Thompson, Department of State, re: Consultation and Authorization Agreement with Canada. Top Secret.

150 (Draft date 27 May 1965) memorandum for McGeorge Bundy, National Security Council, Subject: Nuclear Air Defense Weapons, Release to and

Employment by Canadian NORAD Forces. Top Secret.

151 (Ibid.

152 Ibid.

153 (Draft date 27 May 1965. Dated as having been signed on 17 September 1965) Authorization for the employment of air defense nuclear weapons by United States and Canadian NORAD Forces under the operational control of CINC NORAD. Top Secret. (Entire text) Attached to memorandum for McGeorge Bundy, National Security Council, Subject: Nuclear Air Defense Weapons, Release to and Employment by Canadian NORAD Forces. Top Secret.

154 27 July 1967, memo for Prime Minister Pearson from secretary of state for External Affairs, re: Agreement on Anti-submarine Warfare Nuclear Weapons at Argentia. Top Secret.

155 McMullen, ADC Historical Study No. 14, *History of Air Defense Weapons, 1946-1962.* Historical Division, Office of Information, HQ Air Defense Command. Top Secret, Restricted Data.

156 Ibid.

157 Technical information on the W25 warhead, unless otherwise noted, comes from the following sources: W. Arkin, et al., *US Nuclear Weapons Databook.* p. 41; J. Gibson, *The History of the US Nuclear Arsenal,* p. 78; C. Hansen, *US Nuclear Weapons,* p. 176-178; and C. Hansen, *Swords or Armageddon.*

158 McMullen, ADC Historical Study No. 14, *History of Air Defense Weapons, 1946-1962.* .

159 27 November 1950, Memorandum to the Cabinet Defence Committee from the MND on U.S. Air Operations over CanadianTerritory. Cabinet Document D264. Secret.

160 1 December 1950, Cabinet Defence Committee Minutes, "United States Air Operations over Canadian Territory," Section 68, Subsection III. Top Secret.

161 Ibid.

162 11 September 1951, Memo to Col. Sherrard, ADODO/CONAD from Col. C.W. McColpin, ADOOT-B/CONAD, subject: Interceptor by USAF-RCAF. CONAD Historical File 720. Secret.

163 Ibid.

164 19 December 1956. Cabinet Defence Committee Minutes, "Canada-United States Agreement on Overflights," Section 112, Subsection I. Top Secret.

165 Ibid.

166 Ibid.

167 8 January 1957, Memorandum for the files, of a meeting of Canadian embassy staff and State Department staff, subject: Canadian Revisions to Draft Note on Use of Air-to-air Nuclear Weapons over Canadian Territory by the United States Air Force. Secret.

168 Ibid.

169 A/V/M M.M. Hendrick, daily diary, Washington, D.C., Monday, 27 October 1958. Top Secret.

170 8 January 1957, Memorandum for the files, of a meeting of Canadian embassy staff and State Department staff, subject: Canadian Revisions to Draft

Note on Use of Air-to-air Nuclear Weapons over Canadian Territory by the United States Air Force. Secret.

171 21 August 1957, letter to Marcelis Parsons, director, Office of British Commonwealth and Northern European Affairs, U.S. State Department, from Livingston Merchant, U.S. ambassador to Canada. Top Secret, Official-Informal.

172 A/V/M M.M. Hendrick, daily diary, interview with General Loper, Washington, D.C., Monday, 27 October 1958. Top Secret.

173 19 February 1957, Canada - United States "Agreement on Carrying Air-to-Air Nuclear Rockets on U.S. Fighters in Canadian Air Space," signed by Ambassador A.D.P. Henney and U.S. secretary of state J.F. Dulles.

174 Ibid.

175 12 December 1957, Memorandum of conversation between Canadian embassy staff, U.S. State Department staff, and U.S. Department of Defense staff, subject: Incorporation of Nuclear Weapons in United States-Canadian Defense Arrangements. 742.5/12-1257. Top Secret. 12 December 1957, to External Affairs from Canadian embassy in Washington, re: U.S. Proposals re Closer Integration of Atomic Capabilities in Defence of North America. Top Secret/Canadian Eyes Only.

176 A/V/M M.M. Hendrick, daily diary, Washington, D.C., Monday, 27 October 1958. Top Secret.

177 31 October 1957. U.S. State Department, Memo, to EUR Elbrick, from BNA, Parsons, re: Closer Integration of Atomic Capabilities in Defense of the North American Continent. Top Secret.

178 16 April 1959, Aide -memoire, United States Requirements for Storage Facilities in Canada for Nuclear Weapons. Canada, DJCP/DJP2. Secret.

179 27 June 1959, Cabinet Defence Committee Minutes, "Agreement with the United States on Carriage of Atomic Weapons over Canada by Interceptor Aircraft," Section 124, Subsection I, Top Secret.

180 Ibid.

181 Ibid.

182 Ibid.

183 Ibid.

184 30 June 1959, Canada-United States "Agreement on Carrying Air-to-Air Nuclear Rockets on U.S. Fighters in Canadian Air Space," signed by Ambassador A.D.P. Henney and R. Murphy for the U.S. secretary of state. Canadian note No. 390. Top Secret

185 28 May 1964, External Affairs memorandum to Ross Campbell from Kirkwood in DL(1) Division, re: Authorization and Consultation. 27-1-1/USA, and 3-2-2-11-2. Secret.

186 14 January 1965, memorandum for the president from the secretary of state, subject: Visit of Canadian Prime Minister Pearson. Secret.

187 25 January 1965, External Affairs outgoing message No. 242, from R.P. Cameron, Canadian embassy in Washington, to Ottawa, re:

Authorization and Consultation. 3-2-2-11-2. Secret.

188 26 January 1965, Letter to L. Cardin, acting MND, from Paul Martin, secretary of state for External Affairs, re: Authorization and Consultation and the MB-1 Agreement. 27-1-1-USA-3. Secret.

189 26 February 1965, letter to M. Cadieux, under-secretary of state for External Affairs, from Air Chief Marshal R.F. Miller, chairman, Chiefs of Staff, re: Consultation Concerning and Authorization for the Use of Nuclear Weapons by NORAD. S3310-1 (DCPlans), Secret.

190 23 March 1965, Memorandum for the minister (secretary of state for External Affairs), from DM, re: Authorization for the Use of Nuclear Weapons by NORAD Forces. 27-1-1/USA-3. Secret.

191 26 March 1965, External Affairs telex No. DL-605 to Canadian embassy in Washington, from secretary of state for External Affairs Martin in Ottawa, re: Authorization and Consultation, 27-1-1/USA-3. Secret

192 27 June 1962, Memorandum for Mitchell Sharpe, secretary of state for External Affairs, from H.B. Robinson, re: MB-1 Agreement. Top Secret.

193 Office of the Historian (SAC), *The Development of Strategic Air Command 1946-1986.* Offutt AFB, Nebraska, 1986.

194 Ibid. Office of the Historian (SAC), *Alert Operations and the Strategic Air Command, 1957-1991.* Offutt AFB, Nebraska, 1991.

195 14 June 1951, Agreed Minute on

Procedures for Handling U.S. Atomic Requests. Top Secret. 6 August 1951, to Mr. Arneson, special assistant to the U.S. secretary of state, from W.D. Matthews, chargé d'affaires, Canadian embassy in Washington, re: WISER letter No. 11. Procedures for Handling U.S. Atomic Requests. Top Secret.

196 6 August 1951, to Mr. Arneson, , re: WISER Letter No. 11.

197 29 June 1951, to U.S. ambassador to Canada, from A.D.P. Heeney, under-secretary of state for External Affairs, re: WISER letter No. 4. Methods of Handling U.S. Atomic Requests. Top Secret.

198 8 November 1951, to L.B. Pearson, secretary of state for External Affairs, from H.H. Wrong, ambassador in Washington, re: WISER letter No. 14. Procedures for U.S. Requests - Distinction Between Flights of Political Significance andOthers. Top Secret.

199 Ibid.

200 Office of the Historian (SAC), *The Development of Strategic Air Command 1946-1986; Alert Operations and the Strategic Air Command, 1957-1991.*

201 15 November 1951, to H.H. Wrong, ambassador in Washington, from L.B. Pearson, secretary of state for External Affairs, re: WISER letter No. 15. Procedures for Handling Urgent U.S. Requests- Distinction Between Flights of Political Significance and Others. Top Secret.

202 17 November 1951, to L.B.

Pearson, secretary of state for External Affairs, from H.H. Wrong, ambassador in Washington, re: WISER letter No. 16. Procedures for Handling U.S.Requests. Top Secret.

203 15 November 1951, to H.H. Wrong, , from L.B. Pearson, re: WISER Letter No. 15. Procedures for Handling Urgent U.S. Requests.

204 20 September 1954, Cabinet Defence Committee, Document No. 14-54, Movement of Service Aircraft Across the Canada - United States Border, Strategic Air Command Training Flights. Secret.

205 20 September 1954, Cabinet Defence Committee, Document No. 14-54,. Appendix "B." Secret.

206 12 November 1954, Cabinet Defence Committee, Movement of Service Aircraft Across the Canada - United States Border, Strategic Air Command Training Flights. Section 101, V. Top Secret.

207 Office of the Historian (SAC), *The Development of Strategic Air Command 1946-1986*, pp. 48-49.

208 SAC Historical Study No. 87, History of the Canadian Refueling Base Program. Secret. p. 4. This was called a Yo-Yo tactic.

209 SAC Historical Study No. 87, History of the Canadian Refueling Base Program. Secret. p. 2.

210 18 March 1955, Memorandum of conversation between Secretary of State John F. Dulles, and Secretary of State for External Affairs Lester B. Pearson, re: Continental Defense. Secret.

211 13 June 1956, Cabinet Defence Committee Minutes, "United States Air Force Request for

Preliminary Surveys for Strategic Air Command Tanker Bases in Northern Canada," Section 110, para 14. Top Secret.

212 SAC Historical Study No. 87, History of the Canadian Refueling Base Program. Secret. p. 5.

213 13 June 1956, Cabinet Defence Committee Minutes, "United States Air Force Request for Preliminary Surveys for Strategic Air Command Tanker Bases in Northern Canada." .

214 6 February 1957, Cabinet Defence Committee Minutes, "U.S. Air Force Request for Tanker Base Facilities in Canada," Section 113, paras 3-6. Top Secret.

215 16 July 1956, to Special Assistant to the Secretary of State, from Colonel Easley, USAF HQ, Deputy Director of the Directorate of Operations, re: List of USAF Officers Authorized to Contact State Regarding Overflight Clearance for Canadian Territory. Top Secret

216 2 November 1960, Memo to the under-secretary of state for External Affairs, deputy under-secretary of state for External Affairs, assistant under-secretary of state for External Affairs, and senior duty officers, from Bill Barton of DL(1) Division, re: Action in Event of "Special Message" from Washington. 50195-40. Restricted.

217 Office of the Historian (SAC), *The Development of Strategic Air Command 1946-1986, Alert Operations and the Strategic Air Command, 1957-1991.*

218 03 October 1956, Memorandum for the files by Philip Farley,

deputy to the special assistant to the secretary of state, Subject: SAC Overflight of Canada. S/AE 433/1A. Top Secret.

219 08 November 1956, Memorandum for the files by Philip Farley, deputy to the special assistant to the secretary of state, subject: Canadian XYZ Procedures — Operations Roadblock and Pinegrove. S/AE 467/1A. Top Secret.

220 19/23 November 1956, Memorandum for the files by Gerard Smith, special assistant to the secretary of state, and Philip Farley, deputy, Subject: Canada - Overflight. S/AE-478/1A. Top Secret.

221 19 December 1956, Cabinet Defence Committee Minutes, Establishment of a Bombing Range in James Bay for Use by the U.S.A.F. Strategic Air Command. Section 112, III. Top Secret.

222 1 March 1957, Memorandum for the files by Philip Farley, deputy to the special assistant to the secretary of state, Subject: Canadian Overflight. S/AE 608/1A. Top Secret.

223 8 November 1956, Memorandum for the files by Philip Farley, deputy to the special assistant to the secretary of state, subject: Canadian XYZ Procedures — Operations Roadblock and Pinegrove. S/AE 467/1A. Top Secret.

224 28 May 1957, Memorandum for the files by Philip Farley, deputy to the special assistant to the secretary of state, Subject: NN Canada - Operational Requests. S/AE 777/1A. Top Secret. 27 July

1957, Memorandum for the files by Philip Farley, deputy to the special assistant to the secretary of state, Subject: NN Canadian Operational Requests. Top Secret.

225 SAC Historical Study No. 87, History of the Canadian Refueling Base Program. Secret. p. 14.

226 26 May 1958, Cabinet Defence Committee Minutes, "U.S.A.F. Requirements for Refuelling Facilities in Canada," Section 118, paras 1-4. Top Secret.

227 Ibid.

228 23 October 1957, to Mr. Murphy, deputy under-secretary of state, from John Irwin, assistant secretary of Defense for International Security Affairs, re: Closer Integration of Atomic Capabilities and Methods of Clearing Flights over Canada. SecDef Cont. No. TS-1356. Top Secret.

229 26 November 1957, Memorandum for the files by Raymond Courtney, Office of the Special Assistant for Atomic Energy Affairs, Subject: SAC Canadian Overflight Requests. S/AE 1165/1A. Top Secret.

230 26 November 1957, Memorandum for the files by R.F. Courtney, Office of the Deputy to the Special Assistant for Atomic Energy Affairs, Subject: SAC Canadian Overflight Requests. S/AE 1165/1A. Top Secret.

231 Office of the Historian (SAC), *The Development of Strategic Air Command 1946-1986, Alert Operations and the Strategic Air Command, 1957-1991.*

232 13 September 1958, Memorandum for the files by Philip Farley, deputy to the

special assistant to the secretary of state, Subject: Strategic Air Command Exercise "Headstart." S/AE 2584/1A. Top Secret.

233 11 September 1958, to Raymond Courtney, Office of the Special Assistant for Atomic Energy Affairs, from Saul Rae, minister, Canadian embassy in Washington, re: SAC Overflights of Canadian Territory. S/AE 2575/1A. Top Secret.

234 5 February 1959, Letter to Ambassador A.D.P. Heeney, from Robert Murphy, deputy under-secretary of state, re: SAC Overflights of Canada for March-June 1959. Plus Enclosure. S/AE 2801/3A. Top Secret.

235 4 February 1959, to Foy Kohler (EUR), deputy under-secretary of state for European Affairs, from W. Willoughby (BNA), subject: Request for Canadian Approval Under "XYZ Procedures" of SAC Exercise "Airborne Alert." Top Secret.

236 2 March 1959, to acting secretary of state from L. Merchant (EUR), subject: Canadian Attitudes Toward U.S. Politico-Military Policy. Top Secret (and) 13 February 1959, Memorandum of conversation between Willoughby, Courtney and Parker from State Department, and Saul Rae and Jim Nutt from the Canadian embassy, subject: Request for Canadian Clearance of SAC Exercise "Airborne Alert" under the "XYZ Procedures." Top Secret.

237 13 February 1959, Memorandum of Conversation, subject: Request for Canadian Clearance of SAC Exercise "Airborne Alert" under the "XYZ Procedures."

238 07 March 1959, Memorandum of conversation between Mr. L. Merchant and the Canadian ambassador, subject: Permission for SAC Overflights. Top Secret.

239 22 March 1959, Memorandum of conversation at Camp David between the acting secretary and the British foreign minister, done by G.F. Reinhardt, subject: Canadians. Top Secret, Limited Distribution.

240 6 March 1959, Note to the acting secretary of state from A.D.P. Henney, Canadian ambassador in Washington, re: Overflights of Canada by SAC on Exercise "Airborne Alert." Top Secret.

241 9 March 1959, Memorandum of conversation between the acting secretary of state, the Canadian ambassador, Saul Rae, and L.T. Merchant, subject: SAC Overflights." Top Secret.

242 3 April 1959, Letter to the ambassador of Canada from the acting secretary of state, re: Publicity of Overflights of Canada. Top Secret.

243 17 March 1959, to Mr. Livingston Merchant (EUR), deputy -under secretary of state for European Affairs, from W. Willoughby (BNA), subject: Proposed Revision of XYZ Procedures Governing Nuclear Overflights of Canada in Other Than Interception Missions. S/AE 5134/1A. Top Secret.

244 18 June 1959, Letter to the ambassador of Canada from the acting secretary of state, re: SAC Airborne Alert Training Exercises in Canada in 1959. S/AE 2980/3A. Top Secret.

245 1 July 1959, Memorandum to the secretary of state from Philip Farley, special assistant to the secretary, subject: USAF Airborne Alert Training Exercises Involving Overflight of Canada. S/AE 2993/1A. Top Secret.

246 9 July 1959, Note No. 415 to the secretary of state from A.D.P. Heeney, Canadian ambassador in Washington, re: SAC Airborne Alert Overflights of Canada up to 31 October 1959. Top Secret.

247 8 January 1964, Memorandum to R.S. McNamara, the secretary of Defense and W.J. Howard, assistant to the secretary of Defense for Atomic Energy, from Major General C.V. Clifton, Defense Liaison Officer, White House. Top Secret.

248 23 September 1959, to Secretary of State Herter from Deputy Secretary of Defence Gates, re: Overflights of Canada during "Steel Trap" Exercises. Secret.

249 5 October 1959, Note to A.D.P. Heeney, Canadian ambassador in Washington, from C. Herter, secretary of state, re: SAC Airborne Alert Overflights of Canada 1 November through 31 December 1959. Top Secret.

250 25 September 1959, to Mr. Winship (EUR) from H.T. Skofield, Executive Office of the Secretary of State, re: SAC Steel Trap Indoctrination Exercise. S/S 8278. Secret. 15 October 1959, Memorandum for the under-secretary for Political Affairs from Sullivan, special assistant to the secretary of state, subject: Canadian Overflight Clearance for SAC Indoctrination Exercises Through December 31, 1959. Top Secret. 22 October 1959 Letter to Deputy Secretary of Defence Gates from Under-Secretary of State for Political Affairs Murphy, re: Canadian Overflight Clearance for SAC Indoctrination Exercises Through December 31, 1959. S/AE 3081/3A. Top Secret.

251 Office of the Historian (SAC), *The Development of Strategic Air Command 1946-1986 -*, *Alert Operations and the Strategic Air Command, 1957-1991*.

252 27 June 1959, Cabinet Defence Committee Minutes, Section No. 124, II. Revisions of Arangements with the United States on the Clearance of Overflights of Aircraft, Other Than Interceptors, with Nuclear Weapons. Top Secret.

253 10 July 1959, Aide-memoire to the State Department from A.D.P. Heeney, Canadian ambassador in Washington, re: Amendment of PC 2307. Top Secret.

254 8 July 1960, Aide-memoire to the State Department from the Canadian ambassador in Washington, re: Amendment of PC 2307. Top Secret.

255 18 January 1962, Exercise brief "Spring Thaw," Strategic Air Command, Secret.

256 4 March 1960, U.S. Department of State note, re: Logistical flights of aircraft carrying nuclear weapons through Harmon or Goose Bay during March 1960. Secret.

257 7 March 1960, Canadian Note No. 143, re: Logistical Flights. Top Secret.

258 23 March 1960, 3 October 1960, and 9 December 1960,

Memorandum to the Minister (secretary of state for External Affairs), re SAC Overflights. 50195-40. Top Secret.

259 6 December 1960, Memorandum for the Minister (secretary of state for External Affairs) from Norman Robertson, re: Low-level Flight Corridor in Canada for SAC. 50195-40. Secret.

260 21 September 1960, Memorandum for the file by F.M. Tovell, DL(1) Division, re: SAC Emergency War Plan - Operation Skip Out. 50195-40. Top Secret.

261 Office of the Historian (SAC), *The Development of Strategic Air Command 1946-1986, Alert Operations and the Strategic Air Command, 1957-1991.*

262 15 December 1961, Note No. 894 from A.D.P. Heeney to the secretary of state, re: SAC Overflights of Canada, 01 January - 31 March 1962. Top Secret.

263 3 January 1962, Letter to A.D.P. Heeney, Canadian ambassador in Washington, from W.R. Tyler, A/Assistant Secretary for European Affairs, re: SAC Overflights of Canada 1 January through 31 March 1962, Top Secret.

264 4 January 1962, Memorandum to G.C. McGhee, under-secretary for Political Affairs, from H. Burgess, European Affairs, subject: Proposed Reply to Deputy Secretary of Defence Gilpatric's Letter to the Secretary of State Regarding SAC Overflights. Secret. 4 January 1962, Note to A.D.P. Heeney from the Secretary of State, re: Change in Routes for SAC Overflights of Canada. Top Secret. 15 January 1962, Letter to

R. Gilpatric, Deputy Secretary of Defense, from G.C. McGhee, Under Secretary for Political Affairs, re: Canadian Overflight Route Changes. Secret.

265 14 January 1963, Note No. 22, to Dean Rusk, secretary of state, from H.B. Robinson, Canadian embassy, re: Overflights by SAC Aircraft Engaged in Chrome Dome. Top Secret.

266 15 March 1963, SAC Message "Military Relationships in Canada." DPLCA 22774. Secret/NORFORN.

267 Ibid.

268 Ibid.

269 27 June 1963, 340th Bombardment Wing (M), Whiteman AFB, 1 May - 31 May 1963 Monthly Report to Second Air Force, Strategic Air Command, Secret.

270 27 June 1963, Cabinet Conclusions No. 28-63. "Periodic approval in principle of S.A.C. overflights," paras 36&37. Secret.

271 31 October 1963, Memorandum to the Cabinet Defence Committee from the Minister of National Defence, re: Strategic Air Command Low Level Training in Canada. Secret. 8 November 1963, Memorandum to the Cabinet, re: Low Level Training in Canada by R.A.F. and U.S.A.F. bomber forces. Secret.

272 22 May 1964, National Security Action Memorandum No. 302 for the SoD and the SoS, from McGeorge Bundy, subject: Dispersal Plan for NORAD Air Defense Service. Secret.

273 11 June 1964, Letter to R.J. Barrett, Canadian Desk Office,

State Department, from W.J. Howard, assistant to the secretary of Defence (Atomic Energy), re: SAC Overflights of Canada. Top Secret.

274 Office of the Historian (SAC), *The Development of Strategic Air Command 1946-1986, Alert Operations and the Strategic Air Command, 1957-1991.*

275 10 September 1964, Note to Ambassador Ritchie from Secretary of State Dean Rusk, re: SAC Overflights for 01 October - 31 December 1964. Secret.

276 13 November 1964, Official-Informal letter to W.M. Johnson, Counsellor at the United States Embassy in Ottawa, from R.J. Barrett, Canadian Desk Officer, State Department, re: SAC Briefing in Ottawa. Secret.

277 02 March 1965, Memorandum for General Clifton from R.C. Bowman, National Security Council, re: Canadian Overflights. Top Secret.

278 26 February 1965, to R.J. Barrett, Canadian Desk Officer, Department of State, from W.J. Howard, assistant to the secretary of Defense for Atomic Energy, re: Nuclear Overflight of Canada, and Annex. Top Secret - Restricted Data.

279 7 June 1966, Memo for the Acting Under-Secretary of State for External Affairs, from DL(1) Division, re: US Proposals for ASW Nuclear Weapons Storage at Argentia and for Dispersal of Nuclear Weapons to Canadian Bases. Secret.

280 14 June 1966, Memorandum to H.B. Robinson, from DL(1)

Division, subject: ASW Nuclear Weapons. Secret.

281 Ibid.

282 10 September 1966, Memorandum for DL(1) Division, from H.B. Robinson, re: "Dispersal" in Canada of USA Interceptors. 27-16-2-USA-2. Secret.

283 8 June 1966, 6:30 p.m., Memorandum for the president, from W.W. Rostow, National Security Council, re: Rationale for Reduction in Airborne Alert. Secret.

284 14 June 1968, Note for W.W. Rostow, National Security Advisor, from Spurgeon Keeny, National Security Council, re: SAC Overflights of Canada. Top Secret.

285 Office of the Historian (SAC), *The Development of Strategic Air Command 1946-1986, Alert Operations and the Strategic Air Command, 1957-1991.*

286 22 December 1966, Cabinet Conclusions, No. 149-66, re: Low Level Training Flights by Strategic Air Command. p. 4. Secret.

287 Access to Information request for RCMP records at National Archives of Canada, "Protests and Demonstrations re: NORAD," file No. 1027-98-A-00119.

288 4 June 1968, Letter to the RCMP commissioner, from Colonel C. MacFarlane, DND Director of Security, re: Possible demonstration at Broadview, Sask. V2120-6 TD 8155 (DSecur), Confidential. 30 May 1968, Letter to the base commander, CFB Winnipeg, from Lcol. Q.E. Lawson, for DND Director of Security, re: Possible demonstration against SAC unit

near Winnipeg. V2120-6 (DSecur), Confidential.

289 16/17 May 1968, RCMP Memo for the file, re: "Protests and Demonstrations re: US Actions in Vietnam - Saskatchewan." Submitted by Superintendent R.J. Ross, SIS Detachment, F Division, Regina. Confidential.

290 23 March 1968, Airgram No. A-1072, to Department of State and Department of Defense, from U.S. Embassy in Ottawa, subject: Soviet Bombers Off East and West Coasts of Canada. Secret.

291 11 September 1967, Memorandum to H.B. Robinson, re: Your Trip to Washington, September 12, 1967, and nine attachments. Secret.

292 11 September 1967, Memorandum for H.B. Robinson, from J.S. Nutt, External Affairs, re: "Your Trip to Washington, September 12, 1967," and "SAC Refuelling Bases in Canada." Secret.

293 16 September 1977, Canada-USA Exchange of Notes Concerning Emergency Deployment of U.S. Military Aircraft; and Statement of Conditions Governing the Emergency Deployment and Refuelling of United States Military Aircraft at Canadian Forces Bases. Confidential(?).

294 1 October 1983, Memorandum of Arrangement between the Canadian Forces (Host) CFB Edmonton, Edmonton, Alberta, Canada, and the United States Air Force (Tenant) 22nd Air Refueling Wing (SAC), March AFB, California. Confidential.

295 1984 Letter of Agreement between CFB North Bay, Canada, and 42 BMW, Loring AFB, Maine, USA. Re: Dispersal of 42 BMW. No. 84030538. No classification.

296 The 509th Bombardment Wing was used to drop the atomic bombs on Hiroshima and Nagasaki, Japan, in August 1945. It flew B-52 and KC-135 aircraft in Indochina and was later re-equipped with the FB-111 bomber. The 509th is now the only unit operating the B-2 stealth bomber.

297 23 February 1979, Letter of Agreement between Strategic Air Command and Canadian Forces Air Defence Group for Daily SAC/CFADG Intercept/Air Refuelling Training in Canadian Airspace. No. 79020225. No classification.

298 3 June 1963, National Security Action Memorandum No. 248 to the Secretary of State and the Secretary of Defense, subject: Dispersal Plan for NORAD Air Defense Squadrons. Secret.

299 26 May 1964, Department of State Memorandum of Conversation, between External Affairs, RCAF, White House, and State Department, subject: Interceptor Dispersal to Canada. Secret.

300 June 1967, Minutes of 118th Meeting - PJBD, "Fighter Dispersal." Secret.

301 11 September 1967, Memorandum for H.B. Robinson, from J.S. Nutt, External Affairs, re: "Your Trip to Washington, September 12,

1967," and "Fighter Dispersal." Secret.

302 26 May 1969, Memorandum to Cabinet from SSEA and MND, re: Dispersal of US Nuclear-Armed Interceptors to Canada. Cabinet Document No. 554/69. Secret CC.

303 11 December 1957, Memorandum to secretary for DefenceQuarles, from H. Schooley, director, Public Information, re: General Powers Press Statement on Nuclear Weapons Safety in Britain. Secret.

304 27 July 1956, 21:30z. Telex to Curtis LeMay from COMAIRDIV 7, Walsh at USAB South Ruislip, England, re: Crash of B-47 on Bomb Storage Igloos at Lakenheath. Top Secret, Personal, Operational Immediate.

305 19 November 1958, U.S. Department of State, Summary Record of United States - Canada Political-Military Meeting. Top Secret.

306 17 March 1950, Letter to the chairman, Joint Committee on Atomic Energy, from Mgen. Thomas D. White, USAF director, Legislation and Liaison, re: B-36 Crash and Loss of Atomic Bomb. Top Secret, Restricted Data.

307 01 March 1950, Memorandum for Mr. Borden, from William J. Sheehy, U.S. Atomic Energy Commission, re: The B-36 Crash. Secret, Formerly Restricted Data.

308 Arkin, et al., *Taking Stock, Worldwide Nuclear Deployments 1988.* Natural Resources Defense Council, Washington, March 1998.

309 February 1950, U.S. Army Air Forces Report of Major Accident of 14 February 1950. Secret.

310 11 April 1950, Search and Rescue Mission No. 4-C-7-13 February 1950, Flight C, 4th Rescue Squadron, USAF, McChord AFB, USA. Data for 16 February 1950. Secret.

311 Ibid.

312 March 1950, RCAF Report on Operation BRIX, SAR 12 RCC, F/L DG Bell-Irving.

313 Ibid.

314 Ibid.

315 1 March 1950, Memorandum for Mr. Borden, from William J. Sheehy.

316 Ibid.

317 Ibid.

318 SAC, *The Development of Strategic Air Command, 1946-1986.* pp. 13, 18.

319 2 December 1950, MEMCON, Canadian ambassador to the United Staes and U.S. special assistant to the secretary of state on Atomic Matters Gordon Arneson. DEA 50195-40. Top Secret.

320 U.S. Department of Energy, Openness Press Conference, Fact Sheets. 27 June 1994. p. 172.

321 Sandia National Laboratory, Photograph No. SAND D8176. Albuquerque, New Mexico. c. 1949.

322 2 December 1950, MEMCON, Canadian ambassador to the United States and U.S. special assistant to the secretary of state on Atomic Matters Gordon Arneson..

323 2 December 1950, Letter No. 3088 from the Canadian

ambassador to the United STates, to the under-secretary of state for External Affairs. DEA 50195-40. Top Secret.

324 18 August 1950, Cabinet Conclusions, p. 7. Secret.

325 Captain Francis A. Ferko, No. 12267A, was a special weapons officer in the special weapon section of the 43rd Bomb Group. It was his mission to conduct refresher training for bomb commanders and weaponeers.

326 The USAF/SAC 43rd Air Refuelling Squadron, and the 2nd Air Refuelling Squadron.

327 2 December 1950, Letter No. 3038, External Affairs, File No. 50195-40, from the Canadian ambassador to Washington, to the under-secretary of state for External Affairs, re: Proposed U.S. Strategic Air Command Projects at Goose Bay. Top Secret.; 2 December 1950, External Affairs, File No. 50195-40, Memorandum of conversation with Gordon Arneson on 1 December 1950. re: Proposed U.S. Strategic Air Command Projects at Goose Bay. Top Secret.

328 43rd Bombardment Wing History, Operations and Training, August/September 1950. 15th AF Op Oder #18-50.

329 Charts in the August/September/October secret history of the 43rd Bombardment Wing show that the refuellers flew routes out towards Greenland on the Great Circle route from eastern Canada to eastern Europe.

330 28 September 1950, Letter from USAF General Walsh to Mr. Benninghoff, U.S. State Department. The request arrived at External Affairs in Ottawa on 6 October 1950 in teletype Wa-2411 from the Canadian embassy.

331 2 December 1950, Letter No. 3088.

332 2 December 1950, MEMCON, Canadian ambassador to the United States and U.S. special assistant to the secretary of state on atomic matters, Gordon Arneson. DEA 50195-40. Top Secret.

333 "Explosion Shakes Village," *Montreal Gazette.* 11 November 1950, p. 1.

334 "Explosion Shakes Village.".

335 2 December 1950, Letter No. 3088, Top Secret, External Affairs Ottawa file No. 50195-40, from the Canadian ambassador, Washington, D.C., to the under-secretary of state for External Affairs, Canada. Reference USSEA Letters No. D-3376 of 25 October 1950, and No. D-3377 of 3 November 1950. Subject: Proposed U.S. Strategic Air Command Projects at Goose Bay.

336 28 January 1997, Department of Foreign Affairs and International Trade Canada, Anticipated Question and Suggested Reply on U.S. Atomic Weapons Detonation Over Canada in 1950.

337 http://www.flash.net/~pye396/ B36_Home.htm (on 29/11/99).

338 February 1955, USAF Report of AF aircraft accident of 12 February 1955.

339 24 November 1961, USAF Report of AF aircraft accident of 15 October 1961.

340 12 August 1947, Cabinet Defence Committee Minutes, Section A, Secret.

341 9 September 1946, PJBD, Memorandum for the members, subject: Discussion of Canadian-United States Military Situation. Secret.

342 9 January 1947, Cabinet Defence Committee Minutes, Section 25, Secret.

343 2 August 1947, Memorandum to the Cabinet Defence Committee, No. D-133, from the Secretary of the CDC, re: Goose Bay Air Base. Top Secret.

344 12 August 1947, Cabinet Defence Committee Minutes, Section A, Secret.

345 5 May 1948, Memorandum to the Cabinet Defence Committee No. D181, from the Chiefs of Staff Committee, re: Fuel Storage - Goose Bay. Secret.

346 23 July 1948, Memorandum to the Cabinet Defence Committee No. D186, from the Chiefs of Staff Committee, re: Repairs and Extensions to Runways at Goose Bay. Secret.

347 29 July 1948, Cabinet Defence Committee Minutes, Section 45, re: Goose Bay Airport; Repairs and Extensions to Runways. Secret.

348 1 June 1950, Goose Bay Information Folder prepared for visit of PJBD to Goose Bay by the RCAF and USAF. Restricted.

349 13 November 1950, Brief on "Special Facilities - Goose Bay," by Secretary of CSC, BDF.MO.127-5 (DMO&P). Top Secret.

350 13 September 1950, Despatch 2710, to the Canadian ambassador in Washington, from the secretary of state for External Affairs, re: Stationing of 43rd Medium Bomber Group at Goose Bay. Top Secret.

351 6 October 1950, Memorandum by Defence Liaison Division, C.C. Eberts, re: Strategic Air Command Plans Affecting Canada. DEA/50195-40. Top Secret.

352 September 1960, A Brief on the RCAF's Position and Responsibilities at Goose Bay, TS895-200-5/25 (DAirP), Top Secret. 25 October 1950, Letter No. D-3376, to Canadian ambassador in Washington, from R.A. McKay, for under-secretary of state, re: Proposed U.S. Strategic Air Command Projects at Goose Bay. DEA/50195-40. Top Secret.

353 August 1962, History of the 64th Air Division, January-July 1962, USAF, Goose Bay, Secret, Not Releaseable to Foreign Nationals.

354 24 October 1950, Memorandum for Cabinet, from the MND, Cabinet Document No. 241-50. Top Secret.

355 25 October 1950, Cabinet Conclusions, Top Secret.

356 1 December 1950, Enclosure, Memorandum of conversation with Gordon Arneson, subject: Proposed U.S. Strategic Air Command Projects at Goose Bay. Top Secret.

357 2 December 1950, Letter No. 3088, to the under-secretary of state for External Affairs, from H.H. Wrong, Canadian ambassador in Washington, re: Proposed U.S. Strategic Air Command Projects at Goose Bay. Top Secret.

358 7 December 1950, Memorandum for the under-secretary of state for External Affairs, from R.A. MacKay, Defence Liaison

Division, re: U.S. Enquiry as to Appropriate Channel for U.S. Requests for the Movement of Atomic Bombs to Goose Bay. Top Secret. (Marginalia by L.B. Pearson.)

359 1 June 1952, The Historical Outline, 7th Aviation Field Depot Squadron. PRC. Top Secret.

360 1 April 1963, A History of Labrador and Goose Air Base. Historical Branch, HQ 4082nd Strategic Wing, Goose Air Base, Canada. Unclassified.

361 21 June 1951, Letter to A.D.P. Heeney, under-secretary of state for External Affairs, from Hume Wrong, Canadian ambassador in Washington, re: SAC Requirement in Canada. DEA/50195-40. Top Secret and Personal.

362 3 October 1952, Memorandum to the Cabinet Defence Committee from L.B. Pearson re: U.S. Military Activities in the Newfoundland Area. Document No. D-363. Secret.

363 The 59th arrived on 2 November 1952.

364 8 October 1952, Memorandum for Cabinet Defence Committee, re: Background Note: Goose Bay Lease. No. D-364. Secret.

365 9 October 1952, Cabinet Defence Committee Minutes, Section 89-IV, re: Goose Bay Lease. Secret.

366 13 November 1952, Memorandum to the Cabinet Defence Committee, from the MND, re: Canada-United States Military Installations in Newfoundland and Labrador. No. D-384. Top Secret.

367 14 November 1952, Cabinet Defence Committee Minutes, Section 90, Top Secret.

368 5 December 1952, Letter for the acting secretary of state for External Affairs from the U.S. ambassador to Canada, re: Goose Bay Lease Understanding, Confidential.

369 January 1953, *U.S. Operations in the Northeast 1940-1950.* Directorate Historical and Reference Services, Headquarters, Northeast Air Command, USAF.

370 8 January 1953, Memorandum to the Cabinet Defence Committee from the MND, re: Control of Air Defence Forces and the United States Northeast Command Operating over Canada. No. D-2-53. Top Secret.

371 20 January 1955, Memorandum for the Cabinet Defence Committee, from the MND, re: U.S. Military Operating Requirements - Goose Bay. No. D-5-55. Secret.

372 1 April 1963, A History of Labrador and Goose Air Base.

373 24 January 1955, Cabinet Defence Committee Minutes, Section 103. re: U.S. Military Operating Requirements - Goose Bay. Top Secret. The CDC discussed the CDC memo from the MND of 20 January 1955, Document D5-55.

374 24 January 1955, Cabinet Defence Committee Minutes, Section 103. re: U.S. Military Operating Requirements - Goose Bay. Top Secret

375 SAC History, 1957. p. 64.

376 31 October 1957. Memorandum to EUR, Mr. Elbrick, from BNA, Mr. Parsons, Department of State, subject: a. Closer integration of atomic capabilities in defence of

the North American continent; b. Storage of atomic weapons in Canada for air defence and naval anti-submarine use; and c. Storage of nuclear weapons at Goose Bay for SAC. Top Secret.

377 12 December 1957, U.S. State Department, Memorandum of conversation, re: Incorporation of Nuclear Weapons in United States-Canadian Defense Arrangements. Top Secret.

378 Ibid.

379 Ibid.

380 Ibid.

381 12 December 1957, Message to the secretary of state for External Affairs, from N.A. Robertson, ambassador in Washington, No. 2631 OP IMMEDIATE. Re: USA Proposals re Closer Integration of Atomic Capabilities in Defence of North America. Top Secret, Canadian Eyes Only. 12 December 1957, U.S. State Department, aide-memoire, Top Secret.

382 Ibid. 12 December 1957, US State Department, aide-memoire,

383 3 January 1958, Memorandum for Cabinet Defence Committee, no number noted, from the minister of National Defence. Re: "United States Proposal for Closer Integration of Atomic Capabilities in the Defence of North America." Secret.

384 13 January 1958. Memo to the Chiefs of Staff from General Foulkes, chairman Chiefs of Staff, re: United States Proposal for Closer Integration of Atomic Capabilities in the Defence of North America. Top Secret.

385 10 February 1958, Memorandum for Cabinet Defence Committee,

No. 3-58, from the minister of National Defence. "The Deployment of Nuclear Weapons to the Existing Storage Facilities at Goose Bay." Secret. It was discussed at CDC meeting on 28 April 1958. The document is essentially the same as the later CDC Document No. 14-59 of 21 October 1959, except this does not have the introduction or the annex.

386 28 April 1958, Cabinet Defence Committee Minutes, Section 117-IV, re: Deployment of Nuclear Weapons at Goose Bay for United States Strategic Air Command. Top Secret.

387 Ibid.

388 4 August 1959, Cabinet Defence Committee Minutes, Section 125-I, re: Storage of Defensive Nuclear Weapons at Bases in Labrador and Newfoundland for the use of United States Air Force Squadrons. Top Secret.

389 16 April 1959, Aide-memoire, United States Requirements for Storage Facilities in Canada for Nuclear Weapons. Canada, DJCP/DJP2. Secret.

390 15 September 1959, Letter to the minister of National Defence from the chairman, Chiefs of Staff, re: Storage of Defensive Nuclear Weapons at Goose Bay and Harmon Air Force Base. Top Secret.

391 22 September 1959, Record of Cabinet decision, re: Canadian Draft Text on Storage of Nuclear Weapons at Goose Bay and Harmon Field for U.S. forces. Secret

392 21 October 1959, Memorandum for Cabinet Defence Committee,

No. 14-59, from the minister of National Defence, re: "The Deployment of Nuclear Weapons to the Existing Storage Facilities at United States Leased Portion, Goose Bay Air Base." Secret. (Also recorded as CDC Memo No. 19-59, same date.)

393 Ibid.

394 29 October 1959, Storage of Nuclear Weapons in Canada. Department of External Affairs. Three-page summary of policy, events, and issues. Secret.

395 Ibid.

396 5 November 1959, Cabinet Defence Committee Minutes, Section 128-II, re: Deployment of Nuclear Weapons to the Existing Storage Facilities at U.S. Leased Portion, Goose Bay Air Base. Top Secret.

397 Ibid.

398 8/9 November 1959, Meeting of United States-Canada Ministerial on Joint Defense, Camp David, Maryland, Secret.

399 Ibid.

400 Ibid.

401 Ibid.

402 Ibid.

403 October 1963, History of the 4082nd Strategic Wing (SAC) July-September 1963, Wing Historian, HQ 4082nd Strategic Wing, Goose Air Base, Canada. Secret.

404 21 July 1960, Memorandum to Mr. Dillon, Office of the Secretary of State, from the Assistant Secretary, I.B. White, European Affairs, re: U.S.-Canada Defense Ministers Meeting, July 12-13. Secret.

405 5 August 1960, Transcript of talks at the meeting of ministers at the Seigniory Club, 12-13 July 1960. Top Secret.

406 5 August 1960, Summary of decisions and matters requiring follow-up at the meeting of ministers at the Seigniory Club, 12-13 July 1960. Secret.

407 5 August 1960, Transcript of talks at the meeting of ministers at the Seigniory Club, 12-13 July 1960. Top Secret.

408 06 December 1960 Record of Cabinet Decision. Secret.

409 01 April 1963, A History of Labrador and Goose Air Base. Historical Branch, HQ 4082nd Strategic Wing, Goose Air Base, Canada. Unclassified.

410 08 March 1961, MEMCON, President Kennedy and Ambassador Merchant (U.S. ambassador to Canada). Secret.

411 21 April 1961, Memo to Dean Rusk, the Secretary of State, from William Bundy, DoD, International Security Affairs. Secret.

412 29? April 1961? (date unclear on document) Memo to Ross Campbell from DL(1) Division, re: Nuclear Weapons: United States Storage Requirements in Canada. Secret.

413 17 May 1961, MEMCON, U.S. ambassador Merchant and Prime Minister Diefenbaker.

414 26 February 1962, Telegram to Secretary of State, from Ambassador Merchant, U.S. embassy in Canada, No. 807. Eyes Only Secret.

415 August 1962, History of the 64th Air Division, January-July 1962, USAF, Goose Bay, Secret, Not

Releaseable to Foreign Nationals.

416 Ibid..

417 Ibid.

418 October 1963, History of the 4082nd Strategic Wing (SAC) July-September 1963, Wing Historian, HQ 4082nd Strategic Wing, Goose Air Base, Canada. Secret. "September 1963 EWO (Emergency War Orders) Activities."

419 February 1963, History of the 4082nd Strategic Wing (SAC) and 4082nd Combat Support Group (SAC) 1 December 1962-31 January 1963. Wing Historian, HQ 4082nd Strategic Wing, Goose Air Base, Canada. Secret.

420 SAC History, 1963, p. 120.

421 2 November 1962, 17:30z, Message to 59th FIS, from Goose NORAD/CONAD Sector Goose AD, No. 5803. Secret.

422 6 May 1963, Memorandum No. D-3-63 to the Cabinet Defence Committee from the secretary of state for External Affairs and MND, re: Nuclear Policy. Secret.

423 15 May 1963, Meeting between President John F. Kennedy and Prime Minister Lester B. Pearson at Hyannis Port, Mass. May 10-11, 1963. Summary Report, Secret. 13 May 1963, Cabinet Conclusion, No. 8-63. Secret.

424 26 June 1963, 15:03z, Message to 4082nd Strategic Wing, from 45th Air Division, re: Two Officer/Two Man Policies. Secret.

425 09/11 April 1963, the RCAF and USAF sign a letter of agreement on nuclear weapons accidents at Goose Bay. This is also covered in the May 1963, History of the 4082nd Strategic Wing (SAC) 1-

30 April 1963. Wing Historian, HQ 4082nd Strategic Wing, Goose Air Base, Canada. Secret.

426 October 1963, History of the 4082nd Strategic Wing (SAC) July-September 1963, Wing Historian, HQ 4082nd Strategic Wing, Goose Air Base, Canada. Secret. "September 1963 EWO (Emergency War Orders) Activities."

427 12 September 1963. Record of Cabinet Decision, Re: Storage of Nuclear Warheads on Canada for U.S. Forces.

428 12 September 1963, Cabinet Conclusions, pp. 18-19, "Storage of Nuclear Warheads in Canada for United States Forces." Secret.

429 24 September 1963, U.S. Embassy note No. 105 to secretary of state for External Affairs.

430 26 September 1963, Cabinet Conclusions, "Storage of Nuclear Warheads at Goose Bay and Harmon Air Force Base for United States Forces." Secret.

431 Ibid.

432 Order in Council P.C. 1963-1439, 26 September 1963.

433 1 October 1963. Memo for the prime minister, from Norman Robertson, External Affairs, re: Nuclear Agreement Concerning U.S. Forces at Goose Bay and Harmon Air Force Base. Secret.

434 Ibid.

435 8 November 1963, Letter to the chairman, CoS, A/C/M Miller, from the Under-Secretary of State for External Affairs N.A. Robertson, re: Storage of Nuclear Weapons for U.S. Interceptor Forces at Goose and Harmon. Secret.

436 Ibid.

437 21 November 1963, S0030-106
     Vol. 2 (CAS), letter to chairman,
     Chiefs of Staff, from Chief of the
     Air Staff, re: Storage of Nuclear
     Weapons at Goose Bay and
     Harmon - Proposed Service-to-
     Service Arrangements. Secret.

438 26 November 1963, letter to
     Norman Robertson from the
     deputy minister for National
     Defence, re: Storage of Nuclear
     Weapons for U.S. Interceptor
     Forces at Goose and Harmon.
     Secret.

439 21 November 1963, S0030-106
     Vol. 2 (CAS), letter to Chairman
     Chiefs of Staff, from Chief of the
     Air Staff.

440 3 January 1964 Memorandum,
     from DL(1) Division, External
     Affairs, re: Goose Bay and
     Harmon. Secret.

441 16 January 1964, Memorandum
     to the CAS from the VCAS, re:
     Goose Bay. Secret.

442 April 1964, Report of the
     USAF/ADC 59th FIS
     Detachment, for January-March
     1964. Secret. April 1964, Report
     of the USAF/ADC 59th FIS
     Detachment, for January-March
     1964. Secret.

443 7 January 1964, Department of
     National Defence Memo from
     the deputy minister of National
     Defence, Secret.

444 16 June 1965, Letter to the deputy
     minister of Trade and Commerce,
     from the deputy minister of
     National Defence, re: Dealings in
     Nuclear Weapons. Secret.

445 15 July 1965, Memorandum to
     the Under-Secretary of External
     Affairs, from DL(1) Division,
     subject: Import and Export of
     U.S. Nuclear Weapons, Goose
     and Harmon. Secret. 15 July
     1965, Letter to CDS from
     deputy minister of External
     Affairs, re: Import and Export of
     Nuclear Weapons at Goose Bay.
     Secret. 08 July 1965,
     Memorandum for the minister
     (secretary of state for External
     Affairs) from the DM, re: Import
     Permit Application for Shipment
     of Nuclear Warheads. Secret. 30
     June 1965, Memorandum to
     DL(1) Division from Legal
     Division, subject: Export Permit
     Application for Shipment of
     Nuclear Warheads. Secret.

446 18 March 1964, 2049z, telex to
     CANAIRHED from
     CANAIRWASH. Secret, Priority.

447 25 March 1964, Letter to the
     minister of National Defence, from
     the CAS Air Marshal Dunlap, re:
     RCAF/USAF Supplementary
     Arrangements - USAF Interceptors
     at Goose Bay and Harmon AFB,
     S0030-106(CAS), Secret.

448 There is a handwritten note at
     the bottom of letter: "C.A.S. Apl
     7/64 Approved for transmission
     to External Affairs (signed) Paul
     T. Hellyer."

449 27 April 1964, Letter to the
     Chief of the Air Staff, from the
     A/C/M F.R. Miller, chairman,
     Chiefs of Staff, re: RCAF/USAF
     Supplementary Arrangements -
     USAF Interceptors at Goose Bay
     and Harmon AFB, S1100-117-6,
     Secret.

450 Report of the USAF/ADC 59th
     FIS for April-June 1964.

451 23 December 1963, 18:45z,
     Message to CANAIRHED, from

CANAIRWASH, re: Associated Equipment at Goose Bay and Harmon Air Force Base. S1100-114-6 (DAirD). Secret.

452 5 June 1964, 23:24z, Message to 8 AF HQ, from SAC, re: Nuclear Weapons at Goose Bay AB. Secret.

453 10 June 1964, 20:53z, Message to SAC, from 8 AF HQ, re: Support of ADC Nuclear Capability at Goose, Secret.

454 15 June 1964, 13:50z, Message to 4082 SW, Goose Bay AB, from 8 Air Force USAF HQ, re: ADC Nuclear Weapon Storage - Goose. Secret.

455 July 1964, History of the SAC 4082nd Strategic Wing (SAC) 1 April-30 June 1964. Wing Historian, Headquarters, Goose Bay Air Base, Secret.

456 SAC Command History 1964. Secret, p. 126.

457 15 July 1965, Memorandum to the Under-Secretary of External Affairs, from DL(1) Division, subject: Import and Export of U.S. Nuclear Weapons, Goose Bay and Harmon. Secret.

458 23 June 1965, Initial Capability Inspection, 59th Fighter Interceptor Squadron. USAF ADC, ADCIG-O. Secret. This statement of facts covers the results of the initial capability inspection of the 59th Fighter Interceptor Squadron at Goose Bay AB, conducted during the period 20-23 June 1965, by the Office of the Command Inspector General, HQ ADC, Ent AFB, Colorado.

459 25 June 1965. O 3312-23 TD 5175 (DNW), Memorandum to COPR from the A/DNW, re: ICI - 59 FIS Goose Bay Air Base. Secret.

460 Report of the USAF/ADC 59th FIS for July-September 1965.

461 15 July 1965, Memorandum to the Under-Secretary of External Affairs, from DL(1) Division.

462 9 August 1965, Letter to the Under-Secretary of State for External Affairs, M. Cadieux. from the CDS, A/V/M Miller, S3310-3 (DCPlans). Secret.

463 18 November 1965, V3312-23 (DNW), to CFHQ RCAF, from ADCIG-O, USAF. re: Statement of Facts. Secret. 9 December 1965. V3312-23 TD 5343 (DNW), Memorandum for the VCDS from the A/DNW, re: Statement of Facts - CI, Goose Bay AB, Labrador. Secret.

464 22 November 1966, Memorandum for the prime minister from the secretary of state for External Affairs, re: Goose Bay - Deactivation of U.S.A. Interceptor Squadron. Secret.

465 11 July 1966, Memorandum for the secretary of state for External Affairs, re: U.S. Requirement for Storage of Nuclear ASW Weapons at Argentia. Secret.

466 22 November 1966, Memorandum for the prime minister from the secretary of state for External Affairs.

467 Ibid..

468 Ibid.

469 3 August 1967, 17:43z, Telegram to U.S. embassy in Ottawa, from European Bureau, Canada Desk, State Department, subject: U.S. Security Arrangements at Goose Bay AB. Secret. 16 August 1967, Memorandum of conversation, R.Z. Smith and G.P. Kidd, subject: Arrangements for Future

Operation of SAC Base at Goose Bay, Labrador. Secret.

470 9 November 1967, Memo to Military Secretary, from Sec VCDS, re: Goose Bay-Discontinuance of USAF Interceptor Operations. V3010-15 TD 7311 (Sec VCDS). Secret.

471 c.11 October 1952, To Air Marshal Curtis, Chief of the Air Staff, from General Meyers, Chief of Staff of the USAF, Info: Northeast Air Command, Pepperrell AFB, Newfoundland. DEA/50216-40. Top Secret.

472 27 September 1952, Note to secretary of state for External Affairs, from under-secretary of state for External Affairs, re: Posting of U.S. Fighter Squadron to Goose Bay. DEA/50216-40. Secret.

473 17 November 1952, Memorandum to under-secretary of state for External Affairs, from assistant under-secretary of state for External Affairs, re: Posting of U.S. Fighter Squadron to Goose Bay. DEA/50216-40. Top Secret.

474 15 September 1959, Letter to the minister of National Defence from the chairman, Chiefs of Staff, re: Storage of Defensive Nuclear Weapons at Goose Bay and Harmon Air Force Base. Top Secret.

475 Ibid.

476 12 December 1957, U.S. State Department, Memorandum of conversation, re: Incorporation of Nuclear Weapons in United States-Canadian Defense Arrangements. Top Secret.

477 August 1962, History of the 64th Air Division, January-July 1962,

USAF, Goose Bay. Secret, Not Releaseable to Foreign Nationals.

478 http://www.wpafb.af.mil/museum/research/fighter/f89.htm (14/12/1998).

479 5 December 1960, Memorandum to the Cabinet Defence Committee, re: Nuclear Weapons for NATO and NORAD Forces. CDC Document No._7-60. Top Secret.

480 Ibid.

481 July 1961, USAF Air Defense Command, "History of the Air Defense Command, January-June 1961." Secret/NORFORN.

482 A photograph of three aircraft of the 59th FIS Goose Bay S/N 52-1959, 52-2141, 52-2138, is available electronically at: http://www.wpafb.af.mil/museum/research/fighter/f89-17.jpg (14/12/1998).

483 http://www.wpafb.af.mil/museum/air_power/ap54.htm (14/12/1998).

484 August 1962, History of the 64th Air Division, January-July 1962, USAF, Goose Bay. Secret, Not Releaseable to Foreign Nationals.

485 Historical Record of the 59th Fighter-Interceptor Squadron (ADC) for the Period Ending 30 September 1963. Secret.

486 Ibid.

487 Ibid.

488 28 September 1963, Draft Report of Staff Visit Goose Bay AB, 26-27 September 1963. By Captain (USAF) W.K. Gobble, Team Chief.

489 Historical Record of the 59th Fighter-Interceptor Squadron (ADC) for the Period Ending 31 December 1963. Secret.

490 16 February 1964, HQ GADS Historical Report by Lt. Alan Buell, director of Manpower and Organization. Secret.

491 The technical information on the W54 is taken from the following works: Gibson, *The History of the US Nuclear Arsenal*; Hansen, *U.S. Nuclear Weapons*; Hansen, *Swords of Armageddon*; ADC, *History of Air Defense Weapons, 1946-1962*; and a data sheet from the U.S. National Atomic Museum.

492 17 January 1964, Memorandum to Kirkwood, Defence Liaison Division, from J.R. McKinney, Economic Division, External Affairs, subject: Export of Nuclear Weapons to the United States. 27-11-CDA/USA. Secret.

493 Ibid. (See handwritten note in margin.)

494 14 January 1964, Department of Trade and Commerce, re: Export Permit Application No. 486695, Export of nuclear weapons to USA. Secret.

495 30 April 1964, to the Air Member, Canadian Joint Staff Washington, from A/V/M C.L. Annis, vice chief of the Air Staff, re: Signature of RCAR/USAF Supplementary Arrangement for USAF AD forces at Goose Bay and Harmon AFB. S1100-117-6 (VCAS), Secret.

496 5 June 1964, RUCSER 35 05/2324Z (1964), Telex to Westover AFB, Massachusetts, from SAC. Re: Nuclear Warheads for Goose AB. Secret.

497 Historical Record of the 59th Fighter-Interceptor Squadron (ADC) for the Period Ending 30 June 1964. Secret.

498 Ibid.

499 23 June 1965, HQ USAF Air Defense Command, Office of the Inspector General. Subject: Statement of Facts, Initial Capability Inspection, 59th Fighter-Interceptor Squadron. Secret/NORFORN Except Canada.

500 18 November 1965, HQ USAF Air Defense Command, ADCIG-O, Subject: Statement of Facts. Secret/NORFORN Except Canada.

501 9 December 1965, Memorandum to VCDS, from W/C Z.R. Charko, acting director of Nuclear Weapons, re: Statement of Facts - CI Goose Bay Air Base. V-3312-23 TD 5343 (DNW). Secret.

502 25 June 1965, Memorandum to COPR and DGAF, from W/C Z.R. Charko, acting director of Nuclear Weapons, re: ICI - 59 FIS Goose Bay Air Base. 0-3312-23 TD 5175 (DNW). Secret.

503 Ibid.

504 Ibid.

505 Historical Record of the 59th Fighter-Interceptor Squadron (ADC) for the Period Ending 30 September 1965. Secret.

506 15 March 1966, Det 1, 59th FIS (ADC), subject: Historical Report (RCS: AU-D5), 01 January-25 March 1966. Secret.

507 Ibid.

508 Historical Record of the 59th Fighter-Interceptor Squadron (ADC) for the Period Ending 31 March 1966. Secret.

509 9 November 1966, Outgoing telegram No. 82236, to U.S. embassy in Ottawa, from Bureau of European Affairs, Canada Desk, R.Z. Smith. Secret.

510 16 November 1966, Telegram to C. Ritchie, Canadian ambassador to the United States, from U.S. secretary of state, re: Goose Bay: Deactivation of USAF 59th Fighter Interceptor Squadron. Secret. 16 November 1966, Telegram to External Affairs from C. Ritchie, Canadian ambassador to the United States, re: Goose Bay: Deactivation of USAF 59th Fighter Interceptor Squadron. Secret.

511 22 November 1966, Memorandum for the minister from the Chief of the Defence Staff, re: Deactivation of USAF Fighter Squadron at Goose Bay. V 3010-15 (DConP). Secret.

512 22 November 1966, Memorandum for the prime minister from the secretary of state for External Affairs, re: Goose Bay - Deactivation of U.S.A. Interceptor Squadron. Secret.

513 Ibid.

514 9 November 1967, Memorandum to the MILSEC from the Commander Samson, SEC VCDS, re: Goose Bay - Discontinuance of USAF Interceptor Operations. V 3010-15 TD 7311 (SEC VCDS), Secret. General Allard saw the note on 21 November 1967.

515 31 October 1967, Department of State telegram to secretary of state from U.S. embassy in Ottawa, subject: Discontinuance ADB Fighter Interceptor Squadron Deployment to Goose AB. Secret.

516 3 November 1967, Department of State telegram to U.S. embassy Ottawa, from secretary of state, subject: Discontinuance ADB Fighter Interceptor Squadron Deployment to Goose AB. Secret.

517 Historical Record of the 59th Fighter-Interceptor Squadron (ADC) for the Period Ending 30 June 1968. Secret.

518 Wayne Ray, *US Military Bases in Newfoundland, Harmon AFB Construction*.http://www.mirror. org /groups/cpa/constrct.html (09 July 1998).

519 History of the Strategic Air Command, Historical Study No. 73A, *SAC Targeting Concepts*. Historical Division, HQ SAC. Top Secret.

520 17 June 1952, Memorandum for the file, State Department, subject: Use of British and Canadian Facilities for Atomic Weapon Strikes. Top Secret, Security Information. Four pages.

521 22 September 1959, Storage of Defensive Nuclear Weapons at Goose Bay and Harmon Air Force Base Negotiating Draft and Annex. S003-104. Secret.

522 13 October 1959, 18:34z, Message to CANCOMARPAC, from CANAVHED, re: Request Authority for Swordfish to Attend ASWEX and TRANSITEX. Secret.

523 2 November 1959, Memorandum for the CAS from the VCAS, re: International Agreements - Draft Agreement on Storage of Defensive Nuclear Weapons at Goose Bay and Harmon Air Force Base. S 003-104 (VCAS). Secret.

524 12 September 1963, Record of Cabinet decision, re: Storage of Nuclear Warheads in Canada for United States Forces. Secret.

525 02 October 1963, Outgoing message DL-1281, to the

Canadian ambassador to NATO, from External Affairs, subject: Storage of Nuclear Weapons at Goose Bay and Harmon. Secret.

526 10 October 1963, Message to External Affairs, from the Canadian ambassador to NATO, subject: Storage of Nuclear Weapons at Goose Bay and Harmon. Secret.

527 15 October 1963, Memorandum to the MND from the CAS, re: Storage of Nuclear Weapons in Canada for United States Forces - Harmon and Goose Bay. Secret.

528 15 November 1963, 15:49z, Message to CANAIRHED from CANAIRWASH, re: Nuclear Weapons at Harmon and Goose Bay AB. Priority, Secret.

529 9 January 1964, HQ Goose Air Defense Sector, Quarterly Historical Report. Secret.

530 25 November 1963, Message to Canadian embassy Washington, from External Affairs, subject: Nuclear Weapons Storage at Goose Bay and Harmon. Secret.

531 13 February 1964, Letter to the air member of the Canadian Joint Staff in Washington, from CAS, re: Delivery - Nuclear Weapons to USAF Bases in Canada. S0030-109 (DAFM). Secret.

532 2 December 1963, Letter to the president of the Atomic Energy Control Board, from E.B. Armstrong, deputy minister of National Defence, re: Nuclear Weapons for U.S. Forces in Canada. N.14-2 Vol 3 (JAG/G1). Secret

533 3 January 1964, Memorandum to the CAS from the JAG, re: Canada-U.S. Exchange of Notes

28 and 30 September 1963, Storage of Nuclear Weapons - Harmon and Goose Bay. N.14-2 Vol 3 (JAG/G1). Secret.

534 29 November 1963, Memorandum of meeting, to ADSI from ADSI 2-4, re: Nuclear Weapons Goose Bay - Harmon. S0030-101(DADSI). Secret.

535 17 November 1964, Letter to CAS from the air member of the Canadian Joint Staff in Washington, re: Nuclear Storage at Goose Bay and Harmon. 49-07-01 (AM). Secret.

536 11 October 1963, Airgram to the Department of State, from the U.S. Consulate, St. John's, Newfoundland, re: Nuclear weapons: Newfoundland Opinion Reaction to Installation of Weapons at Two Bases Here. Unclassified.

537 Ibid.

538 04-11 May 1964, ADC HQ ORI.

539 Historical Record of the 59th Fighter-Interceptor Squadron (ADC) for the Period Ending 30 September 1964. Secret.

540 Ibid.

541 9 June 1965, Memorandum for the minister (secretary of state for External Affairs), re: Harmon Air Force Base, Newfoundland. Confidential.

542 Ibid.

543 Ibid.

544 October 1965, History of the 4081st Strategic Wing 1 July - 30 September 1965, Wing Historian, Ernest Harmon AFB, Canada. Secret.

545 11 August 1965, 13:40z, Message to 4081 Strategic Wing, from 8

AF HQ, re: Ernest Harmon
Mission. Secret, NORFORN.

546 January 1966, History of Eighth
Air Force, July - December 1965,
Volume III, Exhibits 104-215.
SAC Historian, Offutt AFB,
USA. Secret, No Foreign Release.

547 17 November 1965, 22:59z,
Message to 4081 Strategic Wing,
from SAC, re: Closure of Ernest
Harmon AFB. Secret,
NORFORN.

548 21 October 1965, Memorandum
for the record, by Bgen. J.W.
Kline, USAF Chief of Staff, re:
Harmon. January 1966, History
of Eighth Air Force, July -
December 1965, Volume III,
Exhibits 104-215.

549 Ibid.

550 07 January 1966, Memo for the
record, HQ Eighth Air Force
(SAC). Subject: Harmon Closure.
January 1966, History of Eighth
Air Force, July - December 1965,
Volume III, Exhibits 104-215.

551 October 1965, Report of the
USAF/ADC 59th FIS for July-
September 1965. Secret.

552 7 January 1966, Memo for the
record, HQ Eighth Air Force
(SAC). Subject: Harmon Closure.
January 1966, History of Eighth
Air Force, July - December 1965,
Volume III, Exhibits 104-215.

553 17 November 1965, 22:59z,
Message to 4081 Strategic Wing,
from SAC, re: Closure of Ernest
Harmon AFB. Secret,
NORFORN.

554 25 November 1965, Message to
Canadian embassy in
Washington, from External
Affairs, subject: Closure of
Harmon Air Base. Confidential.

555 7 December 1965, Note No. 247
to the Honourable Paul Martin,
secretary of state for External
Affairs, from Walt Butterworth,
U.S. ambassador in Canada, re:
Closure of Harmon Air Force Base.

556 8 December 1965, Message to
SAC from 8 Air Force, re:
Closure of Harmon AFB. Secret,
NORFORN.

557 22 November 1966,
Memorandum for the prime
minister from the secretary of state
for External Affairs, re: Goose Bay
- Deactivation of U.S.A.
Interceptor Squadron. Secret.

558 3 March 1966, Cabinet
conclusions, re: Disposition of
Harmon Field, Stephenville,
Newfoundland. Secret.

559 Ibid.

560 11 August 1949, Cabinet Defence
Committee Meeting Minutes,
Section "C," III. U.S. Bases in
Newfoundland. Top Secret.

561 29 December 1952, Note from
Privy Council Office to clerk of
the Privy Council, re: Defence
Relations in the North. (Plus
Enclosure.) DEA/50046-40.
Secret. (*DCER* 1952, p. 1195.)

562 26 October 1966, Briefing note
from External Affairs, re: United
States' Request for Storage of
Nuclear Weapons at Argentia. 27-
16-2-USA-2. Secret.

563 31 October 1957. U.S. State
Department Memo, to EUR Mr.
Elbrick, from BNA Mr. Parsons,
re: Storage of Atomic Weapons in
Canada for Air Defense and Naval
Anti-Submarine Use. Top Secret.

564 21 August 1957, Letter to
Marcelis Parsons, director, Office
of British Commonwealth and

Northern European Affairs, U.S. State Department, from Livingston Merchant, U.S. ambassador to Canada. Top Secret, Official-Informal.

565 31 October 1957. U.S. State Department Memo, to EUR Mr.. Elbrick, from BNA Mr. Parsons.

566 12 December 1957, U.S. State Department, Memorandum of conversation, re: Incorporation of Nuclear Weapons in United States-Canadian Defense Arrangements. Top Secret.

567 12 December 1957, External Affairs telegram No. 2630, to Ottawa, from N.A. Robertson at the Canadian embassy Washington. "USA Proposals re Closer Integration of Atomic Capabilities in Defence of North America," Top Secret, Canadian Eyes Only.

568 3 January 1958, Memorandum for Cabinet Defence Committee, no number noted, from the minister of National Defence. "United States Proposal for Closer Integration of Atomic Capabilities in the Defence of North America." Secret.

569 13 January 1958, Letter to the Chiefs of Staff from the chairman, Chiefs of Staff, re: United States Proposals for Closer Integration of Atomic Capabilities in the Defence of North America. Top Secret.

570 16 April 1959, Aide-memoire United States Requirements for Storage Facilities in Canada for Nuclear Weapons. DJCP/DJP2. Secret.

571 29 October 1959, Storage of Nuclear Weapons in Canada. Department of External Affairs

three-page summary of policy, events, and issues. Secret.

572 5 November 1959, Cabinet Defence Committee Minutes, "Storage of Nuclear anti-Submarine Weapons at Argentia." Secret.

573 8/9 November 1959, United States-Canada Joint Ministerial Meeting on Joint Defense, Camp David, USA. Top Secret.

574 Ibid.

575 5 August 1960, Transcript of talks at the meeting of ministers at the Seigniory Club, 12-13 July 1960. Top Secret.

576 Ibid.

577 5 August 1960, Summary of decisions and matters requiring follow-up at the meeting of ministers at the Seigniory Club, 12-13 July 1960. Secret.

578 21 April 1961, Memo to Dean Rusk, U.S. secretary of state, from William Bundy, DoD, assistant secretary of Defense for International Security Affairs. Secret.

579 19 November 1962, 18:37, Department of State outgoing telegram, to U.S. embassy in Ottawa, from Dean Rusk, secretary of state, re: Opening Negotiation in Ottawa on 21 November. Secret.

580 (June-August) 1963, U.S. draft from Secretary of State Rusk on storage of nuclear weapons in Canada for the use of U.S. forces. Secret.

581 01 June 1962, BUWEPS INSTRUCTIONS 5451.7A, to commanding officer, U.S. Naval Station, Argentia, Newfoundland, from chief, Bureau of Naval

Weapons. Subject: U.S. Naval Station Argentia; Mission and Tasks of.

582 5 September 1963, Memo for the secretary of state for External Affairs re: Preparation for Meeting with SoS Dean Rusk on Canada-US Defence Questions, Nuclear Storage Requirements, U.S. and Canadian Maritime Forces. Secret.

583 9 September 1963, Memorandum to the Cabinet from L.B. Pearson, chairman of the Cabinet Defence Committee, re: Storage of Nuclear Warheads in Canada in Support of United States Forces". Secret.

584 12 September 1963, Cabinet Minutes, pp. 18-19, "Storage of nuclear warheads in Canada for United States Forces." Secret.

585 20 October 1964, Memorandum for the president, from the secretary of Defense, subject: Recommended FY 1966-FY 1970 Anti-Submarine Warfare Forces. Top Secret.

586 Ibid.

587 17 November 1964, Command History Report, U.S. Naval Station Argentia, 1 January-31 December 1964.

588 2 March 1965, Memorandum for the under-secretary of state for External Affairs, from H.B. Robinson, re: Possible Contraction of United States Base at Argentia, Newfoundland. Secret.

589 7 April 1965, Memorandum for Paul Martin, the secretary of state for External Affairs, from Marcel Cadieux, deputy minister for External Affairs, re: Possible Contraction of United States Base at Argentia, Newfoundland. Top Secret.

590 Ibid.

591 7 October 1965, Memorandum for Head of DL(1) Division, External Affairs, from H.B. Robinson, re: Storage of Nuclear Ammunition for USA Use at Argentia. Secret.

592 4 November 1965, letter to R.S. McNamara, U.S. secretary of Defense, from Paul Hellyer, minister of National Defence, re: Election Thank You and Argentia. Secret.

593 11 December 1965, letter to Paul Hellyer, minister of National Defence, from R.S. McNamara, secretary of Defense, re: Election Thank You and Argentia. Secret.

594 23 December 1965, Memorandum to the prime minister from the minister of National Defence, re: Argentia. Secret.

595 22 January 1966, letter to R.S. McNamara, secretary of Defense, from Paul Hellyer, minister of National Defence, re: Argentia. Secret.

596 20 January 1966, Memorandum for the minister, from the deputy minister for External Affairs, re: Nuclear ASW Weapons for Argentia. Secret.

597 20 January 1966, Memorandum for the minister, from the deputy minister for External Affairs, re: Nuclear ASW Weapons for Argentia. Secret.

598 20 January 1966, Memorandum for the prime minister, from the secretary of state for External Affairs, re: Nuclear ASW Weapons for Argentia. Secret.

599 25 January 1966, Memorandum to the minister, from the deputy

minister for External Affairs, re:
Nuclear ASW Weapons for
Argentia. Secret.

600 25 January 1966, Memorandum
to the minister, from the deputy
minister for External Affairs, re:
Nuclear ASW Weapons for
Argentia. Secret.

601 3 March 1966, Cabinet Meeting
Minutes, re: Disposition of
Harmon Field, Stephenville,
Newfoundland. Secret.

602 USN Naval Aeronautical
Organization FY 1966, Argentia,
Newfoundland.

603 26 February 1966, Letter to the
prime minister from D.L.
Wilgress, re: Meeting of PJBD.
Secret.

604 7 June 1966, Memo to acting
under-secretary, from Defence
Liaison (1) Division, subject:
U.S. Proposals for ASW Nuclear
Weapons Storage at Argentia and
for Dispersal of Nuclear
Interceptors to Canadian Bases.
Secret.

605 14 June 1966, Memo to H.B.
Robinson, from J.S. Nutt,
Defence Liaison (1) Division, re:
ASW Nuclear Weapons. Secret.

606 18 August 1966, Memorandum
for DL(1) Division, from H.B.
Robinson, re: "Dispersal" in
Canada of USA Interceptors.
Secret.

607 29 September 1966,
Memorandum for the prime
minister, from the secretary of state
for External Affairs, re: United
States Request for Storage of Airborne Nuclear Anti-Submarine
Weapons at Argentia. Secret.

608 23 June 1966, Aide-memoire on
ASW nuclear weapons at Argentia,

from the U.S. embassy, initialled
by Ambassador Butterworth.
Secret. 15 August 1966, Memo to
the Canadian embassy in
Washington, from the under-
secretary of state for External
Affairs, subject: United States
Request for Storage of Nuclear
ASW Weapons at Argentia. Secret

609 27 June 1966, Memorandum for
the minister, from deputy minister
for External Affairs, re: Canada-
USSR Air Agreement and United
States Request for Nuclear ASW
Weapons at Argentia. Secret.

610 29 October 1959, Storage of
Nuclear Weapons in Canada.
Department of External Affairs
three-page summary of policy,
events and issues. Secret.

611 8 July 1966, Memorandum for
the prime minister, from the
secretary of state for External
Affairs, re: United States Request
for Storage of Nuclear ASW
Weapons at Argentia. Secret.

612 Ibid.

613 11 July 1966, Memorandum for
the minister from the deputy
minister for External Affairs, re:
United States Request for Storage
of Nuclear ASW Weapons at
Argentia. Secret.

614 14 July 1966, Memo to USA
Division, External Affairs, from
J.S. Nutt, Defence Liaison (1)
Division, re: Minister's
Conversation in Washington -
Canada-U.S. Bilateral Defence
Matters. Secret. (For inclusion in
the secretary of state for External
Affairs briefing papers.)

615 29 July 1966, Memorandum for
file, from J.S. Nutt, Defence
Liaison (1) Division, subject:

ASW Storage: Argentia. Secret.

616 18 August 1966, memo of DL (1) Div., re: ASW Nuclear Weapons at Argentia.

617 28 September 1966, letter to DL(1) Division from CDS, re: Weapons Storage at Argentia. V 3310-6 TD 6238 (DConP). Secret.

618 15 September 1966, Letter to the under-secretary of state for External Affairs, from the chief of the Defence Staff, re: ASW Nuclear Weapons Storage - Argentia. V 3310-6 (DConP). Secret.

619 28 September 1966, Memorandum to Cabinet, from the secretary of state for External Affairs, re: Storage of Nuclear Weapons at U.S. Naval Base, Argentia, Newfoundland. For United States Forces. Secret.

620 29 September 1966, Memorandum for the prime minister, from the secretary of state for External Affairs, re: United States Request for Storage of Airborne Nuclear Anti-Submarine Weapons at Argentia. Secret.

621 27 October 1966, Cabinet Minutes, No. 124-66. "Storage of Nuclear Weapons at U.S. Naval Base, Argentia, Newfoundland." Secret.

622 Ibid.

623 01 November 1966, Cabinet Minutes, No. 126-66, "Storage of Nuclear Weapons at US Naval Base, Argentia, Newfoundland, for United States Forces." Secret.

624 24 May 1967, Briefing Note "C," Prime Minister Pearson meeting with President Johnson, re: North American Defence. Secret.

625 11 August 1967, Letter to the USN chief of Naval Operations, from General Allard, chief of the Defence Staff, re Canadian Forces/United States Navy - Service-to-Service Technical Arrangement - Storage of Airborne Nuclear ASW Weapons in Canada. V 3310-6 (DConP). Secret.

626 12 June 1967, 20:05z, Telegram to the secretary of state from the U.S. embassy in Ottawa, re: Dispersal and Argentia and Canadian Vietnamese Views. Secret.

627 13 June 1967, 20:40z, Telegram to the U.S. secretary of state from the U.S. Embassy in Ottawa, re: PJBD Meeting and Walter Gordon Views. Secret.

628 18 July 1967, Cabinet Committee on External Affairs and Defence. Meeting No. 3- 67. re: Agreement Between Canada and the United States for the Storage of Nuclear Weapons at a United States Leased Base in Newfoundland for the United States Forces. Secret.

629 Ibid.

630 18 July 1967, Telegram to secretary of state from U.S. embassy Ottawa, re: Cabinet Agreement on Argentia. Secret.

631 20 July 1967, Cabinet Document 439/67. Memorandum to the Cabinet from the secretary of state for External Affairs, Paul Martin, re: Agreement Between Canada and the United States for the Storage of Nuclear Weapons at a United States Leased Base in Newfoundland for the United States Navy. Secret.

632 Ibid.

633 Ibid.

634 Ibid.

635 Ibid.

636 26 July 1967, Cabinet Minutes, No. 69-67, re: "Agreement Between Canada and the United States for the Storage of Nuclear Weapons at a United States Leased Base in Newfoundland for United States Forces." Secret.

637 26 July 1967, Record of Cabinet Decision, re: "Agreement Between Canada and the United States for the Storage of Nuclear Weapons at a United States Leased Base in Newfoundland for United States Forces." Secret.

638 29 May 1967, Cabinet Document 421/67. Memorandum to the Cabinet Committee on External Affairs and Defence, from secretary of state for External Affairs and MND, re: Agreement Between Canada and the United States for the Storage of Nuclear Weapons at a United States Leased Base in Newfoundland for the United States Forces. Secret.

639 Ibid.

640 18 September 1967, Memo to Legal Division, from DL(1) Division, External Affairs, subject: Storage of Nuclear ASW Weapons at a United States Base in Newfoundland. Secret.

641 18 September 1967, Memo to Canadian embassy Washington, from Gordon Smith, (for) under-secretary of state for External Affairs, subject: Storage of Nuclear ASW Weapons at a United States Base in Newfoundland. Secret

642 11 August 1967, Letter to the USN Chief of Naval Operations, from General Allard, chief of the Defence Staff, re Canadian Forces/United States Navy -
Service-to-Service Technical Arrangement - Storage of Airborne Nuclear ASW Weapons in Canada. V 3310-6 (DConP). Secret.

643 15 August 1967, Memo to DL(1) Division from H. Beesley, Legal Division, External Affairs, subject: Nuclear ASW Weapons Storage at a United States Leased Base in Canada. Secret.

644 25 July 1967. Revenue Canada note, (source unknown).

645 30 January 1968, Memorandum to the VCDS from G/C Henderson, Director Nuclear Weapons, National Defence, re: Canadian Observers/USN NTPI. V 3312-2 (DNW). Secret.

646 3 October 1968, Memorandum to the VCDS from G/C Henderson, Director Nuclear Weapons, National Defence, re: Canadian Observers/USN NTPI. V 3312-2 (DNW). Secret.

647 7 January 1970, 20:50z, Message to CINCLANTFLT Norfolk, Virginia, USA, from CANFORHED, Director of Nuclear Weapons, re: Argentia Inspection. V 3312-2 (DNW). Secret. Major Lowry complains that DNW has not yet received a copy of the September 1969 inspection report. 9 January 1970, 21:09z, Message to CANFORHED from CINCLANTFLT, re: Argentia Inspection. Secret.

648 17 August 1967, Letter to J.S. Nutt, DL(1) Division, External Affairs, from Brigadier Kenyon, DG Int & Sec, DND, re: Storage of Nuclear Weapons. V 2131-0 (DGIS). Secret

649 18 September 1967, Letter to

DGIS Brigadier Kenyon, from Gordon Smith, (for) under-secretary of state for External Affairs, subject: Storage of Nuclear ASW Weapons at a United States Base in Newfoundland. Secret

650 USN/CNO, Naval Aeronautical Organization, OPNAV Notice 05400, FY1969. p. 70.

651 18 February 1969, Airgram to Department of State from U.S. Consulate in St. John's, Newfoundland, subject: Continued Labor Concerns About Possible U.S. Abandonment of Argentia Naval Base. Unclassified.

652 5 December 1969, Telegram to secretary of state, from U.S. embassy, Ottawa, subject: Personnel Reductions at Argentia Naval Station. Confidential.

653 5 December 1969, Telegram to secretary of state, from U.S. Consulate, St. John's, Newfoundland, subject: Argentia Reductions. Confidential.

654 1972 Command Historical Report, U.S. Naval Station Argentia, 1 January-31 December 1972. Secret.

655 Technical information on the Lulu is taken from the following works: Gibson, *The History of the US Nuclear Arsenal*; Hansen, *U.S. Nuclear Weapons*; Hansen, *Swords of Armageddon*; a data sheet from the U.S. National Atomic Museum; and various Internet Web sites dealing with nuclear issues.

656 Technical information on the W57 is taken from the following works: Arkin, *Nuclear Weapons Databook.* 1984, pp. 63-64; Gibson, *The History of the US*

Nuclear Arsenal, p. 95; Hansen, *U.S. Nuclear Weapons*, pp. 164-166; Hansen, *Swords of Armageddon*; a data sheet from the U.S. National Atomic Museum; and various Internet Web sites dealing with nuclear issues.

John Murray Clearwater, BA (Hons), MA, PhD, was born in Winnipeg in 1966. He studied political science at the University of Winnipeg and Dalhousie University. He later received his doctorate in nuclear weapons and war studies from King's College London (UK). John then worked for National Defence headquarters in Ottawa.

His first book, *Canadian Nuclear Weapons,* generated requests for talks in Canada and the USA. The book became the basis for two CBC TV documentaries. John was then consulted on the CNN Cold War series, and provided background to the Pop Up (rock) video company in New York.

Dr. Clearwater now lives in Ottawa where he is a cat-fancier, military analyst, and specialist in nuclear weapons. He can be reached any time via e-mail at: da710@freenet.carleton.ca.